Théodore H. MacDonald

GW00992013

the Super-natural, the Occult and the Bible

the Super-natural, the Occult and the Bible

Gerald A. Larue

Prometheus Books
Buffalo, New York

THE SUPERNATURAL, THE OCCULT, AND THE BIBLE. Copyright © 1990 by Gerald A. Larue. All rights reserved. No part of this book may be reproduced in any manner whatsoever without written permission, except in the case of brief quotations embodied in critical articles and reviews. Inquiries should be addressed to Prometheus Books, 700 E. Amherst Street, Buffalo, New York 14215, 716-837-2475.

94 93 92 91 90   5 4 3 2 1

Library of Congress Cataloging-in-Publication Data

Larue, Gerald A.
    The supernatural, the occult, and the Bible / Gerald A. Larue.
        p.   cm.
    ISBN 0-879755-615-2
    1. Supernatural in the Bible. 2. Occultism—Biblical teaching. 3. Bible—Controversial literature. I. Title.
BS680.S86L37   1990
220-6—dc20   90-40144
                                                                    CIP

Printed in the United States of America on acid-free paper

To

George D. Smith, Jr.
with respect, admiration, and appreciation

Contents

Preface

Critical thinking, logic, and open inquiry are torches lighting the way through the darkness and confusion of superstitions inherited from the past. Human fears of the unknown and of the future produce chimeras that haunt uncritical and uninformed minds and pander to the continuation of supernaturalistic notions conjured up by our ancient ancestors in more primitive times and to the development of New Age occultism promoted by those who rely on magical thinking to solve human problems.

Perhaps the foremost contributions to magical thinking are made by religious organizations that base their authority on "revelations" provided by persons who lived thousands of years ago in ages of tyranny of church and state. Modern occultism draws energy from the pervasiveness of religious supernaturalism and evokes pseudoscience to promote its teachings. In both the old and new supernaturalism, rational and logical thinking are set aside and blind belief and conformity are demanded of adherents. This book addresses some of the problems that arise when notions about the supernatural and the occult are confronted analytically.

The dedication to George D. Smith, Jr., is a token of my respect for his continuing critical inquiry into the origins of the Church of Jesus Christ of Latter-day Saints (Mormons), the faith in which he was raised, for his courage in sharing his findings, and in appreciation of his generous encouragement of my research. He is a rare and very special human being.

Victoria E. Watkins, my research assistant, and Lena Ksarjian provided invaluable aid in the early stages of this book. I am indebted to Jack Foran for editing the manuscript; he has contributed greatly to its clarity. Doris Doyle, my editor at Prometheus Books, is always supportive, cooperative, courteous, and kind. Once again, she has eased me through the problems of publication. Paul Kurtz is more than my publisher. We have shared troubled and triumphant moments. My friendship with him embraces respect and deep caring. Finally, Emily, my wife, is the companion who makes hours, days, months, and years pass in joy and exhilaration. Her love gives meaning to my existence.

*   *   *

The beacons of critical thinking, logic, and open inquiry continue to burn brightly amid the darkness of superstition, and the darkness of supernaturalism and the occult has not been able to extinguish them.

Huntington Beach, California,
June 20, 1990

Introduction

The bishop was right! In 1909, the Right Reverend C. F. D'Arcy, bishop of Ossory, Ireland, wrote, "Christianity is essentially a supernatural religion." He went on to state: "In a world which is doing its best to deny the possibility of the supernatural, the most supernatural of all religions has shown itself the most potent of spiritual forces" (1909, p. 11). He continued:

> If the natural be a name for facts and laws that belong to a higher order of things, this faith may truly be said to be supernatural. And the claim of Christianity has always been that it does speak to us of something higher than our ordinary experience. It has to do with heavenly things and it everywhere supposes the existence of those heavenly things. (p. 18)

The bishop expressed alarm at attempts to explain away happenings such as the New Testament miracles as natural events. He concluded his book by noting the need to trust in God and in faith.

What troubles many modern biblical scholars is that the critical and analytical information concerning the Bible that was available to the bishop and which the bishop was not afraid to discuss openly has pretty much dropped out of sight for the present-day average churchgoer. The important insights into the languages of the biblical world, the results of archaeological research, the continuing literary analysis of the Scriptures, the ever-broadening study of the relationship between biblical concepts and those of its contemporary societies are not usually shared with the general public. There is a reason for this silence and the implications are disturbing.

Of course, the bishop would not approve of the point of view presented in this book. Here the emphasis is on science and reason, on the history of ideas and the findings of research, in the conviction that any faith that is without reason, that insists on "going beyond reason," and that ignores the best scientific information we have accumulated to date amounts to little more than superstition. Such noncritical, nonscientific thinking is not peculiar to modern biblicism only; it lies behind belief in the occult. Consequently, my studies have led me to the conclusion that biblical supernaturalism and the supernaturalism of the occult represent two sides of the same coin, and that from some perspectives they may be viewed as rivals using the same basic premises but employing different cultic and historical settings.

The biblical world, which existed from 1000 B.C.E. (Before the Common Era) to the second century C.E. (Common Era), was characterized by belief in supernatural powers (both beneficial and malignant), mythical monsters, extraterrestrial beings, nonhuman forces, and other occult themes. Because the Bible is a product of its own time, it is not surprising to find supernaturalism threaded throughout its various documents. The supernaturalism of the Bible lies behind the bishop's claim concerning Christianity as the most supernaturalistic of religions.

During the past 2,000 years, in which the Bible has been a powerful and influential religious and social educational instrument, its supernaturalism has been nourished and reenergized over and over again by synagogue, church, clergy, and believing or trusting laity. It is the purpose of this book to examine the influence of the Bible on present, late-twentieth-century beliefs and practices pertaining to the occult and the supernatural.

The Bible referred to in this book will include the Jewish Scriptures, pejoratively labelled "The *Old* Testament" by Christians, the Christian Scriptures, positively called "The *New* Testament" by Christians, and the books placed in the Apocrypha by Protestants and Jews, but included in Roman Catholic and Eastern Orthodox versions of the Bible (see list, pp. 14–15). Reference will also be made to some books in the Pseudepigrapha—a collection of writings composed just prior to and during the early years of Christianity.

Modern occultism is also characterized by belief in supernatural powers (both malignant and benign), mythical monsters, extraterrestrial beings, nonhuman forces, and other mystical themes. The term "occult" signifies not only belief in supernatural powers but also the notion that these powers can be utilized, controlled, or manipulated. In the minds of some, the word has assumed negative overtones because occultism appears to be involved with nonscientific gimmickry or because it represents concepts that are opposed to or are offensive to traditional religions.

The term "supernatural" refers to all beings, events, powers, and so on, that appear not to have an origin in nature as nature is known through the observable and scientifically demonstrable world. To insist that invisible demonic forces are real and are part of nature is to beg the question. What is "real" in our external world is that which is knowable through our five senses (enhanced, of course, by modern technology) and capable of analysis and verification scientifically and logically. We are no longer in the biblical mode of thinking; we live in a different time and place. We have changed and our thinking, and our approach to the phenomena of life, is out of harmony with that of people who lived in biblical times. However, their supernaturalistic and nonscientific notions are still current among us.

For example, we are far removed from the cosmic concepts of the biblical world. "Heaven" is no longer a place just above the observable firmament where angelic beings and God dwell and to which Jesus and later Mohammed could ascend. Our space probes and astronomical studies have demonstrated that such a notion has no basis in reality. Nevertheless, this outmoded way of thinking, which reflects the simplistic views of the past, impacts upon our modern world. We still refer to "sunrise" and "sunset." These terms emerged when humans believed that the sun moved from the east across the sky above the flat disc of the earth and set in the west, and then travelled from west to east through the underworld to rise again next morning. Our language describes an optical illusion that deceived our ancestors. The earth is not a flat disc, although it may appear to be such as we look to our horizons. We know it is because our spherical earth spins on its axis as it orbits a small star, our sun, that we experience day and night. Perhaps the retention of language reflecting ancient misconceptions is rather insignificant, but it serves to illustrate the way in which the supernaturalistic past continues to impose itself subtly upon our scientific present. The imprinting is made dramatically obvious by the gestures of evangelists, like Billy Graham, who point upward when they speak of Heaven. Clearly, they imply that Heaven is a place above the earth! They also point down toward the earth when they speak of Hell. They reinforce the primitive notion that there is a subterranean place called "Hell," which is the realm of the devil and to which Jesus descended during the period between his death and resurrection. Although the core of the earth is believed to be hot and molten, it in no way can be interpreted as the place where the souls of the damned are entertained throughout eternity.

A special problem confronts modern scholars when dealing with Christians who believe and argue with vehemence and often with anger that the Bible as we have it, particularly in the seventeenth-century King James Version, is a divinely revealed and authoritative work and that its truth is for all time and all generations. To deny this concept is, for them, a

The Books of the Old Testament

JEWISH	PROTESTANT	ROMAN CATHOLIC
The Law (Torah)	Genesis	Genesis
Genesis	Exodus	Exodus
Exodus	Leviticus	Leviticus
Leviticus	Numbers	Numbers
Numbers	Deuteronomy	Deuteronomy
Deuteronomy	Joshua	Josue (Joshua)
	Judges	Judges
The Prophets (Nebhiim)	Ruth	Ruth
The Former (Earlier) Prophets:	I Samuel	I Kings (= I Samuel)
Joshua	II Samuel	II Kings (= II Samuel)
Judges	I Kings	III Kings (= I Kings)
I Samuel	II Kings	IV Kings (= II Kings)
II Samuel	I Chronicles	I Paralipomenon (= I Chronicles)
I Kings	II Chronicles	II Paralipomenon (= II Chronicles)
II Kings	Ezra	I Esdras (Ezra)
The Latter Prophets:	Nehemiah	II Esdras (Nehemiah)
Isaiah	Esther	†Tobias (Tobit)
Jeremiah	Job	†Judith
Ezekiel	Psalms	Esther (with additions)
The Twelve:	Proverbs	Job
Hosea	Ecclesiastes	Psalms
Joel	Song of Solomon	Proverbs
Amos	Isaiah	Ecclesiastes
Obadiah	Jeremiah	Song of Songs
Jonah	Lamentations	†Book of Wisdom
Micah	Ezekiel	†Ecclesiasticus
Nahum	Daniel	Isaias
Habakkuk	Hosea	Jeremias
Zephaniah	Joel	Lamentations
Haggai	Amos	†Baruch (including the
Zechariah	Obadiah	Letter of Jeremiah)
Malachi	Jonah	Ezechiel
	Micah	Daniel
The Writings (Kethubhim)	Nahum	Osee (Hosea)
Psalms	Habakkuk	Joel
Proverbs	Zephaniah	Amos
Job	Haggai	Abdias (Obadiah)
Song of Songs	Zechariah	Jonas (Jonah)
Ruth	Malachi	Micheas (Micah)
Lamentations		Nahum
Ecclesiastes	**The Apocrypha**	Habacuc
Esther	*I Esdras (or III Esdras)	Sophonias (Zephaniah)
Daniel	II Esdras (or IV Esdras)	Aggeus (Haggai)
Ezra	*Tobit	Zacharias (Zechariah)
Nehemiah	*Judith	Malachias (Malachi)
I Chronicles	*Additions to Esther	†I Machabees
II Chronicles	*Wisdom of Solomon	†II Machabees
	*Ecclesiasticus	
	*Baruch	
	Letter of Jeremiah	
	*Prayer of Azariah and	
	*The Song of the Three Young Men	
	Susanna	
	*Bel and the Dragon	
	Prayer of Manasseh	
	*I Maccabees	
	*II Maccabees	

---

*Books accepted by the Eastern Orthodox Church but not included in the Jewish Canon.
†Books accepted by Roman Catholics but not included in the Jewish Canon.

denial of the essential nature of the Bible. Bible believers not bound by the authority of a single translation may argue that the writings in the original autographs represent the divine words, and that contradictions found in Hebrew or Greek sources can be blamed on unknown careless translators or copiers. Thus, when in the Torah, which fundamentalists ascribe to Moses, information is provided that could not possibly have been known by Moses, this data is ascribed to later interpreters or copiers who attempted to clarify Moses' ideas. For example, the city called "Dan" is mentioned in Genesis (14:14), the so-called "First Book of Moses," whereas Judges 18:29 makes it clear that there was no such city until long after Moses was dead! It was not until the Danite tribe conquered and renamed the Canaanite city of Laish that Dan came into being. Fundamentalists find no problem here. They argue that some copyist, aware that readers would know of the city of Dan, changed the original name "Laish" in Genesis to "Dan" for clarification! The last chapter (34) of Deuteronomy, the so-called "Fifth Book of Moses," describes Moses' death and burial, states that "to this day no one knows where he was buried," and further comments that "There has not arisen a prophet like Moses since in Israel." The chapter reflects a time later than Moses, and obviously was not written by Moses. Here, the literalists admit that someone added the verses, all the while ignoring the fact that it is written in the same style as the rest of the book. Such examples plus literary analyses demonstrate that the insistence that Moses authored the Torah is simply nonsense!

Where clear evidence of Hebrew copyist errors reproduced in the King James Version is pointed out, those who espouse the King James Version as "the Word" simply disregard these mistakes. The Hebrew text of Lev. 20:10 reads: "If a man commits adultery with the wife of, if a man commits adultery with the wife of." The King James Version faithfully reproduced the dittography and modified the repetitive language to try and make it comprehensible. Modern translators simply place the repetition in the footnotes, recognizing the duplication as an ordinary human mistake. As one contemplates the claim that the autographs were divinely given or inspired, the question arises: Why, if God was so concerned about accuracy in the original autographs, did he disregard the importance of accuracy in the preservation and copying of these divine revelations?

Critical studies have demonstrated that the Bible is a product of the thinking of small groups of people who lived in a corner of the Mediterranean basin in the ancient middle eastern world between 1000 B.C.E. and 150 C.E. Their writings, the products of temple priesthoods, wisdom schools, prophetic circles, hymn writers, letter writers, novelists, biographers, and others, are not always unique, but reflect the social situations as well as the biases, attitudes, beliefs, and the responses to history of their particular time periods. Like those who lived in surrounding nations, they struggled with ethical and moral issues, with finding meaning in life, with problems associated with loss and acquisition, with grief and with joy. Thus, the Bible reflects how particular people, the Hebrews, the Jews, the Christians, interpreted their world and sought to come to terms with it and with their place in it. Like others, they projected into their god-concepts the ethical, moral, and social values that they honored. With some of their concepts we can agree, but there is much that we can no longer accept. Slavery is no longer acceptable. Ancient notions concerning the role of women have been discarded or are in the process of being discarded. Attitudes toward human sexuality have undergone change. The list could be extended.

The Bible is not a unity. It reflects a process which I have called in my *Old Testament Life and Literature* (1968), "a continuing interpretation." Over the more than 1,000 years during which it was composed, human thinking underwent change, just as modern thinking undergoes change. The people of the Bible were influenced by ideas generated in surrounding nations, just as we are today. Many ideas, words, and phrases of the Bible appear to have been borrowed from foreign nations and then adapted to the local life-setting of the Hebrews, Jews, and Christians.

Jews and Christians entertained concepts of the world similar to those of their neighbors in Egypt, Mesopotamia, and the Mediterranean countries. They held similar values. When, in the sixth century B.C.E., the Jews emerged from monolatry (belief that different nations have different deities) to monotheism (belief in a single, universal deity), they moved from parochialism toward universalism. Their god became the sole god, rendering outmoded beliefs in a multitude of deities. At the same time, their parochialism was maintained in the conviction that they alone were the ones chosen by that god as his special people. When Christianity developed, Christians adopted the Jewish notion of being a chosen people. Later Islam was to make similar claims. In each of these monotheistic faiths, particularism was retained within their universalism. Ultimately, the scriptures of these three religions were each to assume the status of unassailable truth in their respective faith communities. Consequently, naive beliefs about the divine and the demonic remained as part of the developing faith systems. In other words, supernaturalism and occultist notions are an integral part of the Bible and the religions that accept its authority.

When belief systems are adopted by powerful rulers and governments, their influence grows and their theology and teachings become the law of the land. Other faiths may be labelled "pagan" and forced underground. At times, these other beliefs may surface as rivals of the central faith system, and when that happens their followers become targets of persecution—as in the case of witchcraft trials. Then, once again, the nonaccepted belief system goes underground, later manifesting itself in new and modified forms.

We are in such a period. "Old Age" religions are being challenged by "New Age" belief systems, some of which are modifications of ancient simplistic folk religions. Both old and new belief patterns are characterized by occult notions. Ancient nonterrestrials are replaced by New Age nonterrestrials. The power of the old priesthoods is challenged by the claims of the new. Old rites are given new form. Both seek support in the findings of modern research and science, even as both appeal to the noncritical, superstitious mind-set of the general public.

In a sense, Old Age beliefs validate New Age ideas, for if supernatural and occultist ideas are found in the Bible, which is the "word of God," then present-day nonbiblical supernatural and occultist notions can claim to have a basis in reality. In other words, by virtue of the authority given to the Bible by synagogues and churches, the Bible sustains and perhaps even justifies the new occultism which both synagogue and church condemn!

Many modern Roman Catholic scholars consider the old supernaturalism to be a relic, and in their thinking and teaching generally disregard such notions. Yet they maintain membership in the Roman Catholic Church, which continues to embrace gross superstitions. To experience this sometimes astonishing dichotomy of thought, one might visit the Roman Catholic Museo del Purgatorio in Rome, Italy. The present curator, the Rev. Renato Simeone, informed Nino lo Bello that the museum was begun by Father Vittore Jouet toward the end of the nineteenth century and was built with the encouragement of popes Pius X and Benedict XV. The curator explained that the exhibits had recently been purged of all but "the most thoroughly authenticated pieces." The collection is now contained in a cupboard in an annex of Sacro Cuore del Suffragio Church. The "authenticated" relics consist of handprints or fingerprints or a cross burned into the surface of some artifact—a book, a garment, a wooden tabletop—by "some soul who came back from purgatory asking for prayers that would release him into paradise." It would be acceptable to modern Catholic scholars if the Roman Catholic Church employed the museum as evidence of antiquated notions. But no! These are "authenticated" artifacts. How embarrassing to some Roman Catholic scholars.

So-called New Age thought, some of which we will examine, became popular in the Sixties, blossomed in the Seventies, and assumed new forms of expression in the Eighties. The late Sixties and the Seventies were characterized by occult and religious experiences induced by mind-altering drugs. New Age persons took hallucinatory "trips" that would, they hoped, send them on journeys through clouds of darkness to realms of light. They experienced intensity of color and sound—an awareness which was often translated into paintings or poetry or descriptive writing or music. While under the influence of drugs, the artists were convinced that they had brought forth new and startling and beautiful expressions. When the effects of the drugs had worn off, they recognized what they had produced as mediocre and inferior. A New Age vocabulary came into being that spoke of different levels of consciousness and sought to provide a different paradigm of the human. Those whose consciousness had been aroused and awakened proclaimed new harmonious relationships with nature or God or the universe.

Meanwhile, those who had been drug-crazed, and those who had experienced the supernatural, now focused on ways and means to deepen their experiences. Some drew from the yoga teachings of the ancient religions of India. Some delved into the superstitions of the Middles Ages and emphasized the mythical effect of planetary positions at the moment of one's birth. Some studied Tarot cards and palm reading. Some declared, on the basis of Kirlian photography, that humans exuded auras which sensitives could discern and translate into meaningful analyses of life-patterns. Some exploited out-of-body and near-death experiences and through hypnotic suggestion helped clients explore "former lives"—a notion borrowed from reincarnation beliefs. Some stated that rocks and minerals in the form of crystals had magical power.

Of course, both church and synagogue condemned New Age occultism, but simultaneously practiced parallel patterns which could be termed Old Age occultism. Within the Christian church ecstatic experiences such as glossolalia, which was associated with Pentecostal religion, entered traditional denominations under the banner of charismatic religion. Charisma implied the input of the Holy Spirit. The babbling of voices "speaking in tongues" was proof positive of personal contact with the divine—proof positive of a trip into another dimension. Television evangelists exploited naive viewers with magical or supernatural divine healing carried on in a circus environment. Hallucinatory experiences proliferated as visions of the Virgin Mary were announced at sites throughout the world. The sales of religious amulets expanded and miracles associated with various holy persons placed dead religious leaders on the pathway to sainthood.

For both New Agers and Old Agers (the church), supernaturalistic emphases paid off. Televangelists became millionaires. Crystals and colored stones soared in price, while believers bought religious artifacts. New Age séances channeled voices from other dimensions and attracted thousands of followers, while claims of visions and messages from heavenly beings brought millions to new sacral and revelatory sites. Some channelers became millionaires; some churches prospered. It is clear that money is at least one of the fruits of claims of the occult, the magical, the supernatural. So long as some are willing to pay, others will be ready to provide for this market.

New Age belief in the occult and in psychic phenomena implies acceptance of the notion that there are invisible powers that lie outside the natural, the normal, and the human, and it is assumed that, for weal or for woe, these powers may directly affect the individual, the group, the nation, and, ultimately, the world. For example, hidden powers may lie behind disastrous natural phenomena such as earthquakes, storms, floods, tornados, and so forth. It is also believed that the intention or will or direction of these unseen powers may be discerned through the use of scrying devices, or through the skill of seers who by one means or another can foretell the future or unravel the developing patterns of that which is yet to happen. Furthermore, there is the belief that it is possible to sway these unseen forces in positive, life-enhancing ways, so that misfortune may be averted and positive results will occur. At the very least, if one knows in advance the good days and the bad days, one may take precautions to thwart the lurking evils that threaten human well-being.

Of course, what can be said about belief in the occult may be said about many modern religious beliefs, which also entertain the conviction that there is power residing outside the human or natural spheres—power that is supernatural and which may be labelled either "God" or "the devil," depending upon whether the influence is discerned as benign or malignant. These positive or negative powers can affect the individual, the group, the nation, and the world. It is also believed that something of the intention and will of these opposing powers may be determined from the study of the ancient texts found in the Bible, where the god-power has revealed to ancient seers not only the will of the deity, but also the deity's final solution concerning human problems. These sacred texts provide insight into the workings of the demonic so that satanic influences may be recognized. Furthermore, there is the belief that it is possible to sway the divine powers in positive or life-enhancing ways through rituals and prayers and specific religious activities that are pleasing to the god-power. Thus, evil may be averted and good may result.

In this volume we will examine these parallel concepts. Traditional religions rigorously oppose the claims of those who accept the reality of the occult and psychic phenomena on the basis that within the Bible there are texts that warn against extrabiblical occultism. For example, in Lev. 20:6, the deity announced, "I will set my face against the individual who wantonly turns to mediums and wizards." Nevertheless, occultism is popular.

As church and synagogue oppose modern occult patterns, they endorse the old occultism embedded in their faith systems.

It has been suggested that the widespread belief in the occult and the supernatural represents a reaction against the scientific worldview and a return to elementary concepts of earlier times. Perhaps modern humans are overwhelmed by the immense amount of data from communication media, from popularization of research findings, from computers and books. Confronted by such a deluge of information, the average person simply gives up and takes refuge in simplistic answers. Perhaps modern life has become too confusing for the average person. Individuals lose their way in the maze of complex problems associated with survival. They turn to magical thinking. They gamble on state lotteries where the odds are 14,000,000-to-one against their winning and succumb to advertising that suggests that because someone does win, perhaps they will be the next lucky person, thereby accumulating the instant wealth that will solve their problems. To help them choose the lucky numbers they resort to all sorts of devices, once again trusting in magic or the occult to make their dreams come true. Obviously, the findings of modern scientific and societal research have not displaced beliefs in the world of magic or spirits or ghosts or demons or otherworldly powers. What is, perhaps, more distressing is to learn that there are police officers, educators, social workers, therapists, nurses, doctors, and others who work directly with human safety, human health, and human learning who believe in demonic powers and the ability of psychics, the curative magic of certain herbs and mental procedures, and so on.

There is further irony in the fact that in our most reputable universities, colleges, and seminaries, critical thinking, logical analysis, and the basis for a methodology of scientific inquiry are taught to men and women some of whom will be prepared as clergy. These religious leaders-to-be are exposed to classes in geology, astronomy, philosophy, psychology, logic, and history in their undergraduate preparatory courses. In the liberal seminary they are taught biblical criticism and biblical history. After seminary training, when these same persons enter a pulpit or conduct religious education classes, the critical information they have learned about the cosmos, the world, and human beings, and the literary history of the Bible is ignored. They fail to challenge primitive and superstitious ideas found in the Bible. They teach denominational brands of religious supernaturalism and in so doing make magical thinking acceptable and prepare the minds of parishioners to accept occult concepts. Why?

There are at least three reasons why the clergy fail to share with their congregations the best information concerning the Bible. The first is that they really do not accept the results of critical inquiry. Such a choice is, of course, personal, and should be open to challenge by fellow clergy and by biblical scholars. The second reason, which appears to me to be more operative, is that they are afraid of confrontation by and lack of support from the conservative members of their congregations who reject critical inquiry, who prefer to accept the Bible as a divinely revealed document, and who threaten to withdraw their support and contributions or to split the congregation if the clergy does not confrom to their ideas. One need only read the news reports of the constant struggles between ultraconservative and more-or-less liberal elements in the Southern Baptist and Lutheran denominations and also in Roman Catholicism to become aware of the conflict. Divisions in Judaism reflect similar battles. In other words, the liberal, critically trained clergy demonstrate a failure of nerve and a desire to continue in their profession without controversy. To some degree one may empathize with them, for they have devoted years of their lives to preparation for the ministry, and now, despite their training and expertise, they are not permitted to share the best of scholarship with their parishioners. The educational potential of the pulpit is betrayed—a most disturbing situation.

The third reason for clergy silence on critical examination of religious notions reflects personal insecurity—an insecurity that goes beyond the fear of divisiveness in the congregation, but which suggests fear of challenge to the authority of the pulpit. Perhaps a personal example will illustrate the point. A number of years ago I persuaded a liberal, well-trained minister to open his Sunday evening service to discussion of his morning sermon. He agreed that this idea had interesting possibilities. When I visited with him several months later he acknowledged that he had experimented with the procedure for two Sundays and had then dropped it. The experience was, he admitted, too unsettling, too threatening. He put a lot of effort into the preparation of his sermon. To have his ideas challenged was reminiscent of having his papers graded in college classes. After the first evening session, he was so disturbed that he could not sleep. Before the second session he was so nervous that he stumbled and fumbled through his responses to the questions posed by the congregation. For him and for many others, the pulpit represented a fortress from which he could safely make his proclamations. As he greeted his congregation as they filed from the church each Sunday morning, he was familiar with the cliche: "enjoyed your sermon." To have this response withdrawn undermined the security he needed as he stood before his parish members each Sunday. It is far safer to stay within doctrinally accepted boundaries and not question the faith. When, as a college student, I questioned a learned priest-educator concerning his acceptance in the classroom of certain Roman Catholic ideas, he admitted that he had entertained questions about these matters "until I learned to accept the authority of the Church." I pointed out to him that it was clear that he could not teach me anything I couldn't learn from Roman Catholic faith books and that therefore I would drop the class.

This book will seek to point up some popular occult themes that can find support in the Bible. If it serves to encourage the laity to challenge the clergy and to urge pastoral leaders to employ the best educational tools in their ministry, then it will have served a useful purpose. If it leads to the application of critical thinking skills to issues of faith and belief in present-day occultism and encourages the asking of analytical questions, perhaps it may stimulate growth in the application of logic and science to popular belief systems. If it encourages those who have been confused about New Age occult and supernaturalist claims, to examine, to question, to challenge, then perhaps it will help in the development of a new generation that will be proud of its skepticism, unwilling to be fooled or misled, and willing to stand firmly on the basis of ideas and beliefs that have been thought through but which are still open to growth.

References

D'Arcy, Charles F., *Christianity and the Supernatural.* London: Longmans, Green and Co., 1909.

Jones, Rufus M., *A Call To What Is Vital.* New York: The Macmillan Company, 1948.

Larue, Gerald A., *Ancient Myth and Modern Life.* Long Beach, Calif.: Centerline Press, 1988.

———, *Old Testament Life and Literature.* Boston: Allyn and Bacon, 1968.

Lo Bello, Nino, "Rome's Occult Museum Draws Curiosity Seekers," *The Los Angeles Times,* May 22, 1988.

The World of Magic

And the magicians said to Pharaoh, "This is the finger of Elohim."
Exod. 8:19

Ancient simplistic attempts to explain the confusing aspects of the world and of life in time became highly sophisticated. The environments of our ancestors confronted them with problems that today we explain scientifically. What causes a hot spring to produce water so different from springs of cool water? Why are some creatures born deformed? How does one decide whether to take the path to the left or the right? Why was a certain person at the wrong place when a rock dislodged from a cliff and struck him or her? Are there good days and bad days? Do the flight patterns of birds contain secret information? As our forebears pondered their relationship to their world, magic was born and it took the form of both a philosophy, or way of looking at life and living, and a means of controlling life.

Magical thinking rests on human conjecture concerning the nature of things. It fantasizes wondrous powers in objects and in nature and then attributes human emotions and attitudes to these mysterious conjectured powers. It reflects the belief that humans can make contact with spiritual and supernatural beings and influence these nonhuman powers on their behalf. It rests upon the notion that the observable forces in this world upon which humans depend for their well-being are under the control of spiritual agents which must be conciliated and appeased and persuaded by words or petitions and by acts or rituals. Ethical concerns may be subordinated to practical considerations. What is most important is the proper performance of ritual, the use of correct terminology and language and formulae. Sacrifices may supersede morality.

Of course not everyone was proficient in the practice of the essential rites; experts emerged—chosen because of their knowledge of that which was believed to be effective in cajoling the unseen powers to act beneficently. These shamanic priests possessed the art of compelling unseen powers to act according to the wishes expressed in the incantation or in the rites. Their abilities were magical—not in the sense of open deception for the purpose of entertainment as practiced in our modern nightclubs and on television—but magical and also deceptive because they are and were based on that which cannot be proven or tested and which calls for noncritical belief and blind acceptance. Where the intention of the magical rite was for the benefit of the person or the community, the magic was good or perhaps "white" magic. Where the purpose was to bring hurt or destruction, the magic was evil or "black" magic. However, whether the shaman intended to cure an illness or place a curse, the procedure could be effective because the participants or the victims believed in the efficacy of the words or ritual.

Magic in the Bible and Religion

According to Christian Scriptures, Jesus transmitted magical power to his disciples: "I tell you this: whatever you bind on earth will be bound in heaven and whatever you loosen on earth will be loosened in heaven" (Matt. 18:18).

The Gospel of John recorded that the post-resurrection Jesus gave even greater authority to his disciples: "If you forgive anyone for their sins, they are forgiven; and if you do not forgive anyone's sins, they are not forgiven" (20:23).

Such magical power, akin to the shaman's ability to place or remove curses, is reflected in the confessional rites of Roman Catholicism, where priestly exorcists hear "confessions" of actions believed to have offended the deity. They then prescribe penitential acts which guarantee forgiveness if the penitent's intention is honest and sincere.

Christian theology embraced the notion of "original sin," which is supposed to be the stain inherent in every person from birth because our primal ancestors, Adam and Eve, disobeyed Yahweh. According to this theology, Jesus, the Son of God, became a sacrificial victim to appease the offense to the Father of man's sin. The Gospel of John declares that: "God loved the world so much that he gave his only son, so that whoever believes in him will not perish but will have eternal life" (3:16).

The death of Jesus and the blood of Jesus have magical significance. However, the magic of Jesus' shed blood, did not, apparently, remove the stain of original sin. According to Roman Catholicism, a special ritual is needed to accomplish that, namely the rite of baptism. When the priest takes from the baptismal font water which has been transformed into "holy water" by virtue of a priestly blessing, and applies this to the forehead of an infant or a child or an adult, and pronounces the formula: "I baptize you in the name of the Father, and the Son, and the Holy Ghost (or Spirit)," the original sin is magically erased and the individual at that moment is free from sin and acceptable to the deity. The words, the water, the gestures, have power and are in themselves compelling and effective. The invisible sin is gone. The stain is removed. No one has ever seen original sin; its existence depends on faith. One believes, the rite is performed, and the sin disappears!

The ceremony does not remove the potential for, nor the consequences of, future sin. The church maintains control over the parishioner by insisting that because humans are, by nature, sinners, other violations of divine laws will occur, creating a need for further confession, penance, and forgiveness. Thus, the potential sinner is encouraged to return again and again for forgiveness, and in so doing automatically comes under the control of the clergy and of clergy magic.

Within Protestantism baptism has a different significance. In some churches only adult baptism is performed. The rite signifies a personal confession of faith and marks an initiation into the fellowship of believers. In other congregations infant baptism constitutes a parental pledge made on behalf of an infant that the child will be raised in the faith. When the child reaches maturity (usually associated with puberty), it is anticipated that the child will make a personal confession of faith and "join the church." There is nothing magical associated with the ritual.

Because only specially endowed or chosen individuals could make contact with the supernatural power, it was important that they retain for themselves the secrets of their craft. To conjure up the power of a demon or a deity it was necessary to call up the spirit by name. When the priests of the Canaanite god, Ba'al, sought Ba'al's power to bring rain, they called out "Oh Ba'al, answer us" (1 Kings 18:26). The invocation of the divine name could be precarious. God should not be disturbed for frivolous concerns. Hence the biblical command, "You must not use the name of Yahweh, your Elohim, for empty reasons" (Exod. 20:7). So powerful was that proscription that the name "Yahweh" was used in temple services only on the Day of Atonement, when the high priest intoned the sacred name seven times in what must have been a most solemn and tense moment. In modern Judaism, the divine name is never used. When the Jewish Scriptures are read and the god's personal name is given in the text, the Hebrew letters Y-H-W-H are not read as "Yahweh" but are read as the Hebrew word *adonay*, which means "lord" or "master." Indeed, the vowels of *adonay* are inserted or pointed in the Hebrew text so that should the reader read literally, the divine name will be mispronounced as "YaHoWaH," or in popular usage "Jehovah." Inasmuch as this is not the name of the deity, Yahweh is not called forth. In synagogue schools, children are taught to avoid writing the word "God" and instead write "G-d." In other words, the primitive fear of improper use of the personal name of a deity is alive in our modern society.

In ancient Egypt, funerary offerings were made to the dead. In the ritual, the lector priest would pronounce a formula by which the material elements were transformed to assume a spiritual dimension. The food that was presented, therefore, had both material and spiritual qualities. The dead partook of the spiritual or divine good; the priests and relatives of the deceased consumed the material food. The ritual brought the living into communion with the deceased and with the gods.

The concept is familiar in Roman Catholicism. In the ritual of the Holy Communion, the wafer held in the hands of the priest and elevated, and the wine contained in the chalice and elevated, are magically transformed at a spiritual level into the body and blood of the dead Jesus. The worshippers consume the material wafer (which is simply flour and water) but at the same time receive the spiritual food which is the body of Christ. The priest consumes both wafer and wine, consuming the material and the spiritual elements of both species. Through the power vested in the clergy by virtue of their ordination and by the laying on of hands by a church superior, they have received spiritual power, which like that of the Egyptian lector priest, enables them to transform the ordinary into the extraordinary, the profane or common into the sacred.

In most Protestant churches the Holy Communion or Last Supper ritual is performed as a remembrance rite. There is no hushed awe as the bread and grape juice are distributed to the congregations, for these elements are not transformed, but remain what they are: simply bread and juice.

Getting the Word

Magical thinking may also include beliefs in divination which, according to T. W. Davies, is "the attempt on man's part to obtain from the spiritual world supernormal or superhuman knowledge. This knowledge relates for the most part to the future, but may also have to do with the present, such as where some hidden treasure may be found" (Davies 1969, p. 6). Biblical divination encompasses everything from the attempt to discern the divine will by use of sacred lots, to oracles of the prophets concerning national well-being, to predictions of seers concerning the end of the world. Sometimes animals were offered to placate the deity and to encourage divine response (Num. 23:1, 2, 14). This giving or offering principle, known as *do ut des* (I give so that you may give), constitutes a tit-for-tat arrangement with supernatural powers.

Various methods of tapping the divine will were employed. An oak tree near Shechem was known as "the Diviner's Oak." Deborah, the prophetess, sat beneath a palm tree for her oracles. Whether messages were transmitted through the rustling of the branches, as some have contended, or by other means, she was believed to be in touch with Yahweh, who provided plans for battle strategy (Jud. 5). Ezekiel noted that the King of Babylon "shakes the arrows, consults the teraphim, examines the liver," all of which were modes of divining. King Saul used sacred lots and visited a necromancer to get answers from Yahweh.

Little information is provided about the techniques used by the prophets to obtain their messages from the deity. The phrase "The word of Yahweh came to me" provides no hint as to how the message was heard or received or what may have been done to invite it. No matter what technique was employed, the conviction remained that certain persons had the ability, the skill, the know-how to break the barriers between the normal and the supernormal.

Of course the deity might desire to communicate with humans without the use of rituals or shamans. One channel was the dream, which was believed to have symbolic significance. The writer of Job had Elihu, the young man who interrupted Job's conversations with his consolers, state that the deity communicated in two ways: through dreams and through physical pain (32:14–30). Concerning dreams he noted:

> In a dream, in a night vision
> When deep sleep falls on men
> As they slumber on their beds,
> Then he [God] opens men's ears
> And terrifies them with warnings
> To turn a man away from evil
> And keep a man from pride
> To spare his life-force from the Pit [the grave]
> And keep him from crossing the river [of death].
>
> (33:15–18)

Dreams might require interpretation, and Daniel, as a dream interpreter, was able to tell King Nebuchadnezzar the meaning of the royal dreams when the national sorcerers failed (Dan. 2). On the other hand, the dream might be so specific that its message required no professional exposition (Matt. 1:20–21, 2:13, 20).

Messages from the nonnatural world might be conveyed through natural phenomena. Stars might provide supernatural information (see chapter on Astrology). The deity might use clouds and a rainbow to communicate. In the flood story, the priestly writers had the deity state that these natural phenomena constituted a reminder of the divine promise never to flood the earth again:

> Here is the symbol of the agreement which I am making between myself and you including every living creature and all future generations: When I set the rainbow in the clouds, it will be the sign of my covenant with the earth and when I cause clouds to gather and the bow is seen in the clouds, then I will remember the agreement between me and you and all life forms that never again will a flood of waters destroy the earth. When the bow is in the clouds, I will see it and remember the eternal covenant between Elohim and all living creatures on earth. (Gen. 9:12–16)

Obviously, the deity did not trust his memory. The rainbow constituted a kind of string tied around the divine finger to ensure memory of the promise. At the same time it communicated to humans the divine intent.

At times the deity sent personal messengers to convey messages (see chapter on Angels). At other times the deity himself might materialize as a human. Abraham not only heard the voice of Yahweh (Gen. 22) and experienced Yahweh in a vision (Gen. 15) but was visited by the deity and two supernatural companions (Gen. 18).

The biblical worldview encompassed the seen and unseen, the known and unknown, the divine and the human, the supernatural and the natural. Because the supernatural, the unseen, the divine, and the unknown impinged upon the human world in mysterious ways, it was important to seek ways to compromise with these mysterious forces. Special people—the seers, prophets, diviners, soothsayers, priests, and wise men and women—provided the channels. Because of the important role the Bible plays in modern society, these ancient notions continue to prevail, encouraging nonanalytic acceptance of supernaturalism and the continuance of magical thinking.

Objects can have magical properties. The wand of the magician is a "magic" wand as opposed to an ordinary stick. The supernatural manifests itself to specially "gifted" persons. Channelers may claim that the spiritual entity with whom they are in communication took visible form and confronted them (see chapter on Channeling). Others may claim to get messages from their spirit guides.

Modern Evaluation of Psychic Communication

Either there are or there are not supernatural entities that exist outside of the natural world. Most of those who claim to hear voices and experience apparitions fit into a category of mental illness known as schizophrenia. In some manifestations of this disorder, the person loses rational contact with the "real" world. For many, medications or chemicals can restore balance and return the person to "normalcy." Most of us view with caution the claims of those who argue that they have experienced visions or who hear voices, even when these claims are made by members of the clergy, and certainly when they are made by persons whose behavior makes us uneasy.

It is possible that the ancient Hebrew prophets suffered from some sort of mental imbalance. However, it is quite clear that individuals like Amos and Isaiah and Jeremiah were in rational contact with their society and their world. They were deeply involved in current social, national, and international problems and practices. Most biblical scholars believe that Jesus' claims to be God are to be considered to have been placed in his mouth by writers for whom Jesus was God incarnate. Modern channelers appear to be either deeply disturbed individuals or charlatans, with the latter appearance predominating. The same can be said for those religious leaders and modern psychics who claim to have made astral trips to heaven or to other worlds. Mass hallucinations can be induced, and what is perceived during the altered state of consciousness rests upon evidence that cannot be sustained either logically or scientifically.

It is possible that the ancient seers were able to move into some sort of trance or meditative state in which the problems of the day became clarified in their thinking and out of which came the statements that they attributed to the deity. There is absolutely no way to test the claims of the past other than by the experiences that we know. On the other hand, if we are prepared to accept the claims of communication with the divine that appear in the Bible, there is absolutely no reason why we should not accept the validity of similar claims by nonbiblical persons extending from Mohammed to the Mormon Joseph Smith to Mary Baker Eddy to Oral Roberts. Uneasiness with the testimony of nonbiblical individuals who believe they have made contact with spiritual entities invites uneasiness with similar claims made by biblical characters.

References

Davies, T. Witton, *Magic, Divination and Demonology Among the Hebrews and Their Neighbors*. New York: KTAV Publishing House, 1969 (first published in 1898).

Thomas, Keith, *Religion and the Decline of Magic*. New York: Charles Scribner's Sons, 1971.

Thorndike, Lynn, *The Place of Magic in the Intellectual History of Europe*. New York: Columbia University Press, 1905.

Wax, Murray and Rosalie, "The Notion of Magic," *Current Anthropology*, Vol. 4, No. 3, December 1963, pp. 495–518.

Channeling—Ancient and Modern

Find me a woman who is a medium so that I may inquire of her.
1 Sam. 28:7

Our ancient ancestors lived in a world peopled with unseen forces, powers, and spirits. Mystical energies were everywhere inhabiting springs, trees, caves, high mountains, and deep valleys. Indeed, the Semitic terms *il* or *ilu*, which appear in the Bible as *el* or *elim* and *elohim* in the plural, signified power or energy outside of human control that could animate or energize a thing or an area. Combining local "els" into a single "El" ultimately produced the idea of a single supreme power-source or "God."

Another biblical term used to identify local power sources is *ba'alim* (*ba'al* in the singular). The term signifies ownership or control. Some place names mentioned in the Bible include reference to the ba'al of the locale such as the ba'al of Mount Hermon (Judges 3:3) or the ba'al of Hazor (2 Sam. 13:23). For example, in Num. 25:3 it is noted that the Hebrews worshipped the ba'al at Pe'or. In each instance, the reference is to the manifestation of the power that owns or controls the area. When local ba'alim were fused into one supreme spiritual force they could be addressed as the deity Ba'al, the god who controlled fertility and the life-sustaining rains. At the same time, the local ba'al could be viewed as the regional manifestation of the supreme Ba'al.

Specially endowed or ordained individuals were believed to be able to make contact with the spiritual powers and act as mediators for those seeking an oracle or a message or an answer to some pressing question. Those who acted under the aegis of a given divinity were recognized as seers, priests, or prophets. They are represented in belief systems throughout the ancient world. In the Hebrew cult they received their oracular responses from the Hebrew god Yahweh.

Several words are used to describe these inspired persons in the Hebrew Bible. The terms *horeh* and *ro'eh* both mean "seer," that is, one who sees that which is hidden, such as the future. The Hebrew word *nabi* means "prophet." At times these several terms meld. The prophet Samuel is identified as a *ro'eh* (1 Sam. 9:19). In this instance he acted as a clairvoyant able to envision events happening at a distance. He informed Saul that the missing asses Saul had been seeking had been found. An editor added a note concerning the identity of Samuel as a *ro'eh:*

> In former times in Israel, when a man went to inquire of Elohim, he said, "Come, let us go to the seer (*ro'eh*)", for he who is now called a prophet (*nabi*) was formerly called a seer (*ro-eh*). (1 Sam. 9:9)

The prophet Amos was called a *hozeh* (Amos 7:12), and some scholars have suggested that perhaps, in this instance, the term was used in a derogative sense. Both the prophet (*nabi*) and the seer (*hozeh*) issued warnings of divine judgment to Israel and Judah. Finally, the seer (*hozeh*) and the diviner (*qasam*) are mentioned together as those who get messages from Yahweh (Micah 3:7).

Just how these inspired persons received their messages is not clear (see chapter on Exorcism). Some appear to have engaged in ecstatic frenzy and have become "spirit crazed" as R. B. Y. Scott phrased it. They were labelled "mad" (2 Kings 9:11 and Hosea 9:7), and the prophetic frenzy could be contagious. King Saul's messengers encountered a group of ecstatic prophets and were caught up in the movement and failed to deliver his messages. When the king himself met this same band,

> . . . the spirit of Elohim came upon him also, and as he went he prophesied, until he came to Naioth in Ramah. And he too stripped off his clothes, and he too prophesied before Samuel, and lay naked all that day and all that night. (1 Sam. 19:23–24)

Apparently the king's prophesying included ecstatic raving. Mediums who functioned outside the Yahweh cult were outlawed, first by King Saul (1 Sam. 28:3) and again later by subsequent legislation (Deut. 18:10–11).

The Modern Seer

If seer power existed in the ancient past and was recognized in the Bible, there is no reason why that same seer power or a variation of it should not exist today. It is not surprising to find that many modern seers declare their belief in the Bible and in Christianity. They are recognized in our time as mediums.

Present-day channeling is a variation of mediumship. Channelers' most recent predecessors were spiritualists who conjured up spirits of dead relatives or friends for their clients. These spiritual entities would provide information or offer advice. There were always risks in calling up familiar friends or family members in that these persons were supposed to have intimate, personal, familial memories and knowledge to share. Should the medium provide incorrect or faulty information, he or she might be labelled a fraud or be accused of inadequacy.

Many prominent and famous people consulted psychics in efforts to renew contact with some dead person. Many were persuaded that the contact had been made. Some mediums introduced visible "spiritual" matter, known as ectoplasm, into the seances. This filmy materialization of the dead person would appear suddenly in a darkened room where the sitting was in progress. Sometimes it floated about. Answers to queries seemed to come from it. Despite the fact that time after time the ectoplasmic presence was proven to be a product of the medium's deliberate deception, there were those who remained convinced that some real spiritual manifestation had taken place.

A more recent aspect of mediumship is spirit writing. The process is rather simple. The medium sits at a desk or typewriter or computer and a spirit of some long dead person takes possession of the medium's mind and body, so that what is written or typed represents the words and thinking of the spirit. For example, in *The Book of James* by Susy Smith the reader is informed that Smith was introduced by the spirit of her dead mother to another inhabitant of the spirit world identified as "James Anderson." This James Anderson is supposed to be the true author of the book. Later, James Anderson turns out to be the famous American psychologist William James. Subsequently, Smith discovered that a British medium, Maude V. Underhill, had produced a manuscript which also claimed the spiritual author to be William James. Smith solved the dilemma nicely. She wrote:

> . . . why should it not be possible that many of his pupils, trained specifically in his techniques and as determined as he to spread information about life in future planes of existence (franchised, one might say, to use his

name) are the ones who communicate so widely as William James—much
like the numerous Fred Astaire dancing schools in which the great Fred
has never tapped a toe. (p. 6)

Thus, while Smith could not claim that William James was personally in
direct contact with her, she could write, simply, that her contact was "James."
It is clear that she believes that her "James" is William James.

Should one ask why his writing style from the spiritual realm differs
so markedly from his earthly writings, Smith acknowledged "that's my fault,
not his." If his unearthly perspective does not agree with that espoused
during his earthly sojourn, Smith explains ". . . why should it? He has
now a completely new perspective on existence. And he is much more
dogmatic in his opinions than he ever was in his writings on earth. He
seems to know more for sure now than he did then."

Why was Smith chosen as transmitter of these sublime truths? James
informed her that she was chosen because she had given up on philosophy
and religion and had not read in either subject since her college days. Now
this may strike one as a very odd attitude to be held by an educator and
psychologist of the caliber of William James.

In his work, *The Varieties of Religious Experience*, James stated that
he had never experienced mystical religious experiences of the type known
to Smith, even though he discussed these phenomena objectively. Smith
might argue that he has perceived new dimensions since his entry into
the spirit world. James, as a psychologist, was keenly aware of the impact
of childhood experiences, and despite Smith's rejection of her religious
upbringing, the ideas, the concepts were still part of her. Her experience
of the psychic world made real, or brought into reality, concepts buried
in her mind. The notion of the spiritual world became actualized for her
and manifest in what she believes is "real life" or reality. All of this William
James would accept—that is, he would accept the reality of her experience
for her. He would not accept her experiences as reality for anyone else.
In other words, the spiritual James that Smith claims is writing through
her is quite alien to the psychologist-philosopher William James who lectured
and wrote during his lifetime.

The experience of the spirit possession trance is widely known. Erika
Bourguignon in the Preface to *Trance, Healing, and Hallucination* (Goodman et al. 1974) notes that it has been observed in the Haitian culture,
where it plays an important role in the Afro-Catholic religion called vodu.
In Bali, the trance state is known as Belo. It has been observed in the
zar cult of Ethiopia. Within American culture, she notes the growth of charismatic movements with trance states and the speaking in tongues phenome-

non. Sects have come into being including such as the Krishna Consciousness Movement and Transcendental Meditation derived from Hinduism. The popularity of mind-altering drugs has a relationship to the religious trance states. What separates the drug experiences from those associated with religions is that the latter purport to be organized and controlled.

The Training of a Medium

Kaja Finkler (1985) reported that spiritualist healers in Mexico enter into trance states themselves and also help their patients experience mild trances. The temple services commence with the singing of hymns. During this period, the medium goes into a trance by means of heavy breathing. When the hymns stop, an invocation is pronounced and commandments are recited. The temple becomes quiet and the medium delivers the messages received from God (irradiations) in "rhythmic cadences." The messages appear to follow a set formula. Meanwhile, the congregation has been affected and has entered a mild trance state, caught up, so to speak, in the ritual. The service concludes with an orderly departure.

During the week novices are trained to enter trance states. During rhythmic recitations by the temple head, the novices sit silent and motionless, with closed eyes and hands resting, palms down, on their knees. They then listen to long exhortations pertaining to doctrine, rules of obedience, submission to the spirit world, and so on. In this ritual, trained mediums may, in trance state, call out the names of dead persons whose violent deaths resulted in perturbed souls. In this manner, the restless souls of the unhappy dead are given peace.

It is clear that during the period when the novice sits with eyes closed and in a relaxed position and listens to the rhythmic voice of the teacher he or she is being inducted into cultic thinking. There are no distractions. Concentration is not diverted by external sights. The voice of the inductor instructs and conditions the student.

Spiritualist healers believe that the medium's spirit protector can bring healing. These protectors are impersonal beings that have contact with the medium or channeler only during trances, not during the waking state. During a trance, the medium sits quietly, for any dramatic display is considered unbecoming conduct. Should a novice cry out or twist his or her body, it is assumed that he or she has been possessed temporarily by a dark spirit, which is immediately expelled on command by the trainer.

Some of these programming patterns are practiced by cults that may be religious, psychological, or political. Deprivation of social contact with the outside world, indoctrination by an authority figure, reinforcement by cult adherents are all part of the induction process. The cult promises new awareness of the self, more power for the self, new meaning to life, and some sort of magical connection with whatever supernatural, divine, or sacral power is believed to be associated with the cult. Those who deny the validity of the experience in the cult or who challenge the authority or teaching of the cult are labelled demonic. Where cult leaders encourage large gatherings of potential adherents, disbelief and questioning is discouraged and those who would disrupt the smooth flow of indoctrination are invited or compelled to leave.

Modern Channeling

Channeling has been advertised as a powerful tool for accelerating personal growth. The channeler sees himself or herself as a bridge between the tangible world of matter and the invisible world of the spirit. By entering a trance state, the channeler is supposed to be possessed by a specific spirit or personal guide, or perhaps a consortium of extraterrestrials. The channeled spirit may claim to be someone who lived on earth in another century. For example, several claim to have been Jesus; others purport to have been followers or lovers or friends of Jesus. On the other hand, the channeled entity may claim to have lived in Atlantis or be from another galaxy.

Those entities that claim to have lived on earth in another century can be challenged. For example, an entity that lived in the time of Jesus should be familiar with Aramaic and perhaps Greek. He or she should be able to augment knowledge gained from archaeological research with reliable, verifiable information about Palestine in the first century C.E. Those who claim to have lived in Egypt in the royal court at the time of the building of the Sakkara pyramid should be able to tell archaeologists where the tomb of the architect, Imhotep, is to be found. So far, no such information has been forthcoming from these entities. Indeed, just the opposite has been manifested. The psychic-directed search for ruins associated with ancient Alexandria is testimony to the waste of time, money, and energy on nonscientific intervention into the realm of archaeology, a discipline that is based on scientific research and tested methodologies. What is even more pathetic is the psychic-directed search for Atlantis, whether the searchers follow the misdirections of the so-called seer Edgar Cayce or some other misguided medium.

Those who claim to channel spirits from other galaxies or other worlds are relatively safe. Perhaps they could be questioned by competent astronomers, but because so little can be determined about planets that may be orbiting some star in space, these persons appear to be beyond challenge concerning their supposed place of origin.

An entity named Ramtha is channeled by R. Z. Knight who lives near Seattle, Washington. Ramtha claims to have lived on the island of Atlantis some 35,000 years ago. No archaeologist has located for certain the island of Atlantis. Some have suggested that the island of Santorini, now under excavation, may have been Atlantis, but to date no substantiating evidence has been found—that is, no road signs saying "You are now entering Atlantis," or more seriously, no boundary markers like those found at the site of ancient Gezer.

We do know something about humans who lived 35,000 years ago. They were our stone age (Upper Paleolithic) Cro-Magnon ancestors, who were still nomadic. But Ramtha, according to Knight, was a warrior and wise man who lived in a city! Through Knight, this primitive wonder offers guidance on everything from buying horses (from Knight, of course, at exorbitant prices) to real estate investment, to personal questions. One wonders at the rationality of those who not only contribute to Knight's millionaire fortune but who seek advice from a man from the Cro-Magnon age.

Of course it can be argued that such a person, having entered into the spiritual world, is privy to all sorts of wisdom hidden from mere mortals. However, the messages that Ramtha provides, like the messages given by other channelers, are combinations of modern pop psychology rephrased in the awkward language of the channeled being and guesses by the channeler about various matters. Recent investigation of the language patterns of so-called channeled beings demonstrates that accents and inflections are not constant and vary widely from time to time. The implication is that the language patterns are chosen by the channeler to give the impression that the entity is not familiar with modern English.

Some channelers offer to enable individuals to discover their own personal spirit guides. They teach clients how to channel, how to get in touch with their inner selves or with their personal guide. The channeler claims to contact a group of spirit guides or teachers who speak while the channeler is in a trance state. By learning how to channel, an individual can make contact with these spirits to discover his or her personal destiny and true human potential, learn how to remove personal (psychological?) blocks that inhibit growth, and find the answers to personal problems—answers that lie within each of us.

How Is It Done?

Research on the methods of training mediums in Mexico provides some clues as to how channelers can come to believe they are conduits for the voices and thoughts of those who lived in other ages or in distant galaxies. Modern psychology recognizes the reality of what have come to be known as altered states of consciousness, which are often induced by drugs. Modern psychology also recognizes the reality of self-hypnosis. Through self-hypnosis, the channeler moves into a state of altered awareness, deliberately induced, and under his or her control. With proper training and practice this state can be entered in a matter of a few seconds.

As one observes channelers as they change from who they are in present time to who they believe they are in other time, many employ deep breathing exercises. They breathe deeply, hold the breath, and expel it. They may bend over to face the floor, twist the body as they straighten, perhaps extend their arms, or make grotesque movements. These breathing and physical exercises are part of the ritual of inducing an emotion that enables moving into the altered state. Because these exercises have been practiced repeatedly over a considerable time period, what may in the beginning have taken several minutes to achieve now takes only a few seconds.

Breathing techniques are a well-known part of hypnotic induction. Clarke and Jackson (1983) explain that in yoga, for example, the expulsion of air from the lungs is done in a series of strong, sudden, explosive, rhythmic patterns controlled by the diaphragm. They quote B. Jencks, who wrote:

> In general, long, slow, deep exhalations bring about relaxation with the accompanying sensations of sinking, widening, opening up, and softening; the feelings of comfort, heaviness, warmth and moisture; the moods of patience and calmness. Inhalations evoke invigorations, tension, or levitation; and they are related to feelings of lightness, coolness and dryness, and to the moods of courage, determination and exhilaration. (p. 85)

Many channelers employ such breathing patterns. As they bend the body they focus on the floor or they relax with closed eyes. The hands or the fingers may be held in specific positions to assist in focusing. These behaviors are components of both hypnotherapy and yoga. The channeler's brief prechanneling exercises include all the facets important to self-hypnosis or to entering an altered state of consciousness. What takes place in the channeler's mind cannot be known for certain, but certainly it must include some focus on the role he or she will be enacting or on the entity that is supposed to be speaking through him or her. Whereas in directed hypnosis there is input from the hypnotist who provides guidance for entering the hypnotic state, for the channeler who has practiced his or her art the guidance is in the self-directed mental-physical acts.

As the channeler does the personal exercises, he or she imagines the role to be enacted. He or she moves into the personality of the person being dramatized. He or she believes that for that moment he or she has become this other entity. The posture, voice, attitude, personality become part of the entity as the channeler imagines it. It is as though the channeler is on the stage (which he or she certainly is) and has moved into a role.

Many years ago I participated in a play directed by an elderly woman who had been a disciple of actress Ellen Terry in England. Our makeup and costuming had to be completed at least one half hour before we went on stage—preferably longer. In that prestage interval we were permitted no scripts. We were expected to withdraw, to meditate, to move into the role we were to play. We were to become that other person. We were not to act as if we were that character, we were to become the character. Because of my own self-awareness, I was never completely at ease with the procedure and never became a serious performer.

Channelers can and do move into the roles they have selected, and through self-hypnosis may actually come to believe in the reality of what they are experiencing and portraying. They feel the part. They experience a self-induced hypnotic feeling-response to a mental image. Obviously, the most successful channelers will be those who have developed a rich fantasy life. They are people who have spent a good portion of their lives daydreaming or fantasizing or imagining. Some will have kept the fantasy part of their life secret from others, but as channelers they can indulge in their fantasies openly and with the support and approval of believers.

In self-hypnosis the individual has complete control over mental and emotional states. At some point the sincere channeler, who initially may truly have believed he or she was in touch with another dimension of time and space, might be expected to question the reality of possession by an outside entity. In other words, how long does it take before the channeler realizes that what is taking place is pure fantasy—a mental and emotional response to self-induced hypnotic imagery? It can be argued that for those committed to psychic explanations belief in the fantasy may persist and even deepen. On the other hand, many have developed a lucrative business as channelers. Thus, the desire to question one's integrity and the reality of the experience may be avoided for financial reasons. In other words, many of the channelers are acting, they are on stage. Some of them are or have been actors—including Shirley MacLaine. To many of us, when they are in the trance state, they are still acting.

Whether channeling is recognized as a form of neurotic fantasizing or as an exercise in creative imagination, the character assumed by the channeler is purely a product of his or her mind. The number and variety of characters adopted by channelers is truly amazing. In each instance, we are confronted by the individual's notion of what the fantasized entity may have been like and might say to the present world. The similarity of the messages suggests borrowing of concepts and points up the blandness of the platitudes uttered by channelers.

What Is the Message?

Because the self-hypnosis utilized by channelers provides an awareness of self-control of emotion and thought, it is not surprising to find that the teaching attributed to the disembodied spirits stresses the importance of the self. In its most simplistic form—and the messages are admittedly bland and even naive—the channelers tell their audiences that each individual is his or her own god. There is a denial of the supernaturalism of traditional Jewish and Christian thought, which postulated a divine being in charge of life, a being that existed independently of the individual. The new supernaturalism echoes the New Age emphasis on self—an emphasis that has been labelled narcissistic by some. Followers are told that they are in charge of their own lives, that they have the power to achieve. It is a message of positive thinking. The external spiritual guides are available for assistance in confronting life, they are not, like the god-power in traditional religions, in charge of life.

Of course there is the usual fortune-telling sort of emphasis wherein the channeled entity, like astrologers and tarot card readers, may advise the client concerning good and bad omens and make suggestions about everything from love affairs to investments. For example, Ramtha advised one very wealthy woman that she should buy a horse named "Mystic," which just happened to be one of the Arabian horses raised by Ramtha's channeler, J. Z. Knight. One might become uneasy about the link between Ramtha and Knight despite Knight's claim that she does not know what Ramtha advises. Knight's mind is in charge, and it is possible Knight's needs and desires could be indulged through her self-hypnotic trance state, assuming of course, that the trance state is genuine.

The Future of Channeling

One might speculate that channeling, like spiritualism, will lose its novelty and will be replaced by some other supernaturalistic claim. However, there will still be those who will cling to channelers, just as there are those who continue to consult spiritualists and astrologers. Human insecurity and the desire to make contact with the supernatural, in combination with uncritical thinking, provide a ready market for humbug. Many of those who consult with so-called psychics have moved away from church and synagogue. They are usually quite frank in stating that in the traditional religious setting they never felt that they came into contact with the divine. One young woman, raised in the church, commented that prayer was like speaking into a telephone without being sure that the person on the other end of the line had picked up the receiver. Even the introduction of charismatic sessions into traditional churches begins to pale as so-called spiritual experiences become routine. Only by closing the mind to awareness of boredom do true believers continue to attend services.

Most of us live our daily lives on a routine basis. The regularity of our behavior patterns is in accord with our work, our family habits, and with what is personally satisfying. When we make important decisions, we do so on the basis of experience or after consulting with experts. It is the insecure, the dissatisfied, and those who have been lured into thinking that there exists an occult world, who seek the services of channelers, mediums, and others claiming to have some insight into or power with regard to the supernatural—including some clergy.

References

Clarke, J. Christopher, and J. Arthur Jackson, *Hypnosis and Behavior Therapy*. New York: Springer Publishing Co., 1983.

Donnelly, Ignatius, *Atlantis; The Antediluvian World*, edited by Egerton Sykes, revised edition. New York: Gramercy Publishing Co., 1949.

Ferro, Robert, and Michael Grumley, *Atlantis, The Autobiography of a Search*. New York: Bell Publishing Co., 1970.

Finkler, Kaja, *Spiritualist Healers in Mexico*. New York: Praeger, 1985.

Goodman, Felicitas D., Jeannette H. Genney, and Esther Pressel, *Trance, Healing, and Hallucination*. New York: John Wiley & Sons, 1974.

James, William, *The Varieties of Religious Experience*. New York: Macmillan Publishing Co., 1961.

Kuhl, Curt, *The Prophets of Israel*. London: Oliver and Boyd, 1960.

Lasch, Christopher, *The Culture of Narcissim*. New York: W. W. Norton, 1979.

Ley, Willie, *Another Look at Atlantis*. New York: Bell Publishing Co., 1969.
MacLaine, Shirley, *Out On a Limb*. New York: Bantam Books, 1983.
Murphy, Gardner, and Robert Ballou, *William James on Psychical Research*. New York: Viking Press, 1960.
Napier, B. D., *Prophets in Perspective*. New York: Abingdon, 1962.
Scott, R. B. Y., *The Relevance of the Prophets*. New York: Macmillan Co., 1944
Schwartz, Stephan A., *The Alexandria Project*. New York: Dell Publishing Co., 1983.
Smith, Susy, *The Book of James*. New York: G. P. Putnam's Sons, 1974.

Astrology

We have observed his star at its heliacal rising and have come to pay him homage.

Matt. 2:2

Our ancient ancestors responded to their world. They contemplated seasonal changes. They studied the heavens. They were aware of the phases of the moon and the movement of the stars. They knew that there were cyclic patterns. They were aware that much of life responds to sunlight—from the flower that opens its petals to the sun, to humans who live life in response to the solar day. Out of their observations there arose the beginnings of the science of astronomy and belief in the nonscience of astrology.

The Stars in Ancient Egypt

In ancient Egypt the most important star was Sirius, the Dog Star. The Egyptian year began when Sirius appeared on the horizon at dawn, July 19. At that moment, the Egyptians knew that the inundation of the Nile was about to begin. This mighty river, fed by rains at its headwaters in the Mountains of the Moon in central Africa, annually swelled and overflowed to revitalize the black soil bordering its banks in Egypt. The event was heralded by festivals dedicated to the goddess Isis. The succeeding twelve months were grouped in three seasons of four-month duration known as the Inundation, the Germination, and the Warm Season.

The Egyptians knew the courses of the planets (Jupiter, Saturn, Venus,

Mars, and Mercury), which they characterized as the Tireless or the Unwearied because they moved endlessly across the skies. The circumpolar stars were called the Imperishables, and the fixed stars were known as the Indestructibles. Thirty-six Indestructibles governed the thirty-six ten-day periods (dekans) of the Egyptian lunar calendar. There was also a solar calendar by which agricultural festivals were determined.

In the Egyptians' star maps, the constellations were known by such names as the Crocodile or the Hippopotamus. They had no fear of eclipses. They conducted no rituals to give protection from the heavenly bodies. As early as the twelfth dynasty (nineteenth century B.C.E.) and perhaps earlier they cast nativity horoscopes.

The Stars in Ancient Mesopotamia

The roots of present-day astrology reach back to ancient Mesopotamia. Little is known of the ancient Sumerian studies of the heavens. The interpretation of a dream experienced by King Gudea (twenty-second century B.C.E.) instructed the monarch to build a temple in accordance with "the holy stars." Some twenty-five stars were mentioned in Sumerian texts, but it is in ancient Babylonian texts recovered from excavations that the relationship of the stars to human destiny is made clear.

In the Babylonian creation epic, *enuma elish,* it is stated that after Marduk had defeated the forces of chaos, he formed the heavens and earth. The earth was the counterpart of the heavens, so that whatever occurred in heaven would have its echo on earth. In his next act,

> He created stations for the great gods
> and formed their astral likenesses as zodiacal signs.
> Having partitioned the year and made divisions,
> He arranged three constellations for each of the twelve months.
> Having defined by constellations the days of the year,
> He established the Nebiru [Jupiter] station to mark the
> heavenly zones, so that none should err or fall short.
> On either side of it he set up the stations Enlil [the north]
>   and Ea [the south].
>
> (*enuma elish,* Tablet 5, lines 1–8)

Having made Jupiter the central star and having placed the northern sphere under the aegis of the wind god and the south under the earth god, Marduk created the moon and determined its four phases. Humans were created to perform the work that would set the gods free. They were expected to stand in awe of these divine creatures and to provide the essentials for worship in the respective temples.

Inasmuch as the stars are created before the sun and moon and humans, it is clear that in the minds of the myth writers these celestial lights had especial significance. Because they were the stations of the gods, the places where the gods dwelled, and because it was the destiny of humans to serve the gods, it is not difficult to understand how the movement and the position of the stars came to be interpreted as revealing something of the divine wills. The twelve-fold division of the zodiac was probably suggested to Babylonian astrologers by the twelve full moons appearing in successive parts of the heavens during the course of a year.

The earliest forms of Babylonian astrological divination appear to have been associated with attempts to make forecasts concerning the well-being of the king or the nation, even to the extent of predicting earthquakes and floods. Astrological omens can be traced back to the end of the third millennium B.C.E.

Unlike the Egyptians, the Babylonians did fear eclipses. For example, during a lunar eclipse, the priests were to gather at the altar of their god so that "when the light fails they should pray that catastrophe, murder, rebellion and eclipse should not approach Erech, the palace, the shrine of Eanna . . . and until the eclipse is clear they should cry out" (Saggs 1962, p. 455).

The conjunction of heavenly bodies was believed to have meaning. For example, when:

> In the night Saturn comes near the moon. Saturn is the star of the sun.
> The interpretation is: it is favorable to the king as the sun is the king's star. (Saggs 1962, p. 455)

Individual horoscopy arose when the locations of visible stars at the time of birth were noted in the belief that celestial phenomena were somehow related to a particular individual. Horoscopic astrology assumes there is a relationship between the position of the stars and an individual's moment of birth that determines both personality and behavior patterns. The divining technique can be traced back to at least the fifth century B.C.E., when it became linked to the zodiac. The practice of horoscopy entered into the Graeco-Roman world and Europe. During the second century C.E. the Greek mathematician-astronomer Ptolemy wrote *Tetrabiblios* ("Four Books") in which he discussed the influence of the stars. His writing became the textbook for astrology for more than fifteen centuries.

The Stars in Ancient Israel

In Hebrew thought the innumerable stars (Gen. 15:5; 22:17, etc.) and other celestial bodies were the creation of Yahweh (Gen. 1:14–16; Neh. 9:6; Pss. 74:16, 136:7–9; etc.) who named them (Isa. 40:26; Amos 5:8) and determined their courses (Jer. 33:25). They were set in place to separate day and night, to give light, and to serve as "signs," which clearly indicates their astrological significance (Gen. 1:14–15). Constellations are mentioned. For example, the Pleiades and Orion are referred to as creations of Yahweh (Job 9:9, 38:31; Amos 5:8). The writer of Job appears to be familiar with the Greek myth of Orion, for he mentions loosening Orion's bonds. According to this myth, Orion, a human of tremendous strength, was at death taken to the sky and bound there to become a constellation.

The zodiacal motif may lie back of the dream Joseph related to his brothers: "Listen, I have had another dream. In it the sun and moon and eleven stars were bowing down to me" (Gen. 37:9). Inasmuch as Joseph was one of the twelve sons of Jacob who were to be the founders of the twelve tribes of Israel, this pompous, egocentric dream was angrily resented by Joseph's brothers. In the zodiacal interpretation, the eleven stars symbolize the non-Joseph tribes acknowledging the supremacy of the Joseph tribe.

Zodiacal inferences discerned in Jacob's final testimony concerning his sons (Gen. 49) are unconvincing and appear to be based on selection of verses and the ignoring of others. For example, Reuben, associated with the water sign Aquarius, is described as "unstable as water" (49:4). The two brothers, Simeon and Levi, listed under Gemini, are presented together (49:5ff.). Part of Jacob's description of Judah fits Leo, Judah's sign:

> Judah is a lion's whelp, my son who has returned from the kill.
> He crouches and stretches like a lion and like a lioness,
> Who will dare to arouse him?
>
> (49.9)

Zebulun, who "dwells by the seashore" (49:13), is represented by Cancer, the crab. Issachar, the gelded ass who "rests in cattle pens," to use the New English Bible interpretation of a difficult Hebrew verse (49:14), is under the sign of Taurus, the bull. Dan, who was to "judge his people" (49:16), belongs to Libra, represented by the scales of justice. Jacob's comments about Gad, who is under Scorpio—a sign associated with sex organs, but also with death and deceit—and Naphtali, who is under Capricorn, don't seem to fit the zodiacal interpretation. Saggitarius, the archer, is supposed to be represented by Joseph, concerning whom Jacob remarked:

Hostile archer's attacked him, shot at him and harassed him,
But his bow remained unmoved, their arms were unstable.
(49:24)

Finally, the statement about Benjamin, who is associated with Aries, the ram, simply does not fit. The zodiacal interpretation does not embrace the complete statements concerning the patronymic founders of the tribes, nor do some of the references apply. Nevertheless, as we shall see, the zodiac notion was to play a significant symbolic role in the development of Judaism.

At times, stars represented angelic powers. Indeed, the poetic parallelism in the Book of Job equates the stars with the sons of Elohim:

. . . when the morning stars sang together
and all the sons of elohim shouted with joy.
(38:7)

In Psalm 148, heavenly beings, angels who are part of the heavenly host, and the sun and moon and stars are told to praise Yahweh. These celestial units were believed to have personalities.

The so-called "Song of Deborah," one of the earliest fragments of Hebrew literature (tenth–eleventh century B.C.E.), depicts the stars fighting on the side of Yahweh and the Hebrews against the Canaanite general Sisera:

The stars fought from heaven
They fought from their courses against Sisera.
(Judg. 5:20)

The Hebrew god is often labelled *Yahweh sabaoth,* "Yahweh of hosts" (Isa. 47:4, 51:15; Jer. 10:16, etc.). The hosts refer to the heavenly army under divine command. In the fictional account of the siege of Jericho, the Deuteronomic editor (seventh century B.C.E.) indicated that Yahweh's army had an angelic commander who could suddenly appear to Joshua and promise divine guidance and support so that the city could be taken by magical procedures rather than by battle (Josh. 5:13–6:7). Yahweh's heavenly host could be envisioned standing about him (1 Kings 22:19) or as stars and sun and moon. These celestial bodies were worshipped by surrounding peoples, but according to the Deuteronomic code (17:3), such worship was tabu for Israel. Nevertheless, star, sun, and moon worship was practiced throughout Israel in the latter part of the eighth century during the reign of King Hoshea (2 Kings 17:16) and throughout Judah and in the Hebrew temple in the seventh century during the reign of King Manasseh (2 Kings 21:5). In other words, the Hebrew people believed that the stars had personalities and formed part of Yahweh's army. Moreover, despite the prohibition against star worship, the Hebrews did engage in celestial worship when under Assyrian domination.

The heavenly hosts included the sun and moon. Sometimes the sun was male and sometimes female, and the term *shemesh* (sun) is given both male and female designations in the Hebrew Scriptures. There is clear evidence of a sun cult and a moon cult in ancient Israel. Clear indications of the presence of the sun cult are found in place names such as Beth-shemesh "house of the sun" (Josh. 15:10; 1 Sam. 6:9, etc.) and En-shemesh, "spring of the sun" (Josh. 15:7, 18:17). Because prohibitory laws are never formulated to protect against what does not exist, the prohibition of sun worship in ancient Israel (Deut. 4:19, 17:3) indicates that the practice was current. References to the worship of the sun during the reigns of King Manasseh of Judah and his immediate successors are found in 2 Kings 21:2–4; Jer. 8:2; Ezek. 8:16.

The Deuteronomic prohibition of moon worship indicates that the Hebrews, like their Semitic neighbors, worshipped the moon. During the reign of Manasseh, the moon cult was officially established in the Jewish temple.

The phases of the moon as calendrical guides are mentioned in Psalm 81:3, "Sound the shofar at the new moon, at the full moon, on our feast day." It has been suggested that the blowing of the ram's horn not only signaled the initiation of the feast but also served to drive away or warn away demonic powers.

There was some fear of the potentially baleful influence of both the sun and the moon. Hebrew worshippers were assured:

> Yahweh is your protector,
> Yahweh is your shade on your right hand
> The sun will not strike you by day
> nor the moon by night.
> (Psalm 121:5–6)

To what degree the Hebrews consulted astrologers can be debated. They were aware that neighboring nations called upon astrologers for omens concerning human well-being. Jeremiah's advice that the Hebrews ought not be "troubled by heavenly signs because [other] nations are troubled by them" (10:2) suggests that there were some who thought that astrological forecasting had importance. The Babylonian Jew presently called "II Isaiah" wrote a mocking indictment of Babylonian beliefs:

Perhaps the astrologers (those who chart the heavens) will save you, the star gazers, the monthly prognosticators. (Isa. 47:13)

Clearly the Jews knew of astrology and some practiced it. At the same time, astrology was not considered to be a legitimate part of Yahweh worship.

Heavenly bodies were involved in prophetic forecasts of destruction by Yahweh. For example, the prophecy concerning the downfall of Babylon in Isa. 13 states that when Yahweh initiated the desolation:

The stars in heaven and their constellations will not give light
The sun will be darkened when it rises and the moon won't shine.
(Isa. 13:10)

A similar image is used by Ezekiel in foretelling the death of the Pharaoh (32:7).

There are some biblical references to the magical manipulation of the sun and moon. In the account of Joshua's conquest of Canaan, a quotation from the lost "Book of Jashar" is mentioned:

On the day when Yahweh delivered the Amorites into Israelite hands Joshua spoke to Yahweh and he said in the presence of Israel:

Sun, stand still in Gibeon!
And moon, in the valley of Ajalon.

Then the sun stood still and the moon stayed until the nation had taken vengeance on its enemies, as this is recorded in the Book of Jashar. The sun stopped in mid-heaven and made no haste to set for about one whole day. There has never been a day like it either before or since when Yahweh listened to the voice of a man, for Yahweh fought for Israel. (Josh. 10:12–14)

Of course, the account is fictional. For either celestial body to pause or halt in its course would mean that there was a pause or stoppage in the earth's revolution, which would have destroyed the world.

Despite the nonscientific nature of this legend there are those who will argue "Couldn't God do this if he wished?" The answer must be "No," because to do this would be to violate natural laws as we know them and result in the destruction of life on earth. In addition, the whole idea trivializes whatever notion of the deity one may hold. In the discussion of the Marian cult it will be pointed out that gyrations of the sun are common hallucinatory occurrences related to this cult that are often justified and declared to be real on the basis of this fiction in the Book of Joshua.

Pictorial evidence of the importance of the zodiac in Jewish worship was found in the excavation of the synagogue at Beth Alpha. There the mosaic floor contained three panels. The first or upper panel shows a Torah shrine together with accouterments. In the lower panel the near-sacrifice of Isaac by his father Abraham is depicted. The central and largest panel contains purely astrological symbols. The central figure was a zodiacal disc portraying the familiar signs such as the crab for Cancer, called in Hebrew "Sartan," the lion for Leo, in Hebrew called "Aryeh," and so on. At the center of this disc is a sun symbol portraying a helios figure driving a sun chariot pulled by four horses. A crescent moon and stars are also shown. In the four corners of the panel are depictions of the four seasons. These panels cannot be dismissed as simple floor ornaments. They represent teaching through art just as stained glass windows and paintings in synagogues, churches, and cathedrals today serve instructional purposes. Inasmuch as the Beth Alpha synagogue is dated in the fifth century C.E., it is clear that at least up to the time of the Muslim conquest of the area zodiacal symbolism and horoscopy were part of the Jewish cult. The Jews also related the twelve tribes to the twelve zodiacal signs. For example, in the Talmud Judah, Issachar, and Zebulun corresponded, respectively, to Aries, Taurus, and Gemini (*Yalkut Shimoni,* Lev. 418).

The six-pointed star, the hexagram, the so-called "Magan David" or Star of David, was an ancient design consisting of two equilateral triangles superimposed at their centers. It was widely used by civilizations from Mesopotamia to Britain during the Bronze Age. It appeared in India during the Iron Age, and was used together with pentagrams on the seals of the tenth- to eleventh-century monarchs of Navarre. It did not become a widely accepted symbol of Judaism until the nineteenth century C.E. It was officially adopted at the first Zionist Conference in 1897 and was later incorporated into the flag of Israel. (For further discussion, see chapter on Satan.)

The Stars in Christian Scriptures

One star plays an important role in Jesus' birth story. We read in the Gospel of Matthew that *magoi*

> came from the east to Jerusalem, asking "Where is the one who has been born king of the Jews? We have observed the heliacal rising of his star and have come to pay homage to him." (Matt. 2:2)

The magoi were, according to Herodotus, a Median tribe that had lost political influence and had ended up as a sacerdotal caste within the Median empire. They were associated with the Persian religion of Zoroaster and with divination, soothsaying, dream interpretation, and astrology. Therefore, according to the gospel writer, Jesus' birth was discerned by Median astrologers, and thus astrological elements automatically became part of the Jesus tradition.

Of course, the wondrous star associated with Jesus' birth never existed. The gospel story is fiction. The gospel writer was a man of his era, and there was belief among the Jews that stars signalled important events. Every first century C.E. Jew would know Num. 24:17 and the current messianic interpretation of this passage: "A star shall come forth out of Jacob, a scepter shall arise from Israel." Many Jews would know the Testaments of Levi and Judah, written in the centuries immediately preceding the beginnings of Christianity. In both of these documents, now found in the Pseudepigrapha, messianic expectations were linked to a star (Levi 18:3; Judah 24:1). The community of Jews who lived on the shore of the Dead Sea and who were probably Essenes made the same connection. Other references can be found in the Talmud (cf. Larue 1982–1983).

In the Graeco-Roman world in which Christianity developed, it was commonly accepted that stars heralded events. Virgil, in the Fourth Eclogue, celebrating the birth of a savior of the world, identified the advent of a new star in the peaceful reign of Augustus with the god Apollo. In *de Divinatione* 1:47, Cicero noted that on the birthday of Alexander the Great, magi prophesied, on the basis of a brilliant constellation, that the destroyer of Asia was born. The listing could be continued. It is clear that in the Graeco-Roman world at large as well as in Judea it was generally believed that star portents were available to astrologers. The Matthean writer employed a literary motive common to his era.

Attempts to find astronomical support for the nativity star end in failure. Neither meteors, fireballs, comets, nova, or planetary conjunctions fit the description given in Matthew. There the star is a divine, magical star that moves across the heavens and pauses over the birthplace of Jesus. It is not visible to Jewish astrologers; only the magoi can discern it and trace its course. The account is pure fiction and is based on a belief in astrology.

In the Revelation of John, Jesus identifies himself as the bright dawn star:

I, Jesus, have sent my angel to you to testify to you concerning the churches.
I am the root and offspring of David, the bright and morning star. (22:16)

This passage is directly connected to the promise made in Rev. 2:28 to the church at Thyatira: "I will give him the dawn star." Both passages are related to the first-century Jewish interpretation of Num. 24:17. Indeed, several passages identify Jesus with light (2 Peter 1:19; Eph. 5:14; John 1:9).

Most present-day Jewish and Christian groups reject the claims of astrology. Some would go so far as to identify astrology as the work of the devil. On the other hand, many, if not most, astrologers proclaim themselves to be religious. Many claim that they are "Christian astrologers." The 1988 disclosures that Nancy Reagan and perhaps President Reagan consulted astrologers indicates the mingling of ultraconservative Christian thought and astrology in the White House. Such blending is rather common.

Although Jewish and Christian scriptures do not endorse astrology, and although Isaiah 47 contains a forthright rejection of astrology, astrological notions are present in the Bible. The second chapter of the Gospel of Matthew indicates that there were Jewish astrologers. This is not surprising inasmuch as these writings were composed between 2,000 and 3,000 years ago, in an era when astrological superstitions were widespread. However, because the Bible is interpreted as sacred writing and has been given unique authority by both synagogue and church, it indirectly lends support to beliefs in the relationship between the position of the stars and an individual's birth—a relationship that, according to astrology, affects that person for the rest of his or her life.

Modern Astrology

Our ancient ancestors experienced deep insecurity about and fear of the unknown. They were mystified by the changes of the moon and sought to explain them in terms of myths or stories about the gods. Some environmental changes were heralded by the lengthening or shortening of days; others were associated with the position of certain stars in the heavens. If certain natural events seemed to occur when the stars were in particular positions or relationships, it was natural to assume that coming events could be tied to star positions. Ancient astrology, like other attempts to fathom patterns of events in the future, fed upon fear and superstition. Once it was decided that the stars were associated with divinities, as they still are in our modern parlance (Mars, Venus, Jupiter, for example), then tremendous power was conferred on astrologers. They became important and valuable people who could foretell good and bad days, successes and failures in war and business, and were believed to be able to provide esoteric guidance for their fearful and naive followers.

Of course, the entire schema of astrology is based on a false conception of the cosmos. Astrology is geocentric. It looks at the starry heavens from

an earthbound perspective, as if the earth were the center of the universe—
which is what our ancestors believed. The notion of a small blue planet
circling a rather small star in the infinity of space does not enter into astrological calculations.

The claims of astrology rest not upon tested hypotheses but on rather
vague traditions that have become sanctified through repetition. Upon these
shaky foundations a logical superstructure has been built that can only
be shaken by examination of origins, by evaluating basic premises, and
by testing conclusions (see Kelly 1982).

Modern Western astrology has grown out of European revisions of
Babylonian concepts. During the Middle Ages the services of astrologers
were sought by royalty. Today there are thousands of astrologers who claim
to be able to "read the heavens" and to provide individuals with clues
for life and living based on natal horoscopes. From day by day reading
of these horoscopes, astrologers claim to be able to provide guidance
concerning favorable and unfavorable days, and in some cases even good
and bad hours of the day. In India, the most opportune times for business
arrangements and marriages are often determined by astrologers. In America, individuals from the White House to those engaged in the humblest
tasks either read the popular horoscopic comments published in newspapers
or consult personal astrologers.

There is, however, absolutely no scientific or any other kind of evidence
for astrological claims. Indeed, there is solid evidence that astrological predictions based on natal charts are no more accurate than chance guesses.
A test conducted by Dr. Shawn Carlson (1985) reported in *Nature* has
demonstrated conclusively that astrologers are not able to do what they
claim to do, namely match personalities with horoscopes. Carlson's test
was developed in conjunction with astrologers, and there can be no question concerning his findings. Other tests, including those by M. and F.
Gauquelin, which seemed at first to give some support to astrology, have
simply not held up. (Kelly, p. 52). In fact, the Gauquelins' study of the
notion that success could be related to birth time when Jupiter was at
or near its highest point is meaningless. Such correlations do not occur
any oftener among successful than among unsuccessful persons. Since ancient Babylonian cosmology gave Jupiter a dominant role, it is easy to
see why astrologers could associate this important planet with success. Nor
has the Gauquelin claim to have correlated athletic success with the position
of the planet Mars at birth been verified. Actually, the Gauquelins' research
discredited traditional astrology and produced results so weak as to be
essentially meaningless (Kelly 1982, pp. 64–66).

Nor have the findings of Hans Eysenck, a British psychologist, and

Jeff Mayo, a British astrologer, claiming a correlation between personality traits as measured by the Eysenck Personality Inventory and sun signs, been confirmed. The experiment, in repeated tests, proved to produce results comparable to those resulting from pure chance, and Eysenck retracted his claims of success (Kelly 1982, p. 53).

Present-day astrology preys on incredulity and fear. Blind hope and the belief that somehow someone using the position of planets at one's birth together with zodiacal charts can explain factors of personality or can warn of possible good or bad days cloud rational thinking. As astronomer Carl Sagan noted, the position of the doctor and those present in the delivery room have a greater magnetic effect on a newborn infant than all of the planets together. Most infants are born indoors where neither the light from the stars nor the moon nor the sun can reach the infant or its mother.

Irrational thinking opens the door for those who would prey on the unwary. It induces a form of magical thinking that may have made sense in ancient Babylon when the stars were considered to be the abode of the gods, but which has no place and no relevance in our modern cosmology. Belief in astrology reflects superstitious fear of the unknown. It responds to the question, "Why is this happening to me?" with answers that obscure rational thinking and encourage a dependency upon interpretations of the movements of massive agglomerates of extraterrestrial matter which appear to the naked eye as lights in the darkness of the night, and which are in reality orbs composed of the selfsame materials as our earth. How foolish to attribute power to these inanimate objects, thus reverting to the primitive thinking of those who developed these beliefs several thousand years ago.

Some people believe there is little harm done by astrological forecasts. After all, if some individuals wish to engage in magical thinking, let them. Treat their attachment as a harmless pastime. There is, however, clear evidence that astrological prediction can produce fear and panic. Some astrologers predicted that in May 1988, because of a planetary alignment, Southern California would be shaken by a gigantic earthquake. The Griffith Observatory received thousands of calls from individuals who were upset and even terrified by the prediction. Some persons moved out of state for the month. Teachers in classrooms reported heightened anxiety among their pupils.

Of course, the earthquake never happened. In the first place, there was no such alignment of stars as that promised by the seers. Second, even if there were such an alignment, it would have had absolutely no power to cause an earthquake. The predictors were wrong. They and those who publicized their forecasts were socially irresponsible and unethical. They disrupted lives—emotionally, physically, and financially.

It is time for synagogues and churches to take a strong stand against astrology. They should begin by admitting that their scriptures not only provide a possible basis for belief in astrology but also reflect the nonscientific worldview of ancient Jews and Christians, including naive notions concerning the importance of stars as heralds of important events. The Christmas star has no basis in reality and this fact should be publicly recognized by churches. Rabbis need to inform their congregations that echoes of star worship can be heard in the Jewish salute "Mazel tov." It does not mean "congratulations" when spoken at a wedding, it is a wish for a happy horoscope, for *mazel* means "constellations" and *tov* is the Hebrew word for "good." By their very silence concerning the presence of astrology in the Scriptures, which affects present-day beliefs, both synagogue and church give token acceptance to the validity of astrology. Perhaps they could take a cue from some of the major newspapers, such as *The Los Angeles Times,* that now print horoscopes on the comic pages. The implication is that star charts are presented for amusement and should not be taken seriously.

References

Carlson, Shawn, "A Double-Blind Test of Astrology," *Nature,* No. 318, December 5, 1985, pp. 419–423.

Dean, Malcolm, *The Astrology Game.* New York: Beaufort Books, 1980.

Eysenck, H., "Astrology: Science or Superstition?" *Encounter,* December 1979, p. 85.

Gauquelin, M., and F. Gauquelin, "Series B Hereditary Experiment," *Laboratoire d'Étude des Relations entre Rythmes Cosmiques et Psychophysiologiques.* Paris, 1970, Vols. 1–6.

Gauquelin, M., "Profession and Heredity Experiments: Computer Re-analysis and New Investigation of the Same Material," *Correlation,* 1924, Vol. 4, pp. 8–24.

Gauquelin, M., "Reappraisal of Planetary Heredity in 50,000 Family Data, New Birthdata Series," *Laboratoire d'Étude des Relations entre Rythmes Cosmiques et Psychophysiologiques,* Paris, 1984, Vol. 2.

Heidel, Alexander, *The Babylonian Genesis.* Chicago: University of Chicago Press, 1942, 1951.

Kelly, I. W., "Astrology, Cosmobiology and Humanistic Astrology," in *Philosophy of Science and the Occult,* edited by P. Grin. Albany: State University of New York Press, 1982, pp. 47–68.

Larue, Gerald A., "Astronomy and the 'Star of Bethlehem,' " *Free Inquiry,* Vol.

3, No. 1, 1982–3, pp. 25–28.

Mayo, J., O. White, and H. Eysenck, "An Empirical Study of the Relation Between Astrological Factors and Personality," *Journal of Social Psychology,* 1978, pp. 229–236.

Morenz, Siegfried, *Egyptian Religion.* Ithaca, N.Y.: Cornell University Press, 1973.

Murray, Margaret A., *The Splendor That Was Egypt.* New York: Hawthorn Books, 1963.

Saklofske, D., I. Kelly, and D. McKerracher, "An Empirical Study of Personality and Astrological Factors," *Journal of Psychology,* 1982, p. 275.

Saggs, H. W. F., *The Greatness That Was Babylon.* New York: Hawthorn Books, 1962.

Speiser, E. A., "The Creation Epic," in *Ancient Near Eastern Texts Relating to the Old Testament,* edited by James B. Pritchard. Princeton, N.J.: Princeton University Press, 1950, pp. 60–72.

Trueheart, Charles, "Anticipating Nancy's Book, Astrologer Reaffirms Stake in Reagan's Stardom," *The Los Angeles Times,* September 15, 1989 (reprint from the *Washington Post*).

White, J. E. M., *Ancient Egypt.* New York: Dover, 1970.

Extraterrestrials—Angels and Other Heavenly Creatures

He dreamed of a ladder resting on the earth with its top in heaven, and angels of Elohim were ascending and descending on it.

Gen. 28:12

Long before the recent interest in extraterrestrials, the Bible recorded visits to earth by creatures of another world. Some of these nonearth creatures were called "angels" and they performed a variety of services in the name of the Hebrew and later the Christian deity.

The Hebrew word for "angel" is *malek* and it means "messenger." In New Testament Greek, the term *angelos* also means "messenger." An angel is thus a messenger sent by the deity.

It should be noted that not all ancient Jews believed in angels. The author of the Acts of the Apostles noted that "the Sadducees say that there is no resurrection, nor angel, nor spirit" (23:8). The statement is puzzling. The Sadducees were temple priests and their theology was based on the same Scriptures used by the Pharisees and Jesus. Perhaps they rejected the oral interpretations of the Pharisees concerning angels. Perhaps they believed that angelic visitations were a thing of the past. The sixth-to-fifth-century additions to the Torah, the so-called Priestly or "P" materials, unlike the earlier Torah writings, contain no mention of angels (for P passages, see Larue 1968, pp. 355–363). As inheritors of that tradition, it is possible that the Sadducees were the skeptics of their era—at least with regard to angels.

The Heavenly Scene

Angels were among the extraterrestrial beings who lived in heaven. According to the Bible, heaven, the dwelling place of God and the angels, was located above the blue hemispheric dome that arches over the flat earth. In biblical times, the sky was believed to be solid to prevent the waters above the firmament from inundating the earth (Gen. 1:6-7, 7:11, 8:2). From heaven, God spoke to his people and dispatched his thunderbolts. When he visited the Jews, he "descended" from heaven to earth. Jacob's dream suggests that the Hebrews thought that angels commuted between heaven and earth by means of a ladder connecting the two environs (Gen. 28:12).

The deity did not live in isolated splendor. Like earthly rulers, he had his court composed of a variety of heavenly beings. Indeed, the divine precinct was believed to house a multitude of nonearthly creatures. For example, Yahweh had an angelic army. When Jacob encountered angels he said, "This is Elohim's army!" (Gen 32:2). The prophet Micaiah told King Ahab: "I saw Yahweh sitting on his throne and all the host of heaven standing beside him on his right hand and on his left" (1 Kings 22:19). The heavenly host includes the heavenly armies that Yahweh could use to fight for his people (cf. Josh. 5:13-15). The heavenly host formed the choir at the birth of Jesus (Luke 2:13). At his arrest Jesus claimed that he could appeal to God and "twelve legions of angels" would be dispatched to rescue or defend him (Matt. 26:53).

Yahweh's throne was guarded by four weird zoomorphic beings (Ezek. 1:5, 10; Rev. 4:6-8). In the report of Ezekiel's vision they are described as "having the likeness of four living creatures" (1:5) and, the description continues,

> they had human form, but each had four faces and each had four wings. Their legs were straight, and the bottom of their feet were like calves' hooves, and they glistened like burnished bronze. Beneath their wings on their four sides were human hands. The wings and faces of the four were like this: each one's wings touched the other's and each one went straight forward without pivoting. As for a description of their faces: each had a man's face in front, a lion's face on the right side, an ox's face on the left side and an eagle's face at the back. So much for their faces. Their wings were spread out above and one pair touched the wings of another and one pair covered their bodies [genitals]. (Ezek. 1:5-11)

What were these weird creatures that moved with lightning speed? Ezekiel called them "cherubim" (10:1,20), but they are a far cry from the chubby little winged figures that appear in medieval religious art. Ancient cherubim were the griffin-like figures flanking the royal throne depicted on the sacrophagus of King Hiram of Byblos. They were the huge winged beasts with human faces that protected royal entryways in Assyria, but which now grace the British Museum. In the Bible, they were the monsters that prevented humans from reentry to the Garden of Eden (Gen. 3:24). They were also the gold-plated, carved, wooden figures supporting the divine throne of the Hebrew god who was believed to be invisibly seated between them on the ark of the covenant in Solomon's temple. Each was fifteen feet high with a fifteen-foot wingspan (1 Kings 6:23–28). Cherubim images formed part of the decorative motifs on the wheeled temple carts (1 Kings 7:29,36). Yahweh rode upon cherubim through the heavens (Ps. 18:10).

In the Book of the Revelation, the description of the four living creatures (*zoa*) that flanked the divine throne reflects borrowing from Ezekiel's cherubim. They were:

> covered with eyes in the front and back. The first living creature was like a lion, the second like an ox, the third had a human face and the fourth was like an eagle in flight. Each of the four living creatures had six wings and were covered with eyes both inside and out. (4:7–8)

The writer of Revelation altered certain details of the Ezekiel apparition. Each creature has a single visage, and each has six wings—a detail taken from the description of the seraphim in Isaiah's vision (Isa. 6:2).

The seraphim, mentioned only by Isaiah of Jerusalem, are the six-winged figures that surrounded the throne of Yahweh. The prophet does not indicate how many of these creatures there were, but there were more than one. They are related to the seraph serpents that attacked the wandering Hebrews in the Exodus story (see chapter on Serpents).

Twenty-four elders, clad in white robes and each wearing a golden crown, are supposed to be seated on thrones around the deity (Rev. 4:4). It is surmised that they are meant to represent the twelve tribes of Israel and the twelve apostles. The seven spirits mentioned in Rev. 1:4, 4:5 are not really identified. Theodor Gaster's suggestion that they represent archangels seems more reasonable (Gaster 1952, p. 134) than more mystical suggestions, for example, that they are "a symbolic reference to the manifold energies of the Spirit of God" (Metzger 1965, p. 491).

The biblical image of heaven depicts a noisy and chaotic environment of strange creatures, endless repetitive activity, and a cacophony of choruses:

And the four living creatures, each of them with six wings, are full of eyes all around and within, and day and night they never cease to sing,

> Holy, holy, holy, is the Lord God Almighty who
> was and is and is to come.

And whenever the living creatures give glory and honor and thanks to him who is seated on the throne, who lives for ever and ever, the twenty-four elders fall down before him who is seated on the throne and worship him who is for ever and ever, they cast their crowns before the throne, singing

> You are worthy, our Lord and God,
> to receive glory and honor and power
> for you created all things and through your will
> they existed and were created.
>
> (Rev. 4:8–11)

This tumultuous scene with songs endlessly repeated over and over, with crowns rolling before the divine presence only to be recovered and thrown down again at the next chorus, is reminiscent of a Keystone Cops comedy. The frenzied ritual is augmented when the author introduces the lamb of God into the heavenly court. At that moment, the elders, each holding a harp and golden bowls containing Christian prayers, fall down before the lamb and sing a new song (Rev. 5:8–10). Their actions prompt thousands of thousands of angels to recite in loud voices: "Worthy is the Lamb who was slain, to receive power and wealth and wisdom and might and honor and glory and blessing." One can only imagine the scene!

What Do Angels Do?

Angels appear to have had many roles. Some, as we have noted, formed the choirs that fed the ego needs of God. Some were indeed messengers. When Abraham was about to sacrifice his only son Isaac, an angel sent by God intervened (Gen. 22:11). An angel appeared to Moses in the burning bush on Mount Horeb (Exod. 3:2). An angel was sent to protect and guide the Hebrews during their wilderness wanderings (Exod. 23:20). Often angels appeared in dreams to convey a message (Matt. 1:20). At times they appeared in person, and although their form is not described, the assumption is that it was human (Luke 1:11).

Some were protectors. A psalmist could declare that angels were charged with guarding faithful Jews: "He [Yahweh] will give his angels charge of you to guard you in all your ways" (Ps. 91:11). Angels could be ministering agents. When the prophet Elijah was in danger of dying from thirst and starvation in the wilderness, he was sustained by food and water provided by an angel (1 Kings 19:5–8). After Jesus' temptation in the wilderness, angels ministered to his needs (Matt. 4:11; Mark 1:13). They could intervene in human affairs to help solve problems, as the angel Raphael did in the story of Tobit. They could rescue humans as the angels rescued Daniel in the lions' den by shutting the lions' mouths (Dan. 6:22). Peter was released from prison by an angel (Acts 12:7–10). An angel rolled away the stone that blocked Jesus' tomb (Matt. 28:2–3).

Angels could be sent on destructive missions. When David angered Yahweh by taking a census of the people, Yahweh presented the king with a choice of three punishments. David chose a three-day pestilence which resulted in the death of 70,000 men (2 Sam. 24:1–15). The devastation had not yet reached Jerusalem:

And when the angel extended his hand toward Jerusalem, Yahweh repented of the evil and said to the angel who was delivering the destruction to the people: "That's enough. Withdraw your hand." (2 Sam. 24:16)

In the fifth century rewriting of this fiction, the Chronicler described the angel as holding a sword extended over Jerusalem (1 Chron. 21:15–16). Yahweh sent an angel to kill 185,000 Assyrian soldiers (Isa. 37:36). These angels simply carried out the commands of their master, Yahweh.

Yahweh's final destructive act in freeing the Hebrews from bondage in Egypt resulted in the killing of all Egyptian firstborn children and animals (Exod. 11:4–5). The Hebrew families were spared because of the magic of lamb's blood smeared on the lintels and doorposts of Hebrew homes:

Yahweh will move through to kill the Egyptians, and when he sees the blood on the lintel and the two doorposts, Yahweh will pass over the door and will not permit the destroyer to enter your homes and kill you. (Exod. 12:23, cf. 12:7)

Although the announcement of this act to the Hebrews indicated that Yahweh would be the killer, it is clear that a "destroyer" would be the agent of death. Most commentators recognize the "destroyer" as an angel acting on Yahweh's behalf. Martin Noth has suggested that the term reflects an older tradition in which " 'destroyer' will have been the original name for the demonic power which the Passover sacrifice had the effect of keeping away" (Noth 1962, p. 92). The unknown Christian writer of Hebrews gave the "destroyer" of the Exodus account a separate and perhaps demonic identity (Heb. 11:28). The apostle Paul wrote that the "destroyer" was the destructive element in the wilderness sojourn (1 Cor. 10:10, cf. Num. 16:41,49, 21:5–6, 25:1–18) and seems to refer to a demonic power or perhaps an angel.

An abundance of angelic manifestations are presented in both Jewish and Christian Scriptures. Angels played important roles in the Jesus story. Jesus believed in angels (Luke 12:8–9). His mother Mary and his father Joseph were each visited by angels who announced his conception (Luke 1:26–31; Matt. 1:18–21). His birth was proclaimed to shepherds by an angel and an angelic choir (Luke 2:9–15), who on completing the assignment returned to heaven. After Jesus' death, an angel confronted Mary Magdalene when she visited his tomb (Matt. 28).

Apparently the angels were organized. There was an angelic council (Ps. 89:7). Jesus made reference to this group (Luke 12:8–9). Some of the angels had specific identities and functions. For example, Michael was the angel in charge of the Jews (Dan. 10:13, 12:1). Raphael was the angel who assisted Tobias (Tobit 3:17, 5:5, 12:15). He claimed to be "one of the seven holy angels who present the prayers of the saints and enter into the presence of the glory of the Holy One" (Tobit 12:15). Clearly, by the time Tobit was composed, the Jews had elevated Yahweh to the level that direct contact with the deity by ordinary humans was denied and, as in a modern business executive's office, the divine presence was not to be intruded upon directly by individual prayers from his people but only by way of intermediaries—in this case, angels. The Book of Revelation states that the elders who occupied thrones in the presence of the deity held bowls that contained the prayers of the saints, which were presented in the form of incense (Rev. 5:9). Gabriel, who interpreted Daniel's vision (Dan. 8:15–16) and announced the birth of John the Baptizer, stated that he stood in "the presence of God" (Luke 1:11–20).

One thing angels did not do was have sexual relations. They were, according to Jesus, nonsensuous beings (Matt. 23:30; Luke 20:34–36). However, some Jews considered the "Sons of God" who had intercourse with human women to be angels who became "fallen angels," the result of whose behavior caused the flood (Enoch 6–9).

The Appearance of Angels

In most manifestations, angels took the form and shape of humans. Abraham entertained angels without being aware of their divine identity (Gen.

18). Angels looked like men when they visited Abraham's nephew, Lot (Gen. 19:1). The commander in chief of Yahweh's angelic armies appeared to Joshua at Jericho in the form of a man (Josh. 5:13–14). Jacob wrestled with an angel at wadi Jabbok (Gen. 32:24–25).

Sometimes when angels were recognized they caused terror. Zecharias, the father of John the Baptist, was frightened and upset when visited by the angel Gabriel (Luke 1:12). Mary, Jesus' mother, was also frightened by Gabriel (Luke 1:26–29). The soldiers guarding Jesus' tomb were terrified by an angel (Matt. 28:4), as were the women who came to the tomb (Luke 24:5). Sometimes they appeared in a less frightening manner in dreams (Matt. 1:20, 2:13). No descriptions of the heavenly visitors are given in these encounters.

The Worship of Angels

When John the writer of Revelation fell down before an angel to worship him, he was told:

> You must not do that! I am just a fellow servant with you and your brothers who bear their testimony to Jesus. Worship God. (Rev. 19:9, 22:8–9)

Despite the warning, the Roman Catholic Church has venerated angels from the fifth century. In 493 C.E., an apparition of St. Michael on Mount Garganus occasioned the feast of St. Michael, which is observed in Roman Catholicism on September 29th. This same angel appeared again in France in 706. In *A Catholic Dictionary,* edited by Addis and Arnold, it is noted that the Feast of Angel Guardians was instituted under Paul V, and in 1923 the Feast of St. Gabriel (March 24) and St. Raphael (October 24) were extended to the Universal Church (p. 24). Churches are named after angels promoted to sainthood by the church. Regamey (1960) points out that the veneration of angels is of a lower order than the veneration of God (p. 119). But worship is worship and angels are worshipped within Catholicism.

Angels and the Modern Scene

One might think that references to angelic beings in a document that originated some 2,000 to 3,000 years ago might be thought of now as ancient folklore that has been rendered meaningless by modern science. On the contrary, angels have been attested as real by religious leaders ranging from the Pope to Billy Graham to televangelists. An August 7, 1987, UPI report in *The Los Angeles Times* stated that Pope John Paul II told a crowd of 8,000 pilgrims and tourists that angels are pure spirits who have no bodies and are therefore immortal. He went on to say,

> The angels are gifted with an intellect and free will, like man, but to a greater degree than him. Angels therefore are personal beings and, inasmuch, are also made in the image and likeness of God.

The Pope listed the nine different categories or "choirs" of angels as developed by the medieval church: seraphim (the highest order), cherubim (the second order), thrones, powers, dominions, virtues, principalities, angels, and archangels. Obviously, because angels were said to have existed in biblical times, they continue to exist today.

Because the church continues to promote belief in the existence of angels, there are millions who accept the belief as having a solid basis in fact. When I was a child, my Roman Catholic father placed a framed picture of a guardian angel over my bed. Whether the picture was supposed to have some protective power or whether it was simply an educational tool or merely a wall ornament, I do not know. The winged, robed figure of a long-haired, clean-shaven, youthful angel, bending with a protective outstretched hand over the figure of a child poised at the brink of a cliff and reaching for a flower, was supposed to convey the idea of divine protection through a guardian angel. As a child, I could never understand why this supposed guardian let the infant get into such a precarious and life-threatening position in the first place. Did the protective angelic beings only function when the person was in a desperate situation? Did they not seek to help the person avoid such crises? The picture was less than persuasive. Nevertheless, the churches still teach the presence of guardian angels.

Modern Extraterrestrials

One might argue that if angels, as creatures from another dimension who have visited earth, are to be accepted as real, there is no reason to doubt recent claims of encounters with aliens from outer space. In other words, the Bible serves to authenticate the reality of space creatures.

Modern science has speculated that it is possible that in some distant galaxy life-forms have developed and evolved over millions of years to produce creatures that are more advanced scientifically, and perhaps in other ways, than humans. If these putative creatures that exist on planets millions of light years away could perfect a means to traverse the immense distance from their home to the earth, they might display some interest in the life-forms existing here. These speculations are nothing more than conjectures. At this moment, despite science fiction and mathematical calculations concerning the reasonableness of such a possibility, there is absolutely no evidence of any developed life-forms existing elsewhere in the cosmos. They may be there, but we do not know of them.

Nevertheless, there are those who claim to have had encounters with creatures from outer space—encounters that can be recognized as updated versions of ancient space legends. These creatures usually come in a streamlined, wonderfully mechanized space vehicle (compare the vehicle described by Ezekiel). As in the biblical stories, the nonearth creatures often have characteristics similar to but not identical with those of humans. Ancient visitors were winged; modern space creatures are little green men or monstrous giants with tiny heads, as in the version provided by Russian schoolchildren. Ancient astro-figures could speak the language of humans; modern aliens communicate through thought-transference. The angels had supernatural powers; the spacemen of today have superior weapons and sometimes possess forms of destructive laser energy that emanates from their eyes or finger tips (at least in the films!).

Sightings of unidentified flying objects, assumed by some observers to be vehicles from outer space, have on investigation proved to be weather balloons, fireballs, meteors, and so on. None have been identified as bearing space creatures; none were built on or have come from another galaxy or planet. Modern sightings are in the same literary category as biblical sightings: fiction.

References

Addis, William, and Thomas Arnold, eds., *A Catholic Dictionary,* 16th edition. London: Routledge and Kegan Paul, 1957.

Atwater, Donald, ed., *A Catholic Dictionary (The Catholic Encyclopaedic Dictionary).* New York: The Macmillan Company, 1958.

Broderick, Robert C., ed., *The Catholic Encyclopedia.* Nashville: Thomas Nelson, Inc., 1976.

Carr, Wesley, *Angels and Principalities.* Cambridge: Cambridge University Press, 1981.

Gaster, Theodor H. "Angel," *The Interpreter's Dictionary of the Bible.* New York: Abingdon, 1962, Vol. I, pp. 128–134.

Larue, Gerald A., *Old Testament Life and Literature.* Boston: Allyn and Bacon, 1968.

Metzger, Bruce M., "Annotations on Revelation." *The Oxford Annotated Bible with Apocrypha,* New York: Oxford University Press, 1965, pp. 1491–1512.

Noth, Martin, *Exodus,* trans. by J. S. Bowden. Philadelphia: Westminster Press, 1962.

"Pope Says Angels' 'Intellect Exceeds Humans,' " *The Los Angeles Times,* Thursday, August 7, 1987.

Regamey, Pie-Raymond, *What is an Angel?* trans. by Dom Mark Pontifex. New York, Hawthorn Books, 1960.

Satan—God's Cosmic Enemy

Then Jesus said, 'Go away, Satan!'

Matt. 3:10

Satan is real. According to the Pope, Billy Graham, Oral Roberts, Jerry Falwell, and a host of other well known religionists, the devil and his cohorts are at work in our society. Sometimes this conviction is dramatized. Roman Catholic priests perform exorcisms. Televangelist faith-healers claim they are expelling Satan. When young women in Mexico and Central America reach their fifteenth birthday, they may be involved in a celebration known as Quince Annos. Part of the ceremony calls for the young women to "renounce Satan." Hollywood productions echo such religious customs. During the baptismal scene in *The Godfather,* the child's godfather swears "to renounce Satan and his works." In the film *The Exorcist,* a young girl is possessed by demonic forces and in the exorcism rituals the priest challenges Satan.

Clergy use Satan as an explanation of natural occurrences. When the tragic earthquake occurred in Mexico City in 1985, The Rev. Jess Moody, pastor of First Baptist Church of Van Nuys, California, placed an ad in the Saturday, Oct. 5, 1985, edition of *The Los Angeles Times* in which he stated that the earthquake was not to be explained by reference to God or to science ("physics") but that he believed that "Satan did it." It is clear that in these closing years of the twentieth century there are millions who believe in Satan and the devil and there are clergy who encourage this belief.

Who is Satan?

Satan is the "evil one," the power of darkness, the anti-God, a fallen angel and, according to Protestant reformers like Luther and Calvin, "the Prince of this world." According to some interpretations, it was Satan's temptation of Eve in the Garden of Eden that resulted in the stain of original sin on all humans. According to others, Satan was once in the court of Heaven but he rebelled against divine authority and was ejected. Together with other rebel angels he established a kingdom in Hell. Whereas Heaven constitutes light and joy and peace, Hell represents darkness and pain and punishment. Satan is the devil, the embodiment of evil. It is he and his fellow demonic angels who tempt humans and bring evil and sickness and disruption into society. He is God's cosmic antagonist.

Often he is portrayed as a serpent. Sometimes he has a goat face, with horns, and lips curled back in a frightening grimace. He has cloven hooves rather than feet. He is depicted with a tail and sometimes he carries a pitchfork. It is assumed that he can take many forms, possess individuals, and exert commanding power in the lives of individuals, families, or groups both large and small who acknowledge him as lord or who simply unwittingly come under his spell. Satan is the symbol of evil, the embodiment of destructive power.

How Do We Know of Him?

The source for belief in Satan is the Bible and other religiously authoritative materials related to the Bible including the Koran, Mormon scriptures, the writings of Mary Baker Eddy and other Christian Scientists, the essays of Ellen B. White and other Seventh Day Adventists, Jehovah Witness pamphlets, and so on. In other words, the source of knowledge of Satan is the Bible, writings that draw from biblical notions, and most of all the clergy of the various religious groups that believe in the authority of biblical teachings. Our next major question is: "How did the idea of the devil as a personality originate, and what does the Bible really say?"

Where is Satan?

Satan is everywhere, according to those who believe in him. He has been present from the beginning. As we shall see, he was in the Garden of Eden with Adam and Eve, and he is alive and functioning in our present culture.

His headquarters are located in Hell, which in Christian thinking is the opposite of Heaven. But where is Hell?

Hell is in the netherworld, which the Greeks called Hades and the Hebrews called Sheol, the place of the shadowy dead. Sheol was described as the final meeting place of all the living (Job 30:23) and pictured as a "pit" or a "ditch" (Ps. 30:10; Ezek. 28:8) in the depth of the earth (Deut. 32:22), a place of gloomy darkness (Job 10:21f) where inhabitants are cut off from Yahweh (Pss. 6:5; 88:4–5). Like an insatiable monster, it awaits with open jaws to receive the living (Prov. 27:20, 30:16). In other words, in Hebrew thought, Sheol was the grave, and at no point is it a place of eternal punishment.

The intertestamental period was a time of transition in which apocalyptic notions, derived from Iranian theology, were accepted by some Jewish sects. The Book of Enoch referred to a fiery abyss or valley in which Azazal and guilty angels were punished (Enoch 10:1–16, 18:11–16, 90:20–27). By the time Christian writings appeared the abyss was linked to Gehenna, a term which is simply the Greco-Latin form of the Hebrew word for "valley of Hinnom." The Hinnom valley is a ravine south of Jerusalem in which cultic rites to foreign deities including the sacrificial cremation of children had taken place (2 Kings 23:10; Jer. 7:32, 32:35). With the evolution of the idea of Satan as the devil, Sheol and Gehenna were linked to become something more than the grave and a valley and emerged as Hades or Hell (Rev. 20:14).

Jesus taught that the wicked went to Hell (Hades) where they were tormented by unquenchable fire (Matt. 13:41–42; Mark 9:42; Luke 16:23–24). Indeed, in the afterlife Jesus himself was to pronounce the curse that dispatched the unrighteous to the fires of Hell (Matt. 25:41). For modern Christians, Hell represents the headquarters of Satan—his kingdom, an idea made most popular by Dante and Milton. The fact that the core of the earth is molten may coincide with the notion of a fiery pit below the surface into which the evil are flung, but the geology does not accord with the simplistic theology.

The Presence of Evil

Awareness of the presence of evil, of that which is destructive in human society and in human personality, can be seen in our earliest written records, where the sophistication of the writing suggests a long history of contemplation about the subject before ideas were recorded. Our ancient ancestors asked the questions "how?" and "why?" They sought explanations for what happened in their lives. Not having the advantage of modern science, they explained misfortune supernaturally. When floods or storms destroyed homes, or when rains failed to come and crops died, when plagues devastated villages, or when death struck through accidents or disease, because they had personalized and divinized natural events, they understood such tragedies as behavioral reactions of supernatural powers, that is, as acts of the gods. They reasoned that because humans hurt one another, therefore, when injuries resulted from natural causes, there must be some personality behind the experience.

Temple storytellers recounted mythical adventures of deities. Floods, whether local or universal, were acts of angry gods. When life-sustaining rains did not fall, it was because the rain god was disaffected from the people. For example, Canaanite myth explained that during the dry season of the year, Ba'al, the god of rain and fertility, was in the underworld in the clutches of Mot, the god of death. The coming of the fall rains signified Ba'al's resurrection. If the rains failed, it was because Mot continued to hold Ba'al captive. Something had gone wrong in the seasonal cycle and somehow humans were involved. The situation could only be alleviated through cultic rites and sacrifices. Such a belief system lay behind the Mount Carmel contest of the priests of Ba'al with the Yahwist prophet Elijah to determine which god produced rain (2 Kings 18:25–29).

Behind all events, both favorable and unfavorable, were supernatural forces that had to be pleased and appeased. Such a belief system, affecting personal, business, and national fortunes, gave great power to the clergy as transmitters of the sacred myths and interpreters of the will of the gods. The myths revealed that gods, like humans, expressed themselves emotionally. Like humans, they could become angry and throw temper tantrums, and their fits of pique could result in the extermination of human populations. So long as there were a multitude of gods, and these gods had personalities reflecting the emotions found among humans, unfavorable natural events and social conditions could be attributed to them.

There was no devil, no single personification of evil as such, but evil was considered to result from the complex personalities of the gods in conjunction with the activities of malignant spirits. Artists depicted divine beings in grotesque and frightful forms combining human and animal features. Assyrian priests wore ceremonial garb consisting of bird or animal masks, wings, and even clawed feet. The dragon figure known as the zigrush that adorned the walls of the Ishtar gate in Nebuchadnezzar's Babylon symbolized Marduk, the protective patron god of the city. Monstrous winged animal forms with human faces known as "kerubim" (cherubim) guarded the entry to Assyrian palaces. They can be seen today in the British Museum in London. Hittite monsters were winged lions with twin animal and human heads. Egyptian sphinxes presented human faces on leonine bodies. The goddess Hathor sometimes had cow's ears and sometimes the head of a lioness. The god Horus had a hawk's head, and Thoth could be a baboon or have an ibis head. Nightmarish figures abounded in the ancient world (Pritchard, *Ancient Near Eastern Texts in Pictures,* pp. 212ff.). Supernatural figures were more than human ānd not simply animal. They had frightening dimensions that could only be hinted at through art and in ritual drama. Even protective city and national gods like Marduk had terrifying potentials.

The purely demonic was represented in figures like Pazuzu, whose image was used to symbolize ancient evil in the movie *The Exorcist.* But Pazuzu was not the devil. Pazuzu was a horned, winged, scaly man with a leonine face. Archaeologist M. E. L. Mallowan described Pazuzu's image found on a plaque as depicting:

> an evil genius who brought fever and sickness; he was sometimes referred to as the son of the South Wind, a hot feverish blast which brings depression in its wake. The feathered, winged body of this horrible creature . . . is composed of the tail of a scorpion, a phallus in the shape of a snake's head, and the feet of a bird of prey. (Mallowan 1966, vol. I, p. 118)

Pazuzu's equally frightening mate was Lamashtu, who possessed "a lion's head, human hands, a feathered body and bird's feet." The man from whom she was to be exorcised (depicted in a plaque) was, in Mallowan's estimation, "suffering from *delerium tremens* in the last stages of a sickness which verges on madness" (vol. I, p. 118). Terrifying, malignant powers in the world of our ancient forebears often represented evils that we, today, recognize as sickness and disease and that through medical science we seek to control and eliminate.

Evil in the Bible

The earliest biblical sources, recorded between the tenth and sixth centuries B.C.E., portrayed Yahweh as the author of both good and evil. Because Yahweh had not yet been conceived of as a universal deity concerned with all humankind, his focus was on his own people. The Hebrews alone received his blessing and experienced his wrath. He could destroy an enemy to help them, or withdraw his support and thus use an enemy to punish and destroy his own followers.

Like other gods in the ancient world, Yahweh was subject to fits of anger in which he expressed the demonic or destructive side of his personality. Consequently, individuals, entire families, clans, and tribes suffered when they violated Yahweh's will. Cain was destined to become a nomadic gypsy because in jealous anger he killed his brother Abel whose flesh offering Yahweh preferred to Cain's vegetarian presentation (Gen. 4:11-16; Gen. 4:17 reflects a different, later tradition). Hebrew temple mythology taught that the Canaanites became enslaved to the Hebrews, not only through Hebrew infiltration and settlement or conquest, but primarily because Ham, the Canaanites' ancestor, "saw his father [Noah] naked," thereby offending Yahweh and provoking the curse of subjugation (Gen. 9:22-25). Lot's wife was transformed into a pillar of salt because she disobeyed the warning given by Yahweh's angelic emissaries and turned and looked back at the burning cities of Sodom and Gomorrah (Gen. 19:17, 26). Judah's son Er was killed by Yahweh, who judged him to be wicked, and Yahweh killed Judah's second son, Onan, for refusing to fulfill the law of the levirate (Gen. 38). David's illegitimate son by Bathsheba was killed by Yahweh because David had committed murder and adultery (2 Sam. 12:13-14). Yahweh caused famine and drought when some of his followers turned to the worship of the rival god Ba'al (1 Kings 17). The Deuteronomic priests could threaten national blessing or disaster depending upon the degree to which the people obeyed Yahweh's rules (Deut. 28). The destruction of the northern Kingdom of Israel by Assyria was attributed to an act of Yahweh (2 Kings 17:18). Each experience of hardship or destruction, each individual or national disaster, was the act of Yahweh.

Nor was the disaster always the result of sin or disobedience of divine commands. For personal reasons Yahweh "closed Hannah's womb," preventing her from bearing a child (1 Sam. 1:5). Yahweh made Saul vulnerable by night by causing a deep sleep to fall on him (1 Sam 26:12). Yahweh dispatched a lying spirit to confound King Ahab (1 Kings 22:20-22). As Amos, the eighth century B.C.E. prophet, put it: "Does evil befall a city unless Yahweh has done it?" (3:6).

Natural disasters could be interpreted and utilized for religio-political advantages. King David's clergy claimed that a three-year famine stemmed from "blood-guilt" engendered by David's predecessor, King Saul. Because many Hebrews disliked David and continued to be loyal to Saul, so long as any of Saul's family were alive, David feared the possibility of insurrection to reinstate the line of Saul. At that moment all of Saul's sons by his wives were dead. David used a theological interpretation of the famine as a basis for exterminating Saul's sons born to his concubine Rizpah, and the grandsons born to Saul's daughter Merab (2 Sam. 21). One grandson, Mephibosheth, was spared because he was lame (2 Sam. 4:4) and was thus no threat to David, since only a physically perfect person could assume the throne. Yahweh could dispatch evil spirits to bring discord: "And Elohim sent an evil spirit between Abimelech and the men of Shechem" (Jud. 9:23; see also 1 Sam. 16:14; 1 Kings 22:19–23, etc.).

Like their neighbors, the Hebrews believed that there were unseen powers outside of Yahweh that could affect their well-being. A psalmist promised divine protection so that the people would not fear

> . . . the terror of the night
> nor the arrow that flies by day
> nor the pestilence that stalks in darkness
> nor the destruction that wastes at noonday.
>
> (Ps. 91:5–6)

The terror of the night could refer to nightmares (Gaster 1969, p. 770) or packs of wild dogs (Dahood 1968, p. 331). The arrow and the night pestilence refer to the demonic shafts and the actions of Resheph, the Canaanite god of plague and disaster (Gaster 1969; Dahood 1968). The Canaanite demons of plague (Resheph) and disaster (Deher) became Yahweh's attendants when he went to war (Hab. 3:5). The noonday destruction signified demonic personification of sunstroke. Similar promises were made in Psalm 121, where destructive powers were attributed to the sun and moon (Ps. 121:6).

Lilith (whose identity was obscured in the King James Version by translating her name in Isaiah 34:14 as "the screech owl") was a Mesopotamian female wind spirit, the demon who haunted desolate places. She was feared by the Canaanites as the child-stealer. Subsequently, she became Lilith the child-stealer in Jewish folklore.

Azazel was the Hebrew demon of the wasteland. On the Day of Atonement the high priest of Israel magically transferred the sins of the nations onto the head of a goat selected for Azazel. The scapegoat carried the sins into the wasteland, where, apparently, the animal and the sins were destroyed by Azazel (Lev. 16:7–10, 20–22).

Evil powers could possess individuals. Social and emotional responses were understood in terms of spirit possession. Hosea stated that Yahweh complained

> My people seek answers from a tree
> and their staff gives them oracles [rhabdomancy].
> A spirit of fornication has possessed them
> and they have departed from their Elohim to fornicate.
>
> (Hos. 4:12)

It is clear that the biblical world was supernatural, peopled with demonic powers.

Satan in the Jewish Scriptures

The Hebrew word "satan" means "adversary" or "opponent." When David aligned himself with the Philistines, some Philistine military commanders did not trust his loyalty. When they were about to do battle with the Hebrews, these Philistine leaders suggested that David be excluded from their foray because he could turn out to be "a satan [adversary] to us" (1 Sam. 29:4). Hadad the Edomite was the satan or adversary that Yahweh raised up against King Solomon (1 Kings 11:14). The word "satan" assumed supernaturalistic overtones in the story of Balaam. When Yahweh became angry with Balaam, the seer summoned by King Balak of Moab to curse the Israelites, he prevented Balaam's response and "Yahweh's angel blocked his way as his adversary [satan]" (Num. 22:22). The angel is not "Satan" but is "a satan," an adversary.

It was not until the exilic (sixth century B.C.E.) or post-exilic period that Satan as a supernatural power was introduced. He appeared first as a member of the heavenly court, one of the sons of the Hebrew god Yahweh. Only later did he become the embodiment of evil. How did this happen?

Although Satan is presented as a son of Yahweh (Job 1:6), the mother of Satan or of Yahweh's other sons is never indicated. Perhaps she was the Canaanite mother goddess Asherah, or Ba'al's sister-lover Anat. Satan's role in Job has two dimensions. In one, he represents youth challenging age, the son questioning the father. Yahweh had boasted of Job's righteousness. Satan, Yahweh's son, was suspicious of Job's behavior. He believed that Job's blameless behavior resulted from Job's awareness that obedience paid off handsomely. Job knew that Yahweh would reward him for his constant obedience to divine will. Now, Satan suggested to his father, if the rewards were withdrawn, Job would reveal his true nature and curse, rather than worship, the deity. In this role Satan is the provoker, the skeptic, the social scientist who believed in testing to evaluate testimonies.

Satan's second role was that of an obedient son carrying out his father's decision to test Job (1:12). Satan never acted outside of the divine will. He was not anti-God. All that happened to Job happened because Yahweh ordered and endorsed the experiment.

Later, changes in Satan's role occurred. In the mythic trial of Joshua, the high priest, Satan, stationed at Yahweh's right hand, is in the role of accuser or prosecuting attorney (Zech. 3:1).

When the Chroniclers rewrote the history of the Hebrew kingdom as presented in 1 and 2 Kings, they changed the phrase "Yahweh's anger," which explained why David took a census (2 Sam. 24:1), to "Satan stood up against Israel." Thus, in the revisionist history, it was Satan rather than Yahweh who incited David to initiate a census (1 Chron. 21:1.). In other words, whereas the early writers recognized Yahweh as the source of evil, the Chronicler transferred the responsibility to Satan. Satan took action on his own initiative. The role of Satan and the personality of Satan were in the process of redefinition.

The big change, when it did come, was due to the introduction of Aryan religious beliefs into the Semitic theology of Israel. In the sixth century B.C.E., Cyrus the Great released the Jews from Exile in Babylon. For the next two hundred years, until the conquest by Alexander the Great, the Near East was under the domination of Persia. The teachings of the Persian prophet Zoroaster were adopted by the successors of Cyrus the Great, and the impact of Persian thinking and theology was felt throughout the Persian kingdom.

Aryan monotheistic theology postulated the existence of a single universal god, Ahura Mazda, who represented truth and light and justice. At the same time, the Persians recognized the existence of an anti-God power of the lie and darkness called Ahriman. Each human was free to choose: to follow the way of light, truth, and justice, or take the path of darkness, the lie, and injustice. It was the image of Ahriman that was to impinge upon Jewish thinking and result in the transformation of Satan.

Yahweh was also in the process of change. The unnamed exilic writer known as Deutero-Isaiah, whose writings (Isa. 40ff.) were attached to the work of Isaiah of Jerusalem, proclaimed Yahweh as the sole god of the universe and argued that all other deities were false or not real (Isa. 40:18–20, 41:29, 43:11, 44:6). This marked the beginning of Jewish monotheism. From that point on, Yahweh was transformed—like Ahura Mazda he was a universal god and not merely a tribal or a national deity. However, though he became the universal god, the Jews remained his chosen people.

The Persian religious thesis that evil existed outside of the supreme godhead was borrowed by the Jews. No longer was Yahweh pictured as the author of both good and evil. Like Ahura Mazda, he became the god of righteousness. Evil had another source, and in the development of Judaism Satan became the devil.

During and after the time of Alexander the Great (fourth century B.C.E.), Greek thought impacted directly on the Jews. Some Jews abandoned the notion of the psychic unity of body and spirit and postulated that humans consisted of two principles: body and soul. The true self was the imperishable soul, which inhabited a mortal body during life, but after death, while the body decayed, the soul continued in a separate spiritual existence. The destiny of the soul depended upon the quality of the individual's life. If the person during his lifetime had chosen good, there would be a happy afterlife; if the person had chosen evil, there would be misery. The writer of the pseudonymous Wisdom of Solomon (first century B.C.E.) noted:

> The souls of the righteous are in God's hands, and no torment can touch them. In the eyes of the foolish they seemed to be dead, and their departure was reckoned as an evil fate, and their going from us as disaster, but they are at peace. For though in the sight of men they are punished, they have a sure hope of immortality. After having endured a little chastisement they will receive great blessings, for God has tested them and found them worthy to be his; He tested them as gold is tested in the crucible, and accepted them as whole burnt offerings. (Wisd. of Sol. 3:1–6)

Satan in the Intertestamental Period

Few laymen know what scholars in religion and informed clergy fail to share—namely that between the writing of the last book of the Old Testament (Daniel) and the beginning of New Testament writings, Jewish theologians were hard at work thinking, debating, composing a developing theology, and reinterpreting Old Testament mythology. Some of the intertestamental writings, called the Apocrypha by Protestants and Jews, are included in the Roman Catholic and Eastern Orthodox Bibles. A much larger collection is known as the Pseudepigrapha. Some of the material in the Babylonian Talmud also came from this era. The Dead Sea Scriptures, produced by a sect of Jews that established a monastic community on a terrace on the northwest corner of the Dead Sea, were written in this same time frame. From these writings we can trace some aspects of the development of the role and responsibilities attributed to Satan in the Jewish religion.

In the pseudepigraphical Book of Enoch, Jewish savants reinterpreted the Genesis 6 myth of the sons of Elohim copulating with human women to produce giants. These giants were now recognized as the source of disembodied demonic spirits that emanated from them (16:1). Satan was introduced as the power that led angels astray (54:6). A vast array of demonic powers or satans are named, including Azazel, Samjaza, Armen, Kokabel,

and others whose names were later sometimes called out in magical rites
(6:7f; 69:2f). It should be noted that an equally impressive army of angelic
powers was also identified.

A possible reference to Satan appears in the writings of the wise ben
Sirach, who noted that "When an ungodly man curses Satan [an adversary?], he curses his own soul" (21:27). The first century B.C.E. Wisdom
of Solomon links the serpent of Eden with the devil:

> For God created man for incorruption
> and made him in the image of his own eternity
> but through the devil's envy death entered the world,
> and those who belong to his party experience it.
> (2:23f.)

In 2 Enoch 31 the devil and the serpent become one as the seducer of Eve.

The Old Testament word "belial" was used with reference to lawless
or dissolute personalities. A son of Belial implied a reprobate (Deut. 13:13;
2 Sam. 20:1; etc.). During the intertestamental period, Belial became identified as the prince of evil, and the name Belial became another label for
Satan or the devil. In the Dead Sea Scriptures of the Qumran sect and
in some pseudepigraphical documents (Levi 16:12; Zebulun 9:8; etc.) Belial
is portrayed as in charge of the anti-God forces.

Satan in Christian Scriptures

By the time of the New Testament, Satan had acquired the status of the
devil, the adversary of God, the tempter and seducer of humans, the lord
of demonic powers. It is not surprising to find that ideas generated in
the immediate pre-Christian period were echoed in the Christian Scriptures.
For example, the Apostle Paul asked the Corinthians: "What accord has
Christ with Beliar [Belial]?" (2 Cor. 6:15). Clearly the name Beliar/Belial
is simply another term for Satan. In Matthew's Gospel Jesus substituted
the name Satan for the Pharisees' reference to Beelzebub as the "prince
of demons," and Satan's demonic adjutants were clearly disembodied spirits
(12:24–28). The writer of Revelation identified Satan as a dragon figure
that was cast out of Heaven (Rev. 12:9).

Satan was the tempter and in the wilderness Jesus was tempted by
Satan (Mark 1:12; Matt. 4:12–17; Luke 4:1–13). Satan was identified as
the instigator of evil (Matt. 13:39) and the perverter of men's minds (Luke
8:12; John 13:2). He was the source of illness (Acts 10:38). While the

developing Christian church and some other sects of Judaism emphasized belief in the demonic powers of Satan and the devil, the Sadducees rejected belief in the devil.

From Zoroastrian teaching Judaism borrowed the concept of choice. Ben Sirach, the teacher, observed:

> It was he [the Lord] who created man in the beginning,
> and he left him in the power of his own inclination. . . .
> He has placed before you fire and water:
> Stretch out your hand for whichever you desire.
> Before a man are life and death
> and whichever he chooses will be given to him.
> (15:14,16,17)

In other words, without reference to demonic powers, ben Sirach, like the Zoroastrians, claimed that humans choose whether to follow light or darkness.

Modern religious Jews refer to the *yetzer ha-ra* and the *yetzer ha-tov*—the impulse toward evil and the impulse toward good. Modern Christians, relying on the New Testament, refer to Satan, the devil, Lucifer, Azazel, Belial, and even Old Nick as the source of evil with the power to cause evil to emerge in humans.

Lucifer

The identification of the devil as "Lucifer" rests on an unfortunate translation of the Hebrew word *helal* in Isaiah 14:12 in the King James Version. The word *helal* comes from a Semitic root meaning "to be bright, to shine." In Canaanite mythology, Helal was the Day Star or Light-Bringer. In the Vulgate or Latin version of the Bible, Helal was translated as Lucifer (*lux* = light; *fer* = bringing or carrying). The King James Version followed the Latin, and because the translators were Christian, a supernatural interpretation was imposed, and Lucifer became Satan.

A mocking taunt-poem in the form of a lament over the death of an unnamed world ruler was composed by an unknown author and included in the works of Isaiah of Jerusalem. The poet drew upon an ancient Canaanite myth that told of the attempt by Helal, the Dawn Star, to ascend the Mount of Assembly in the north where the gods met. The effort was thwarted and the star was cast down. The unnamed ruler, like the Dawn Star, failed in his attempt to tyrannize the ancient world. The poem reads:

How you have fallen from heaven
O Helal, son of Shahar [the Canaanite god of the dawn].
You, who devastated nations, are cut to the ground.
In your heart you said,
I will ascend to heaven above El's stars
I will set my throne on high,
I will sit on the Mount of Assembly
in the distant north [Saphon]
I will rise above the highest clouds
I will be like Elyon.

(Isa. 14:12–14)

The Canaanite origin of the allusions cannot be denied. Saphon, the north, was the location of the mountain where Canaanite gods met. The names of two Canaanite deities (Helal and Shahar) known from the Ras es Shamrah texts, and the reference to Elyon, the father god of the Canaanite cult, demonstrate the absorption of Canaanite beliefs into Hebrew theology.

Of course, the references have nothing to do with Satan. The Canaanite myth about Helal, assimilated into Judaism and used to mock the downfall of a tyrant, was transmogrified to become one of the bases for Satanic mythology that postulated the fall of Satan from heaven. The name Lucifer as one of the identities of Satan rests on a seventeenth-century mistranslation.

The Mark of the Beast

One of the catch phrases associated with Christian Satanism is "the mark of the beast," based on the reference in the Book of Revelation 13:8. This particular apocalyptic document envisions a violent, cataclysmic end of the age like that found in similar writings, including Daniel, some intertestamental scriptures, and the Essenic materials discovered at Qumran. The writer believed that the end of time was at hand (Rev. 1:1, 3; 3:11; 22:20).

The Book of Revelation, which was probably written during the reign of Domitian (81–96 C.E.), when emperor worship was being enforced, was designed as a messsage of hope and anticipation in a troubled time when Christians were being tested for their loyalty to the Roman Empire. The message was couched in veiled language because the document could be interpreted as subversive, inasmuch as it promised the violent overthrow of the Roman Empire and the establishment of the Christian Kingdom of God, in which Christians, not Romans, would rule (5:10). Symbols and numbers easily understood by initiates but confusing and unintelligible to outsiders obscured identities. For example, in chapter 4 the author introduced a vision of heaven, and in the next chapter referred to "a lamb standing as though it had been slain" (5:6). This animal was praised: "The lamb who is slain is worthy to receive power and wealth and wisdom and might and honor and blessing" (5:12). The scroll of destiny which contained the secrets of what was to come could be opened only by this lamb.

To the Christian there could be no question: the lamb was Jesus, the lamb of God (John 1:29) who had, according to Christian belief, been killed, but who survived death. To an uninformed, non-Christian reader the statement could only be nonsense. How could a dead lamb open a scroll? Why should it be praised?

The reference to the "mark of the beast" is derived from Revelation 13. The opening verse introduces a beast "from the sea" (Rome) which had destroyed Jerusalem, controlled the known world, and whose purpose it was to persecute Christians (the "saints," 13:7), by imprisonment and death. The author called for perseverance (13:10).

The second beast, from the earth, the imperial priesthood, enforced emperor worship as a testament of loyalty to the state. Those who performed the required rite received a mark, enabling them to buy and sell as patriots (13:17). The identity of this beast, hidden from the casual reader but decipherable by Christian initiates, was concealed in the numerical code 666, or in some manuscripts 616. It is believed that the identity of the beast was further obscured by the employment of the Hebrew-Aramaic number-letter pattern—that is, in the Hebrew alphabet, consonants, and vowels when written in full, have numerical value. The name of the feared Roman emperor who was dead but who many feared would be reborn was Nero. The schema based on the Hebrew consonants in the name CaeSaR NeRON (the "O" in NeRON is written in full and has numerical value) is as follows:

$$C=100 \quad S=60 \quad R=200 \quad N=50 \quad R=200 \quad O=6 \quad N=50, \ = 666.$$

In manuscripts where the final N is omitted the total is 616. Of course, other interpretations have been made. For example, the Greek word LATEINOS, which would refer to Rome, also totals 666. In any case, the reference is clearly to the Roman state or one of its representatives.

During the past 1,900 years, as the promised Christian kingdom failed to materialize, the passage has undergone countless reinterpretations. For example, in the twentieth century Kaiser Wilhelm of Germany, Adolph Hitler, and for some fundamentalist Protestants, the Pope of Rome, have been identified as the beast. When I was a student, some of us, using a Latin base, demonstrated that our New Testament professor's name could be added to total 666. There are many possibilities. It has been pointed out that in the name Ronald Wilson Reagan, each name contains six letters, so ex-President Reagan can be the latest 666!

Fundamentalists insist that the beast is yet to come and yet to be recognized. Therefore, the identification process will probably continue, despite the best evidence that the interpretation of the 666 number was intended to refer just to the first century. But the continuation of the process makes the mystical number fair game for youth who wish to shock their elders by indiscriminate application of the symbol.

Modern Satanism

The media have provided information concerning so-called Satanic cults. Some tales are bizarre and feature a curious lack of solid evidence to support their claims. Most reports are anecdotal.

It is well known that forms of Satanism are sometimes engaged in for fun by teenagers. Some young people inscribe the number 666 or the pentagram symbol or inverted crosses or other symbols in public places and even on tombstones in cemeteries. They may favor T-shirts decorated with Satanic images and wear jewelry with Satanic symbols. Their aim is to defy custom, to declare freedom and independence, and most of all to shock the older or more staid population.

Some persons, usually in the privacy of their own dwellings, experiment with what they perceive to be Satanic rituals. They draw chalk circles and pentagrams, light candles, recite spells found in books of magic, and even prick their fingers to draw blood, as supposedly called for in the rite. Their intent is to win back a lost love, magically to conjure up attractive companions, and so on. Some have confessed that their experiments felt "spooky," and some have admitted to being frightened. Of course, nothing happens as a result of the rituals. No devil responds. The lost love remains lost and no handsome males or beautiful females materialize. Satan fails them. These persons usually mature beyond this stage of magical thinking and hoping.

A few who toy with Satanism get caught up in the process and become completely absorbed. They begin by engaging in ghoulish, macabre rituals. They graduate from torturing and killing small creatures to the murder of a person. Their interests are fed by books and heavy metal music, which sometimes stress Satanism and violence. They are often drug users. As in almost every case of juvenile asocial behavior, familial problems are a factor. Divorce and estranged parent-child relationships contribute to feelings of isolation and the need for something to provide feelings of personal power and control.

Despite popular claims, there is absolutely no evidence of an organized Satanic cult promoting death rituals. Some ethnic voodoo religions, which feature overlays of either Roman Catholic or Protestant religious groups, include secret exorcism practices in which chickens or goats are sacrified, but these are not Satanic practices. The best surveys indicate that Satanism is less a religion than a preoccupation of Christian groups who accept biblical and church beliefs in a demonic power called Satan.

It is not impossible that some child abusers who engage in child pornography may have utilized horrors popularly associated with Satanic rituals, including the killing of animals, to induce silence in their young victims. Children who come from families in which biblical notions of Satan may be present or who are acquainted with "dark powers" through television programs can be terrorized into silence. A molester could claim to have Satanic powers and persuade the victim that what happened to the animal can or will happen to them or their family if they reveal the molestation. By trickery, it can be made to seem that a child or an infant has been killed and that the young subjects of the molestations are responsible for the death. Later, adult manipulators can pretend to magically bring the "murdered" child back to life. By appearing to have the power of life and death at their command, molesters could persuade a child of the danger of telling anyone about what is taking place. Consequently, the child begins to live two lives—an ordinary life with parents and friends, and a secret life of a victim of molestation. Even when outsiders become aware of the discernable signs of trauma and maladjustment, such as sexual acting out, genital and anal bruises and injuries, the traumatized child will continue to deny what has occurred. Cruel, manipulative child abusers are often labelled Satanists, but if they use Satanic notions, including warnings about demonic powers that can affect the child and his or her family, it is to conceal their abusive activities.

It is important to note that there is evidence that some claims of child abuse are inaccurate, that they are based on inadequate or misinterpreted evidence as well as poor investigative procedures. Not all physicians are capable of determining child abuse. Not all doctors are familiar with normal variations in vaginal orifices, and therefore may misread what they see during a pelvic examination. Not all therapists who question children maintain a proper objective approach. In some instances, children have been either led or persuaded or encouraged to give answers to conform to what the questioners want to discover. A six-part investigative report by Tom Charlier and Shirley Downing for the Memphis, Tennessee, *Com-*

mercial Appeal has demonstrated that children not only lie but respond according to what they think the adult wants to hear. When notions about Satanist conspiracies are aired over popular television talk shows and persons who are clearly disturbed tell tall tales about breeding children for Satanist ritual killings, the public is encouraged to find Satanism everywhere. Despite the claims that thousands of children have been sacrificed by Satanists, there is no evidence to justify these assertions. No bodies have been found, no precise details of when, where, or how the ritual killings occurred have surfaced. Just how absurd the panic can become is demonstrated in the analysis of sixty-seven cat deaths that occurred over a two-month period in the Los Angeles area. Some pet enthusiasts insist that the cats were killed by Satanists for Satanic rituals, despite the fact that there is absolutely no evidence to support the claim. A representative of the Department of Agriculture's Animal Damage Control found that the killings were consistent with what a coyote or other wild predator might do (Samuels 1989).

There are, of course, true Satanists who meet in Satan centers. Some individuals are attracted to their rituals out of opposition to traditional religions. Rites may include mirror-performances of ceremonies like the Roman Catholic mass. Black candles rather than white are lighted (the color black is supposed to be related to evil). The so-called "Lord's Prayer" is altered and addressed to "Our Father who art in Hell," and so on. The altar may consist of a nude female, and during the so-called "Black Mass" the chalice of wine and the host (preferably black bread) are employed in parodies of Roman Catholic rites (LaVey 1972, pp. 37–53). Most accouterments are for dramatic effect. There is an element of childlike misbehavior or defiance in the rites, through rejection of that which others hold sacred. There also seems to be some sort of exorcism of the guilt feelings engendered by traditional religions. But there is no connection with heavy metal sounds or music, nor encouragement to inscribe graffiti in public places. There is no doctrine or ritual or practice that would encourage or even tolerate any form of child abuse or human sacrifice.

In 1966, the Church of Satan was founded by Anton Szandor LaVey (Howard Levy) who claims the title "Exarch of Hell." In the ensuing years a number of subgroups have been formed. Satanist churches follow patterns used by other religious groups. They celebrate weddings and conduct funerals for their members. Credal statements, newsletters, and, of course, donations are part of the organization. The Temple of Set, of which Michael A. Aquino is high priest, developed out of the Church of Satan and is based on similar principles.

Some African-Caribbean cults, such as Santeria, have been confused with Satanism. Santeria religious groups incorporated Christian beliefs in-

to belief systems originating in Africa. The merging occurred when Santeria was brought by slaves to the Caribbean and initially was, at least
in part, an attempt to mask the African religion from a Christian culture
that would automatically be hostile to it. A casual analysis suggests that
there are recognizable parallels in magical concepts in Christianity and
Santeria. Both believe in blood rituals. In Christianity the sacrificial blood
of Jesus is represented symbolically; in Santeria the blood of a sacrificed
chicken or goat, mingled with honey and poured over a sacred rock, is
used. Both religions encourage home altars or shrines. Both believe in
exorcism. Christian exorcism can be seen as a thwarting of the devil. Some
Protestant faith-healing ceremonies are often congregation-oriented. They
are dramatic and involve Bible thumping and the use of cross symbols.
Santerian rites involve congregational or group dramatics, dancing, noise,
and the use of symbols. Santerian religion also employs Christian symbols.

Because followers of Santeria have splashed animal blood on tombstones, local authorities often conclude that Satanism is at work. Santerians
eschew Satanism, violence, and antisocial activities. They seek magic that
will provide success, wealth, and health. Because they believe in ritual magic, the followers are often victims of unscrupulous Santerias or priests
who take advantage of the desperate needs and hopes of devotees.

There is anecdotal evidence to suggest that there may be some off-
beat groups of so-called Satanists involved in pathological and antisocial
behavior. These sociopathic groups may engage in animal killing and mu-
tilation. If so, they hide their Satanic affiliation and to the outside world
behave and appear as normal citizens. In secret they meet with fellow Satanists and conduct their rituals. When the sociopaths engage in violence
against humans their activities become public. Charles Manson and his
followers, who are clearly mad, would fit into this category.

What is the Importance of
Satan in the Modern Church?

Inasmuch as Christians have adopted the devil as a symbol of evil and
because Satan is a prominent character in biblical drama, it is easy to
understand how the idea of personified evil remains as part of modern
society. Satan, together with other ancient Jewish semidivine personalities
including "Lucifer," Azazel, Belial, and Beelzebub, become convenient symbols for anything from non-Christian thought and actions to downright
maniacal acts, including murder. But in an age of educated people, in a

time when churches and synagogues are staffed with informed and well-trained clergy, one can only ask why there is failure to deny the reality of the negative spiritual power called the devil? Perhaps the following suggestions might be relevant:

1. The notion of personified evil enables the Christian to maintain the concept of an all-powerful deity that is pure, good, undefiled, above evil, just, honest, trustworthy, and concerned with the well-being of humans. The goodness of God and the presence of evil is a theological issue known as theodicy or the problem of the justice of God. Obviously, it became a major concern in Judaism and Christianity. Jeffrey Russell (1981) posed the problem this way:

> Four logical options exist with regard to theodicy: (1) God is neither all-good nor all powerful (an option usually excluded on the grounds that no one would call this God); (2) God is all-good but not all-powerful; (3) God is all-powerful but not all-good; (4) God is both all-good and all-powerful. The last option, usually adopted in the Judeo-Christian-Islam tradition, is a difficult one requiring some concordance of the existence of God with the existence of evil. (p. 17)

Russell's analysis is presented as a modern theological problem. Such theological arguments do not appear to have been part of early biblical thinking; they reflect the logical rationalism of Greek rather than Semitic biblical theology. However, once the Jews embraced monotheism and felt the impact of Aryan theology, it was no longer theologically expedient to attribute evil to Yahweh. The notion of the devil became a convenient way out of the problem. In other words, evil is dumped on Satan, who represents darkness, the underworld, the malevolent anti-God.

2. The story of Satan provides a simplistic mythological explanation of evil. It provides naive answers to the question of why bad things happen to good people, by explaining that the devil is at work affecting health, work, security, and safety. It reveals why children get into mischief, why businessmen cheat, why men in high office become crooks, why violence, brutality, injustice, crime, degradation, and other noxious influences exist in the world. All these negative factors are the work of the devil. Even disasters that can be explained naturalistically by scientists become the work of the devil.

3. It justifies maltreatment. Christian parents are not cruel and heartless when they beat their children, they are simply beating the devil or hell out of the child, for the child's well-being. Televangelists maltreat their clientele in the name of defeating Satan. They are willing to take money from persons living on the edge of poverty in exchange for promises they know will never

be fulfilled. They justify their behavior because they are engaging in a fight against Satan. The money which is used to enhance the living standards of the clergy is somehow interpreted to be thwarting Satan.

4. Belief in Satan can be used as a motivating force to encourage good behavior. On the other hand, the fear of Hell can be a powerful and frightening teaching tool. A student with a traumatizing fear of Hell explained that his grandfather told him as they sat before a blazing fireplace that the flames demonstrated what Hell was like. The disturbing image continued to haunt him in adulthood.

5. Teaching about Satan encourages magical, nonrational thinking, and consequently places immense power in the hands of the clergy, who are presumed to be experts in matters pertaining to the supernatural.

6. The church, by its insistence that Satan is a personality, and the media, by exploiting the claims of fundamentalist church people who find Satanism rampant, fan incendiary flames that can induce simplistic interpretations of serious crimes and produce fear, overreaction, and a tendency toward violence.

7. Church leaders who violate their marriage vows or fleece their flocks and become millionaires find it very convenient to be able to claim that Satan was responsible for their reprehensible behavior. Thus, among evangelical clergy, a self-confessed sexual deviate like Jimmy Swaggart and an accused rapist like Jim Bakker, divest themselves of responsibility and blame their behavior on Satan. Satan becomes a convenient scapegoat, relieving the individual of responsibility. Like those pathetic mentally and emotionally disturbed murderers who claim that their foul acts resulted from the voice of Satan advising them, these religious leaders take refuge in the same mythology. However, if the evangelists are accepted as truth-tellers and forgiven when they blame Satan, then murderers who claim that they acted under the demonic influence of Satan deserve the same kind of forgiveness. Each hides behind the same defense: The devil made me do it!

References

Anshan, Ruth N., *The Reality of the Devil*. New York: Delta, 1972.
Baskin, Wade, *Dictionary of Satanism*. New York: Philosophical Library, 1972.
Boyd, James W., *Satan and Mara*. Leiden: E. J. Brill, 1975.
Charlier, Tom, and Shirley Downing, "Six-Part Child Abuse Accusations Series, *The Commerical Appeal*. Memphis, Tenn., January 17–22, 1988.
Dahood, Mitchell, *Psalms I, II*, The Anchor Bible. Garden City, N.Y.: Doubleday, 1968.

Davies, T. Witton, *Magic, Divination, and Demonology among the Hebrews and Their Neighbors*. New York: KTAV Publishing House, Inc., 1969.

Driver, G. R., "Lilith," *Palestine Exploration Quarterly*. London: Palestine Exploration Fund, January–June 1959, pp. 55–58.

Fairfax, Edward, *Demonologia*. New York: Barnes and Noble, 1971 (reprint of 1882 edition).

Fontenrose, Joseph, *Python: A Study of Delphic Myth and its Origins*. Berkeley: University of California Press, 1959.

Gaster, Theodor H., *Myth, Legend, and Custom in the Old Testament*, 2 vols. New York: Harper and Row, 1969.

Glock, Charles Y., and Robert N. Bellah, *The New Religious Consciousness*. Berkeley: University of California Press, 1987.

Guazzo, Francesco Maria, *Compendium Maleficarum*, trans. by E. A. Ashwin. Secaucus, N.J.: University Books, 1974.

Jones, Tamara, "Dead Pets to Human Sacrifice," *The Los Angeles Times*. October 19, 1988.

———, " 'Fun' Killers Now Paying Devil's Dues," *The Los Angeles Times*. October 20, 1988.

Kelly, Henry Ansgar, *The Devil, Demonology and Witchcraft*. New York: Doubleday, 1968.

———, *Towards the Death of Satan*. London: Chapman, 1968.

———, *The Devil at Baptism*. Ithaca, N.Y.: Cornell University Press, 1985.

Kinsella, Warren, "Devil's Disciples" and "Satanism Suspected." *Calgary Herald*, March 7 and March 8, 1987.

LaVey, Anton Szandor, *The Satanic Rituals*. Secaucus, N.J.: University Books, 1972.

Los Angeles Times, "3 Convicted of Cutting Heart out of Stray Cat," December 13, 1988.

Maafe, Ken, "Yes Virginia, There is a Devil." *U.S. Catholic*, June 1986, pp. 14–19.

MacKenzie, H. Lincoln, "Who and What is Satan?" *The Churchman*, May 1970, pp. 6–7.

Mallowan, M. E. L., *Nimrud and its Remains*, 2 vols. New York: Dodd, Mead & Company, 1966.

Nauman, St. Elmo, ed., *Exorcism Through the Ages*. New York: Philosophical Library, 1974.

Olson, Alan M., *Disguises of the Demonic*. New York: Association Press, 1975.

Pritchard, James B., *The Ancient Near East in Pictures Relating to the Old Testament*, 2nd edition with Supplement. Princeton, N.J.: Princeton University Press.

Remy, Nicolas, *Demonolatry*, trans by A. A. Ashwin. Secaucus, N.J.: University Books, 1974.

Russell, Jeffrey B., *Satan, The Early Christian Tradition*. Ithaca, N.Y.: Cornell University Press, 1981.

Samuel, Allison, "U.S. Experts Say Coyotes, Not Satanists, Killed 67 Cats." *The Los Angeles Times*, August 10, 1989.

Scott, A. F., *Witch, Spirit, Devil*. London: White Lion, 1974.

Sheed, F. J., *Soundings in Satanism*. New York: Sheed and Ward, 1972.

Wheatley, Dennis, *The Devil and All His Works*. New York: American Heritage Press, 1971.

Zacharias, Gerhard, *The Satanic Cult*, trans. by C. Trollope. London: George Unwin, 1969.

Exorcism—Getting the Devil Out

> Your enemy, the devil prowls about like a roaring lion, seeking someone to devour.
>
> 1 Peter 5:8

Exorcism is an ancient form of mental and emotional healing which involves the expelling of demons or the devil by the use of incantations, conjurations, adjurations, prayers, sacred substances, symbols, rituals, or artifacts. It is based on the assumption that supernatural powers could take possession of an individual. Just as physical illness was attributed to sin or to demonic possession, mentally and emotionally ill persons were believed to be possessed by evil spirits. Because the behavior of some individuals was, on occasion, bizarre or outrageous, it was assumed that another personality had seized control of the individual and was being manifested.

Today, belief in spirit possession is widespread, particularly in countries which many Americans consider backward. At the same time, this notion is alive and current in America and other so-called First World countries. The primary source for the belief in demonic possession in the Western world is the Bible and writings based on the Bible as an authoritative document.

Divine Possession in the Jewish Scriptures

The Bible portrays King Saul as a highly disturbed person. Today he would probably be diagnosed as manic-depressive, suffering from a bipolar disorder. The writer who described Saul's depressed mood did so in the jargon of his time (tenth century B.C.E.):

> Now the spirit of Yahweh had forsaken Saul and an evil spirit from Yahweh would come upon him. (1 Sam. 16:14)

When David played on the lyre, Saul's dark mood left him:

> Whenever the evil spirit from Yahweh came upon Saul, David would take the lyre and played on it, so that Saul was refreshed, became well, and the evil spirit left him. (1 Sam. 16:22)

But music therapy was not always enough. Even as David was playing, Saul's mistrustful, suspicious side manifested itself and he tried to pin David to the wall with his spear. Saul's paranoiac behavior was attributed to "an evil spirit from Yahweh" (1 Sam. 19:10).

Of course, Saul had exhibited extreme behavior while he was still a farmer, prior to becoming king. When told that the people of the town of Jabesh-Gilead were under siege by Nahash, the Ammonite, Saul's emotions went out of control. He hacked up his valuable oxen, dispatched the chunks of flesh throughout the countryside, and threatened to butcher the cattle of those who failed to rally to his call to battle against the Ammonites. His actions are comparable to a present-day person wrecking his new Mercedes Benz and sending pieces to other automobile owners, threatening to destroy their cars if they fail to come when called. The writers who reported his story explained his behavior as resulting from possession by Yahweh's spirit (1 Sam. 11:6ff.).

In each of the above situations, the implication is that at a given moment Saul became ecstatic (*ex-stasis*), standing outside of himself, and another spirit took control of him. In such instances, Saul was no longer his normal self. He became someone else, and depending on the writer's interpretation of his behavior, the occupying spirit was either benign or malevolent—of Yahweh or of an evil spirit.

Mass prophetic ecstasy was also known. Four hundred prophets were apparently enraptured as they gathered before King Jehoshaphat (1 Kings 22:6,10). Saul's ecstatic seizure in response to the activities of Samuel's prophetic group was described as divine possession. This group utilized the harp, tambourine, flute, and lyres to induce frenzy (1 Sam. 10:5). As he came under their influence, Saul stripped, entered into some sort of trance state, and lay naked all day and night (1 Sam. 19:18–24). In response to music, the prophet Elijah was also transported into a prophetic state described as "the hand [power] of Yahweh" possessing him (2 Kings 3:15). It is not surprising that there were those who considered prophets to be madmen (2 Kings 9:11; Jer. 29:26).

Prophets claimed to speak not their own words but words given to them by Yahweh. The prophet Ezekiel, whose prophetic claims are somewhat bizarre, stated that Yahweh's spirit came on him. As a result he was provided with a message for the Jews in captivity in Babylon (Ezek. 11:5). Concerning other prophets, it was said that Yahweh's words "came" to them (Jer. 1:2; Hos. 1:1; Joel 1:1; etc.). They declared positively "thus says Yahweh" (Jer. 23:16; Amos 1:3, 6; etc.). Just how the messages from Yahweh were received is not indicated. Isaiah received his prophetic summons in an hallucinatory experience in the temple precincts (Isa. 6:1–9). Jeremiah seems to have used free association. In what seems to have become a trance state, he focussed on a pot of boiling water that became a symbol of divine action (Jer. 1:13f.). Amos concentrated on a man testing the perpendicularity of a wall (Amos 7:7f.). Some of Hosea's proclamations grew out of his unhappy marriage (Hos 1:2–3:5). Other prophetic utterances appear to be related to what might be termed an "ineffable experience" (cf. Jer. 20:7–9). In any case, for the most part, prophetic oracles were accepted as genuine. Should prophesies be in conflict, the prophets resorted to name-calling and even physical assault (1 Kings 22:1–28). "False" prophets provided messages the king or the public wanted to hear (1 Kings 22). Warnings against those who posed as prophets and delivered untrustworthy oracles are found in both Jewish and Christian Scriptures (Jer. 14:14–15; Matt. 7:15, 24:24). The test of genuineness appears to have been whether or not the oracles came to pass. Divine possession by the deity was not evil in and of itself and did not require exorcism; possession by demonic spirits was another matter.

Of course, there were professional exorcists, although little is told of them. David's use of music therapy might be classified as a form of exorcism in that it relieved Saul of the evil spirit that possessed him. The action of the high priest on the Day of Atonement when the sins of the nation were transferred to a goat by the laying on of hands might also be recognized as a form of exorcism. The demon Asmodeus, referred to in Tobit, was expelled by the foul odor of burning fish (Tobit 6:7, 16–17, 8:3). It is probable that in Israel, as in Babylonia, there were itinerant exorcists who expelled demons by using the name of one god or another. In Israel, exorcism would be performed in the name of Yahweh.

Exorcism in the Christian Scriptures

Demons and exorcists were prevalent in New Testament times. The first-century C.E. Jewish historian Josephus described King Solomon as a master exorcist:

God also enabled him to master the art of expelling demons which is a useful healing science. He composed incantations to alleviate illness. He left behind him exorcism techniques still in use today by which demons are driven away, never to return. Indeed, I have seen a countryman named Eleazer, free the demon-possessed in the presence of Vespasian, his sons, captains and numerous soldiers. This is the way he did it: he placed a ring holding one of the roots mentioned by Solomon beneath the nose of the demoniac and proceeded to draw the demon out through the man's nostrils. Immediately, when the man collapsed, he abjured him [the demon] in the name of Solomon and by the Solomonic incantation to never return. To demonstrate that he truly had such power, he placed a cup or a basin filled with water at some distance. He then commanded the demon, as it left the man, to overturn it, thereby demonstrating to the spectators that it had truly left the man. Thus the skill and wisdom of Solomon was manifested. (*Antiquities of the Jews,* VIII. 2.5)

Jesus is the principal exorcist in the New Testament. He casts out demons by "the spirit of God" (Matt. 12:28), with his own "word" (Matt. 8:16), and by virtue of a personal command:

Now there was in their synagogue a man possessed by an unclean spirit, and he shouted, "What have we to do with you, Jesus of Nazareth? Have you come to destroy us? I know who you are—the holy one of God." Jesus rebuked him saying, "Be quiet! Come out of him!" The unclean spirit convulsed him and with a loud cry came out of him. Everyone was amazed and asked, "What is this? A new teaching? He commands the unclean spirits with authority and they obey him?" (Mark 1:23–27)

The gospel writer has the conversation of the demon move from plural to singular as if the demon had multiple personalities but only one voice. In another situation, Jesus encountered a violent possessed man who lived in a cemetery. When Jesus asked the demon to identify itself, it responded that there were many demons in the man. Jesus exorcised the man and caused the demons to enter a herd of pigs, which ran into the sea and were drowned, presumably destroying the demons along with the swine (Mark 5:2–13). Other instances of possession reflect medical problems such as epilepsy (Mark 9:17–29) and perhaps hysterical blindness and dumbness (Matt. 12:22).

Just as the schools of the prophets learned from their masters, so Jesus' disciples were empowered by him to cast out demons on his authority (Matt. 10:1; Mark 6:7). The power of Jesus' name was used by the Apostle Paul, who healed a woman possessed by a divining spirit by saying,

"In the name of Jesus, I command you to come out of her" (Acts 16:18). When a nonfollower used the magic of Jesus' name to expel demons, the disciples were upset. Jesus said,

> Don't stop him. No one who does a supernatural work in my name will be able to speak evil of me. For he who is not against us is for us . . . . (Mark 9:39–40)

But there could be danger in using Jesus' name. Some itinerant Jewish exorcists attempted to exorcise demons "by Jesus whom Paul preaches." The demon responded, "I know about Jesus and Paul, but who are you?" The possessed man then physically attacked the exorcists (Acts 19:13–16).

Because people were convinced there was such a thing as demonic possession, there were those who claimed the skills, the formulae, and the power to expel demons. These sorcerers, priests, shamans taught and encouraged belief in demonic possession so that they could continue to exploit the gullible. Jesus' role as an exorcist is made to serve two purposes. First, to show that demons, as supernatural beings, recognized Jesus for who he really was—a supernatural being in human flesh. Second, to demonstrate Jesus' compassion. His followers appear to simply follow his leadership and example.

Modern Exorcism

The New Testament exorcism tradition continued through the early Christian era and the Reformation to the present time. Today, it stands in stark contrast to modern medicine and modern psychotherapy. Because the church refuses to relinquish belief in demons and Satanic possession and relegate these notions to the nonscientific era out of which they came, and refuses to point out to Christians that such concepts reflect primitive magic and primitive folkloric medicine, belief in possession remains alive and part of the thinking of the modern world. Perhaps the most popular notions come from motion pictures dealing with possession, witchcraft, and the devil. Those that have been most carefully researched, for example, *The Exorcist,* usually make Satan or satanic influence the basis of the possession, employ imagery from the world of art to portray the demonic invader, and feature exorcism rituals of the Catholic or Episcopal church.

Exorcism is a dependent ritual. It exists only where belief in demons and devils and possessing spirits exists. In rational communities, where such notions are laughed to scorn, neither possession nor hauntings occur and exorcisms do not take place. This is not to suggest that emotionally and mentally disturbed individuals will not exhibit behavior patterns some might describe as possession, but the affliction is best defined otherwise in medical and psychological terms. The witch doctor and the exorcist are replaced by the psychiatrist. The magic is gone. Rationality and the best information from medical and social sciences prevail. Exorcism and the belief in demonic possession are looked at as residues from the past. Their presence in our culture is possible primarily because the Bible says they are real, and uncritical believers accept what the Bible says. They are kept alive and current through the church and synagogue, because these institutions derive their authority from a collection of writings that are 2,000 to 3,000 years old and from commentaries and pronouncements that have been made in the intervening years by theologians who accept the Bible and other writings that are linked to it as divinely revealed truth. Exorcism and belief in demonic possession exist in modern society because the scientific spirit of the twentieth century has not yet dispossessed such ancient notions.

Within the Episcopal Church and Roman Catholicism, there are still official "exorcists." These priests are supposed to be experts in the ceremonial patterns of expelling demons or the devil. They are empowered to act only with the approval of a bishop. They employ language of command not unlike that found in the New Testament, plus gestures such as the sign of the cross, blessed water or oils, prayers, psalm reading, and so forth. There can be no question that the whole ceremony must be impressive and perhaps moving to the possessed individual and his or her family. The rite is rife with magic.

The silly antics of television healers and exorcists are really beneath notice. They prance about the stage, exhorting the devil or demons to come out of sick people. Some go through kicking motions as if they were physically expelling a demon. They shout, they cry, they wail and shriek, and "put on a show" that entertains the audience even as it convinces them that exorcism and healing is actually taking place.

What about the possessed person? It is not impossible that some individuals, feeling isolated, alone, neglected, and misunderstood, and living in an environment or culture where demon possession is accepted as a reality, adopt behavior patterns that imply possession. As such behavior manifests itself, they become the center of attention. The claim of demonic possession is, at least in some instances, a cry for attention, for notice, for help in dealing with feelings of estrangement. Like the channelers, the possessed person acts out the role of the demonic personality purported to have taken possession of them (see chapter on Channeling). The rich ritual performed with the troubled individual at the center alleviates the individual's sense of unimportance and feeds the ego. In other cases, clear manifestation of mental and emotional disorder call for medical as well as psychological treatment.

Many of those who claim or are claimed to be possessed are children at the age of puberty. In this awkward stage of human development they may feel and act out of tune with the world, estranged from family and friends, unappreciated, and misunderstood. Their strange behavior is obviously an effort to acquire attention from those who have, in the child's mind, been indifferent to them. Just as poltergeist activity has been demonstrated to be the action of children in this same age range, so demon possession requiring exorcism is also often associated with adolescent behavior.

Of course, there are those who, in hallucinatory experiences, claim to have conversations with Satan. These sadly deranged individuals are usually found in mental institutions where they may receive treatment and are kept from doing harm to or receiving harm from the public.

Occasionally some person will seek to do violence to others, claiming to be prompted by demonic or Satanic voices. Often these are lonely, isolated persons, whose desire for attention and notice lie behind their antisocial acts. The voices are, of course, of their own making. The attribution of them to Satan is a reflection of modern Christian teaching and influence. These persons do not need the help of an exorcist; they require incarceration and medical and psychological assistance.

References

Ebon, Martin, *The Devil's Bride, Exorcism: Past and Present.* New York: Harper and Row, 1974.

Neaman, Judith S., *Suggestion of the Devil.* New York: Anchor Press, 1975.

Whiston, William, translator, *The Works of Flavius Josephus,* Hartford, Conn.: The S. S. Scranton Co., 1911.

The Occult World of Witches

> You shall not let a witch [sorceress] live.
> Exod. 22:18

Witchcraft today represents a rather naive form of nature religion that seeks to invoke occult powers. By this aim it can be recognized as rivaling traditional religions that seek to do exactly the same thing through socially approved and accepted channels. At certain periods in history, witchcraft, together with astrology, enjoyed recognition in royal courts. Medieval romances tell of powerful wizards like Merlin and evil magicians.

Rivalry between witchcraft and Christianity has a long history and at times resulted in bitter, cruel, unwarranted maltreatment of men and women accused of witchcraft. The records of witch persecutions reflect malevolent manipulation of information and power by church authorities and a startling credulity of both the persecuted and the persecutors.

Much of the reported activities of witches is folkloric and anecdotal, rich in fantasy, imagination, and belief in magic and supernatural powers. Witchcraft as a religion has its own mythology—a mixed bag drawn from various sources and transmitted primarily by oral tradition but also through medieval notebooks, court proceedings, and the writings of those who sought to denigrate the craft. The chief deities are "The Horned One," who is not the devil (although, thanks to the church, such an identification has been made and the devil does feature in some aspects of witchcraft), but represents Pan or other nature symbols, and the moon goddess Diana. Diana is supposed to have seduced her brother Lucifer, the sun, to produce a female child, Aradia, who lived on earth and gave her message to avatars including the Buddha, Krishna, Zoroaster, Christ, and Mohammed before returning to heaven.

Each coven or congregation has its own organizational form and ceremonial patterns. Newcomers, both male and female, go through training and initiation ceremonies that, in addition to rituals, can include scourging. Those selected to become witch queens, high priestesses, or high priests are privileged to receive special training by which they become masters of the secret lore and magical spells of the faith. In all of these procedures of initiation, induction, and elevation, witchcraft parallels the customs of traditional churches.

Practitioners believe that by incantations and charms (some of which were borrowed from the medieval church), spells, the use of certain basic elements (salt and water, which were used in the medieval church to expel demons), secret herbs, oils, and formulae they can effect changes. They seek to "will the power" to manifest itself, thereby indulging in magical thinking enhanced by incantatory commands. For example, they will stand in a circle and by focusing or willing, imagine that they create a cone of power by means of which they can induce change. They assume they can cast spells and conjure up special power through the god or goddess. Some covens seek to draw down the moon goddess to become incarnate in a priestess during a trance, or try to cause the god to inhabit a priest.

Some rites are similar to those performed in traditional religions. For example, there are communal meals involving bread and wine. As in Catholicism and the eastern Christian rites, emphasis is placed on costume. As in traditional Christianity, there is a belief in the sanctity of certain locales (such as Stonehenge). The altar may consist of a nude female lying in a so-called "five-star" position, with arms and legs widespread. Both pentagram and circle patterns are believed to help focus power. There are no angels, but some practitioners claim to have "familiars," elemental spirits that can be materialized and made to act at their bidding.

Ceremonies are performed according to a seasonal calendar that includes the Four Greater Sabats: the winter solstice (which begins the year), the summer solstice, and spring and fall equinoxes, as well as the Lesser Sabats: Hallowe'en or Samhain (Oct. 31), Candelmas or Oimelc (Feb. 1 or 2), May Eve (April 30), or Beltane (May 1), and Lammas or Lugnasadh, the fertility festival (Aug. 1) (Glass 1973, p. 98; Simons 1974, p. 130). According to descriptions, the rites elicit various emotional responses including awe, solemnity, exuberance. The stress on "nature" encourages gatherings in wooded or parklike settings, although covens also meet in homes. Being "skyclad" or nude is favored as representing a closeness to nature as well as signifying social and mental freedom. Some rituals are symbolically sexual, representing the fertility dimensions of the belief system; others are overtly so. Although some rites seem childlike, including a type of circular follow-the-leader ceremony, the practitioners believe that through their performances they evoke powerful forces. Sympathetic magic can be used and may include making wax or clay images of persons or objects the witches hope to affect. Claims include levitation and speaking in a foreign language previously unknown to the utterer (Sanders 1976, p. 16). The religion in its "white" form appears to be harmless, but in its "black" manifestations has a hurtful and malevolent aspect.

Efforts to trace the origins of witchcraft back to Neolithic times are singularly unconvincing. Most arguments are marred by reading into ancient sculptures, cave paintings, and the like whatever the reader wishes. The contention that secrets from ancient Egypt are part of the cultic practice is equally questionable. The use by witchcraft practitioners of various names of divinities that were worshipped in the Nile Valley reflects popular notions, not scholarly findings, about magic and the supernatural. Witchcraft does not seem to be connected to Egyptian religion. Witchcraft practices seem to be more akin to the supernaturalism that was widespread in the Near Eastern and Mediterranean worlds when Christianity came into being. At that time sorcerers and priests of various cults made supernatural claims and worshipped deities that are reflected in some of the beliefs of modern witchcraft. The witchcraft claims were challenged by the early Christian church whose authorities saw in witchcraft a rival to the magical power attributed to Jesus. Of course, there is no evidence that our ancient ancestors possessed any more power to contact and employ unseen powers than any witch or priest today.

Witches appear to have some relationship to ancient local wise men and women who possessed knowledge of plants, herbs, mixtures, incantations, and spells that were medicinal in nature and to which uncanny powers were attributed. The broomstick upon which witches are depicted as flying has been recognized as a fertility pole, or perhaps more simply just an ordinary household broom. The pointed black hat was a common headdress in medieval times. The witch's cat was simply a pet and of no greater significance than the cats and dogs that bring comfort and solace to households today. In other words, popular notions, enhanced by Walt Disney films, keep alive, distort, and popularize medieval nonsense.

Some effort has been made to relate witchcraft to present-day beliefs in psychic phenomena. Telepathic and clairvoyant claims rest on anecdotal, not proven, data. Miraculous healing attributed to covens and circles of witches are in the same unproven category as the faith healings claimed by present-day Christian groups (see chapter on Healing). Perhaps through nudity and body-to-body ceremonies, some of which may involve sexual intercourse, individuals with sex problems may be helped. On the other hand, such behavior can be exploitive—a fact that is freely admitted by witches.

The persecution of witches developed when the Christian church decided to eliminate the popular "old" religion of the common people. The conflict was between the concept of one true god and the belief in multiple powers and non-Christian deities; between the notion of Jesus as the only savior and the acceptance of magical powers outside of the church that would provide help and succor for living; between the church's attempt to be solely in control and the nature religion that had its roots in long-held sorcery practices. At this point, the Christian belief in the devil and biblical antiwitchcraft teachings provided what was considered to be an acceptable theological basis for torture and death for witches.

Witchcraft and the Bible

The biblical world was infected with unseen powers and populated with persons who believed that certain individuals had the means to manipulate these hidden forces. Each nation had its official priesthood and sorcerers who, in the name of one god or another and by the use of secret lore including incantations, spells, and formulae claimed to be able to bind or loose destructive spirits. There can be no doubt that ignorance of the causes of illness and disease and the superstitious beliefs held by a naive public enhanced the power of the exorcists. When the skills of one faith system came into conflict with those of another, the more powerful would seek to eliminate the weaker by pronouncing it anathema. Such a process took place in ancient Israel.

During the reigns of kings Saul, David, and Solomon, Yahwism became the dominant religion in Israel. Immediately it sought to eliminate other existing faith systems. It challenged the fertility claims of Ba'alism (see chapter on Control of Nature) and struggled against the popular appeal of those who claimed to be able to work with demonic spirits.

King Saul outlawed necromancers who worked with "familiar spirits" (see chapter on Channeling). Subsequent legislation outlawed sorcerers (Exod. 22:17; Deut. 18:10). Because laws are passed to regulate current situations, it is clear that sorcery was a prominent aspect of ancient Hebrew-Jewish life (Isa. 2:6, 47:12; Jer. 27:9). However, if Yahweh was considered to be the source of good and evil (see chapter on Satan), then the recognition of any other powers would constitute a denial of Yahweh's supremacy and could be dismissed or challenged as superstitious nonsense. Indeed, the label "sorcerer" assumed a deprecatory status in first-century Judaism: the Pharisees were accused by Jesus of being sorcerers, just as Jesus was accused by the Pharisees (Matt. 12:24–27).

During the intertestamental period, the relationship of women to witchcraft was asserted in certain Jewish writings that were ultimately read by the Christian theologians. For example, the Book of Enoch, a composite work that was supposed to be the revelation of the Enoch who had been "taken" by Elohim (Gen. 5:24), retold the story of the sons of Elohim copulating with earth women. The author noted that the divine beings taught the women "charms and enchantments, the cutting of roots and familiarity with plants" (7:1). H. A. Kelly notes: "Here already in the second century before Christ we see foreshadowed many of the characteristics that will be found in 'Christian witchcraft' " (Kelly 1968, p. 40).

Although the medieval reports of witches flying about on broomsticks has no basis in the Bible, biblical characters were magically transported from place to place. Ezekiel, a Jewish captive in Babylon (Ezek. 1:1), was levitated and carried "in visions" to Jerusalem (8:3). Elijah went by whirlwind from earth to Heaven (2 Kings 2:11). Habakkuk was lifted by the crown of his head and carried from Judea to Babylon (Bel and the Dragon 36). Philip the evangelist was magically transported by "the Spirit" from a spot near Jerusalem to Azotus (Ashdod) near the Mediterranean (Acts 8:39–40). Jesus levitated and disappeared in the clouds after his resurrection (Acts 1:9). Biblical tales of levitation and magical travel were accepted by the church as truly happening; hence, it seemed possible that witches could also possess the magical power to transport themselves through the air.

Witch Trials

Perhaps the greatest testimony to the desire to control and to feelings of threat or imperilment is persecution—whether the fear is of a different political ideology (Communism in America; Democracy in China), social practice (freedom of choice in abortion issues), or education (evolution versus biblical creationism in public school science classes). Oppressive tactics can range from verbal denunciation to violent confrontation, from malevolent mischief to destruction of property and ultimately to killing, whether under the aegis of law or by murder.

During the Middle Ages, the Christian church had not progressed beyond the magical notions inherent in the Bible. Indeed, the idea of supernatural powers existing outside the church was so prevalent that when the bishop of Trèves died during a baptismal ceremony, Jews were accused of placing a waxen image of the bishop in a fire, causing his death (Williams 1941, p. 83). How simple it is to cast blame and induce purging!

In the eyes of some learned clergy, witchcraft was nonsense. But witchcraft came to be viewed as a threat to the supreme authority of the church. The biblical injunction that sorcerers should not be permitted to live provided an authoritative scriptural basis for the elimination of anyone who practiced witchcraft. And when witchcraft was aligned with the influence of the devil, the enemy of God, the church's responsibility became clear. The result was purgation of witchcraft in the form of torture of suspected witches, confessions extracted by torture, and ultimately the killing of witches in the most horrendous modes conceivable.

It is clear from documents of the twelfth and thirteenth centuries that there was at that time some concern in Christian circles about witches and sorcerers. For example, in 1231, Pope Gregory IX gave directions to Conrad of Marburg (and subsequently to the prelates in Germany) that resulted in maniacal persecution of sorcery (Summers 1965, pp. 470ff.).

The witch-hunt craze was instigated by the church in the late fifteenth century. There was no systematized cult of witches at that time. That notion was created by the inquisitors in much the same way that certain groups today argue that there is a nationwide cult of Satan. The practice of witch burning was well under way in 1484 when Pope Innocent VIII, solicited by German Dominicans, issued the bull *Summis Desiderantes Affectibus* that increased the priestly power to persecute witches. The textbook for identification and proper treatment of witches, the *Malleus Maleficarum*, was published about 1489 C.E. It was written by two Dominican inquisitors: the Rev. Henry Kramer, a zealous prosecutor who occupied the chair of theology at the University of Salzburg, and James Sprenger, the Provincial of the German provinces, who became the grand inquisitor for Germany. These two zealots for the protection of the faith were convinced that souls could be damned but could be saved only through the moral and sacramental system of the Catholic Church. The enemy of that salvation system was the devil, whose nature, evil practices, and influences they proceeded to define. Satan influenced men and women to become his followers as wizards and sorcerers or witches. With such gullible people, Satan entered into pacts which included renunciation of the Catholic faith, homage to the devil, the offering of unbaptized children, and the indulgence in carnal lust with incubi or succubi. The most secure of all protections against witchcraft was the name of Jesus, the "word made flesh." Of course, in keeping with the thinking of the time, the church also encouraged the employment of mechanical means to secure protection against the devil. These included the use of holy bread and water and candles, the magical power of the sign of the cross, consecrated herbs, sacred words worn next to the body, and the sound of church bells. Certain prayers guaranteed immunity against witchcraft, disease, mad dogs, and the devil (Thomas 1971, p. 493).

Thus, witchcraft trails opened with the assertion "In the beginning was the word," and included such tests as the tying and hanging of a Bible from a suspect's finger. If the person could not support the book and it fell, it was a significant indication of witchcraft. Witches supposedly had places on the body that were insensitive to pain and the inquisitors attempted to discover these by probing. All magic employed by witches for healing was of the devil. Midwives were suspect because they delivered babies and babies were used by witches (killed, cooked, and eaten) in their rituals. No one was safe. Some disaffected neighbor needed only make an accusation, and no matter how flimsy the evidence, an investigation was undertaken.

The *Malleus Maleficarum* provided procedural guidelines for witch trials. The treatise was composed of three parts. The first set forth Catholic doctrine pertaining to witches. The second discussed how witches could flit from place to place, how an incubus (male demon) copulated with a witch, how witches could change men into animals, slay children, and in horrible rites, offer them to Satan. The third section provided information concerning the punishment of witches, including interrogatory methods and the use of torture to extract confessions. The instructions were followed religiously, resulting in a pattern of persecutions and executions that spanned some two hundred years and numbered in the tens and perhaps the hundreds of thousands of victims. Witch fever spread across Europe. In Protestant countries dominated by Calvinist and Lutheran theology, evidence of witchcraft was also sought out and punished. And from Europe, the infection crossed the ocean to America.

The Puritans, seeking religious freedom for themselves, had brought to America a heritage of superstition concerning witchcraft. In 1641 anti-witchcraft legislation was introduced in Massachusetts; in 1642 in Connecticut; and in 1655 in New Haven. As the anti-witch campaign reached its zenith in England, persecution also increased in America, fanned by the maniacal obsession of influential clergy like Increase and Cotton Mather, reaching panic proportions in Salem, Massachusetts, at the close of the seventeenth century. Ultimately, the furor died down. Rational thinking prevailed, and persecution of witches became no more than a dark blot on the history of the American search for freedom.

Today, witches are emerging from the closet, so to speak. In the present atmosphere of toleration and pluralism, witches are not afraid to declare themselves. Indeed, according to *The Los Angeles Times* (Aug. 9, 1989), "A coven of witches has won tax exempt status in Rhode Island as a legitimate religious group." The coven, known as "Our Lady of Roses Wiccan Church," has some thirty to forty members who meet three times per month.

The potential for a persecutory change of attitude toward witchcraft remains. Roman Catholics continue to believe that there are demons to be exorcised. Fundamentalist evangelical Protestants still go through the motions of expelling Satan and demons from possessed persons. When the public library in San Jose, California, advertised a "Meet a Real Witch" program as an historical service where teenagers could learn about this religion from the witch Zsuzanna Budapest, protests came from clergy and disturbed parents (*The Los Angeles Times*, July 10, 1986). The media exploit public naivete with television programs and newspaper stories about Satanism and Satanic cults. Witchcraft is blamed for inciting persons to commit crimes. In 1986, a convicted murderer explained his brutal acts on the basis of being driven to them by "voodoo, witchcraft and black magic" (Hicks 1986). For many, the Bible is still the word of God, and the Bible contains the command stating that a witch should not be permitted to live. If educational systems abandon the emphasis on critical thinking, the numbers of naive, nonanalytical individuals will increase, and it is to such persons that belief in extraterrestrial beings, demons, spirits, and the power of witches appeals.

Witchcraft is a carryover, in the form of folk religion, of our superstitious past, when all sorts of spiritual powers roamed the earth and when certain men and women had learned the necessary skills to tap these powers. The spells, charms, and invocations of witches are about as effective as the prayers and incantations of the churches. Both are rooted in far-off eras when humans believed in the mystical power of words and rites to affect the unseen world of spirits and deities. Neither has any real power.

References

Boguet, Henry, *The Examination of Witches*. London: John Rodker, 1929; New York: Barnes and Noble, 1971.

Douglas, Mary, ed., *Witchcraft Confessions and Accusations*. New York: Tavistock, 1970.

Glass, Justine, *Witchcraft, the Sixth Sense*, North Hollywood, Calif.: Wilshire Books Co., 1973.

Hamer, Michael J., *Hallucinogens and Shamanism*. New York: Oxford University Press, 1973.

Hicks, Jerry, "Medina Blames Voodoo, Witchcraft for Killings," *The Los Angeles Times*, November 7, 1986.

Kelly, Henry Ansgar, *Towards the Death of Satan*. London: Geoffery Chapman, 1968.

Lea, Henry C., *Materials Toward a History of Witchcraft*. London: Thomas Yoseloff, 1957.

Maple, Eric, *The Dark World of Witches*. Cranbury, N.J.: A. S. Barns; 1962, New York: Pegasus, 1970.

Marwick, Max, *Witchcraft and Sorcery*. Baltimore, Md.: Penguin Books, 1970.

Murray, Margaret A., *The God of the Witches*. London: Oxford University Press, 1931, 1952, 1970.

Remy, Nicolas, *Demonolatry*, trans. by E. A. Ashwin. London: John Rodker, 1930; New York: Barnes and Noble, 1970; Secaucus, N.J.: University Books, 1974.

Roelofsma, Derk K., "Inside the Circle of Witches Modern," *Insight*, June 8, 1987, pp. 59–61.

Seabrook, William, *Witchcraft—Its Power in the World Today*. New York: White Lion, 1972.

Sanders, Maxine, *Maxine, The Witch Queen*. London: Wyndham, 1976.

Simons, G. L., *The Witchcraft World*. New York: Harper and Row, 1974.

St. Leger-Gordon, Ruth E., *Witchcraft and Folklore of Dartmoor*. New York: Crown, 1974.

Summers, Montague, *The Geography of Witchcraft*. Secaucus, N.J.: The Citadel Press, 1965, 1975.

Thomas, Keith, *Religion and the Decline of Magic*. New York: Charles Scribner's Sons, 1971.

Trevor-Roper, H. R., "The Persecution of Witches," *Horizon*, Vol. II, No. 2, 1959, pp. 57–63.

Williams, Charles, *Witchcraft*. New York: Faber and Faber, 1941; Meridian, 1959.

Woods, William, *A Casebook of Witchcraft*. New York: G. P. Putnam's Sons, 1974.

Seers, Clairvoyants, and Psychics

> They are a rebellious people, dishonest sons,
> sons who will not listen to Yahweh's instructions;
> Who say to the seers, "Do not see"
> and to the prophets, "Don't prophecy correctly;
> tell us smooth things, prophesy illusions."
>
> Isa. 30:10

Seers are clairvoyants who are supposed to be able to discern events or happenings that occur at a distance or that are concealed from view. The prophet Samuel was clairvoyant. When Saul, who was to become king of Israel, was seeking for some lost asses, his servant suggested that they consult a seer, that is, one who could see what was hidden and tell them where the lost beasts had strayed. They went to Samuel, who immediately informed Saul that the asses had been found. He went further and predicted the enthronement of Saul as king of Israel (1 Sam. 9). Samuel's information was supposed to have come from Yahweh. Later, when Yahweh became disaffected with Saul, he informed Samuel that he had chosen David to be the successor to Saul, and the seer anointed David before the young man began the journey to the throne (1 Sam. 16).

Elisha the prophet was clairvoyant. He had just healed Naaman, the commander of the Syrian army, of leprosy. Naaman wished to reward the prophet, but Elisha refused. Gehazi, Elisha's greedy servant (the name "Gehazi" means "greed"), decided to capitalize on the healing. As Naaman left, Gehazi followed and received silver and rich clothing as payment. Later, when he met with Elisha, the prophet said: "Didn't my heart go with you?" or "Was I not with you in spirit?" (2 Kings 5:26). The implication is that

Elisha was able to envision in his mind (heart) what had occurred. Gehazi was found guilty and punished.

The king of Israel dispatched a killer to murder Elisha. Before the killer arrived, Elisha, who was sitting in his own house with Israelite elders, informed them that the king's messenger of death was on his way (2 Kings 6:32).

At times in the Old Testament the roles of the clairvoyant, the seer, and the prophet overlap and merge. None of their psychic activities are condemned in the Bible. On the contrary, foretelling is a central theme in biblical literature. There were both seers and prophets in the royal courts, and 2 Chronicles 33:19 indicates that at one time there existed a Seers' Chronicle that recorded the words of the clairvoyants.

Some Bible interpreters feel that the prophets' gift was the gift of seeing events in the distant future—that is, they predicted events that had nothing to do with their own time and place in history. For example, ancient sectarian Jewish groups, like the one that lived at Qumran, Israel, and that produced the Dead Sea Scrolls, believed that references in biblical documents that were centuries older than their time pertained to their present situations. A reference in the book of Habakkuk (written after 605 B.C.E.) concerning the Babylonian threat reads: "Look, I am rousing the Chaldeans, that bitter and restless nation. . . ." (1:6). The Dead Sea Scroll writers in the so-called Habakkuk Commentary reinterpreted the saying and declared that Habakkuk wrote about the "Kittim," that is, a contemporary enemy (probably the Romans).

The writers of Christian Scriptures employed a similar interpretive pattern. The Gospel of Matthew makes constant reference to prophetic utterances in the Jewish Scriptures to demonstrate that the birth, ministry, death, and resurrection as recorded in the Christian Scriptures were foreseen and foretold in the Old Testament prophetic writings. Therefore, it can be reasoned, if the prophets foretold the coming of Jesus, they were indeed seers, perhaps with visions of that which is still to come. Thus, it is not surprising to find that fundamentalist preachers search the prophetic writings of the Old Testament and the New Testament for clues to understanding our present age. These modern interpreters employ what I label the "double bounce theory" of prophecy. For example, in a conversation with one fundamentalist biblical scholar concerning the words of the prophet Isaiah, "Behold, a young woman is pregnant and will bear a son and will name him Immanuel" (7:14), the fundamentalist commented, "Isn't it wonderful that the Holy Spirit could give Isaiah 7:14 one meaning for Isaiah's time and another meaning some 800 years later in New Testament times?" When I asked if the Holy Spirit could give it still another meaning for our time, he acknowledged that this was possible. In other words, my "double bounce theory" could become a "multiple bounce theory," depending, of course, on the whim of the Holy Spirit!

Critical biblical scholars see the prophets in a different light. They note that the Hebrew word *nabi,* which is translated "prophet," means something other than foreteller. William F. Albright and others have related the Hebrew word to the Accadian term *naba'um* (root *nabu*), which means "to call," so that the prophet is one who had received a call or a vocational summons from the deity, much like those reported by Amos (7:14–15) and Isaiah (6), etc. On the other hand, based on the same etymology, B. D. Napier (1962) suggests that the prophet is a "caller" or an "announcer," that is, one who announces the message or the words of the deity. The Greek Septuagint translates *nabi* as *prophetes,* derived from *pro* meaning "for" or "in behalf of" and *phemi,* "to speak." Therefore, the prophet is one who speaks on behalf of another. When Aaron was appointed a *nabi* for Moses, it is clear that he was to be the spokesman (Exod. 7:1), or as Exod. 4:16 indicates, "the mouthpiece," at those moments when Moses acted as a god. Thus the Hebrew prophet can be described as a spokesman for Yahweh, or as one called to serve as a spokesman.

What is more important is that the prophets were people of their own time. If Isaiah was saying to King Ahaz who was worried about a threatening alliance of Syria and Israel, "Don't worry, in about 800 years a woman will bear a child and name him Immanuel," it is doubtful he would have had the king's ear for long. The fundamentalist scholar evaded that issue by saying that the Holy Spirit was responsible for reinterpreting the passage for inspired gospel writers. He would not admit that the Holy Spirit also inspired the monks of Qumran to reinterpret what Habakkuk wrote! The Holy Spirit only seems to work in a Christian context for this kind of interpreter.

Because we do not have the Seers' Chronicle, there is no way of analyzing what they claimed to have foreseen. The few references provided in the Bible link them with the prophets as spokesmen for Yahweh, but they, too, were men of their own time, with no more potential for discerning the distant future than the prophets.

The Dutch clairvoyant M. B. Dykshoorn has claimed that as a child he was able to foretell events. As an adult he is supposed to have helped police in Europe, America, and Australia locate missing bodies, reconstruct crimes, track down criminals, etc. For these exploits he used a dowsing tool—a looped wire that is supposed to twist in the dowser's hands to guide him (see chapter on Dowsing). Interestingly, Dykshoorn does not document the claims in his book by dated newspaper clippings or official letters—all of which he claimed were available. The references are general and the accounts of psychic success are anecdotal.

Police officials with whom I have spoken say that seers or psychics often volunteer their help in dramatic cases of missing persons or property. None of the police with whom I have spoken were helped by these seers. Each of the officers indicated that the psychics tended to become nuisances, interfering with police procedure by insisting that their "revelations" be investigated, wasting valuable time and resources.

Modern seers who label themselves psychics make predictions each New Year. They have a good chance of accuracy when they engage in generalizations such as "There will be trouble in the Middle East," to which one may respond "When, during the recent past, has there not been?" When they predict what will happen to known personalities, they usually fail miserably. Indeed, their failure rate has been calculated at something between ninety-five and ninety-eight percent. Experiments with my university classes had about the same success rate. When I ask the students at the close of the year to predict what will occur during the coming year, they are secure when they make general references to interactions between nations. When they zero in on personalities or specific events such as with regard to the stock market or baseball or football titles, they provide similarly erroneous results as modern seers. Clairvoyants, whether psychic or astrological, have no more insight into the future than any other person.

Many present-day psychic foretellers claim that their "gifts" of clairvoyance and prophecy are God-given. They claim to be Christians, quote the Bible—particularly the Pauline statement on "gifts of the spirit," which include "prophecy" and "knowledge" (which is interpreted as knowledge of that which occurs at a distance).

Some Christian clergy also pose as seers, boasting that by interpreting the Bible they can foretell the shape of things to come. The Rev. Hal Lindsay, for example, by taking scriptural passages out of context and by isogesis (which consists of reading into the text what one wishes to take out of it, as opposed to scholarly exegesis, which is reading from the text), interprets the biblical sources to relate to modern nations that were not in existence and were unknown in the time of the ancient writer. Like the ancient Qumran community and like the early Christians, such interpreters make the Bible into a talisman to be manipulated according to the interpreter's whim. The only problem faced by these modern Christian interpreters is that most of the time they are in error and thus must continually readjust their conclusions. Amazingly, their followers appear to be able to adjust to their continuing variations of false prophecy.

In view of the support given to prophecy by the Bible and by certain

Christian clergy, it is not surprising to find those who are ready to enter the prophetic field in the present time. They use a combination of biblically supported ideas including astrology and channeling as their techniques.

References

Albright, William F., *Samuel and the Beginnings of the Prophetic Movement,* The Goldsen Lecture for 1961. Cincinnati: Hebrew Union College Press, 1961.

Dykshoorn, M. B., *My Passport Says Clairvoyant,* ed. by Russell H. Felton. New York: Hawthorn Books, 1974.

Gaster, Theodor H., *The Dead Sea Scriptures.* New York: Doubleday, Anchor Books, Third Edition, 1976.

Napier, B. D., *Prophets in Perspective.* New York: Abingdon Press, 1962.

The Mysterious Power of Faith Healing

> If one of you is ill, let him send for the elders of the church, and let them pray over him and anoint him with oil in the name of the Lord. The prayer, offered in faith, will save the sick man. The Lord will raise him up and he will be forgiven for any sins he may have committed.
>
> James 5:14–15

The relationship between belief or faith systems and healing has a long and diverse history, and because faith healing has a number of facets, it cannot be defined simply. In general, faith healing is based on a mythologizing of disease. Illness may be attributed to occult powers including Satan or other demonic beings. Sickness may be interpreted as divine punishment for sin. Such explanations reflect ideas generated in a nonscientific age, when supernaturalistic thinking prevailed and each new disease or epidemic spawned exotic rituals and bogus remedies. The pattern is alive today.

Faith healing can be defined as the belief that diseases and other human ailments of any kind, including bodily injuries, may be cured or healed or warded off or overcome by faith, prayer, or the divine power of God without the use of drugs, medications, or surgical intervention of any kind. Through the power of faith and by the healer uttering incantations, including the name of Jesus, demonic forces can be banished from the body, the devil overcome, the sin forgiven, and the suffering individual cured or healed instantaneously and permanently. Obviously, faith healing is based on a belief that religious language possesses mystical power.

Faith healing may also include denial of the reality of illness through rejecting both the concept of disease and the notion of cure in the usual medical sense. Those who embrace belief systems like Christian Science employ such denial. Some faith circles recommend devices or drugs not recognized as useful by medical science as alternatives to or supplements to regular medical procedures. This group includes those who use amulets and herbal mixtures prescribed by so-called psychic healers. Some faith systems accept selected aspects of modern medicine while denying others. The Jehovah's Witnesses reject, on biblical grounds, certain treatments for life-threatening illnesses, including blood transfusions. Occasionally, when on the basis of religious beliefs parents have refused essential lifesaving treatments for their children, the legal powers of the state have been invoked to protect the child. Still others believe that a combination of faith practices, including prayer and meditation, used in combination with modern medicine may facilitate healing and cure. This group would receive some support from modern psychiatric studies that acknowledge that belief in the power of the cure may promote healing.

Fortunately for public health, most people live and act in accord with the findings and teachings of scientific medicine. Children are immunized by vaccination against certain infectious diseases. About-to-be-married couples have blood tests for sexually transmitted diseases. Antibiotics are employed to fight infections. Surgical procedures, hospital machines, and the latest drugs are employed to restore ailing and damaged bodies.

The Nature of Modern Medicine

Professional medicine has many subdivisions. Specialists treat certain diseases or specific areas of the body. Oncologists deal with cancer, heart specialists with diseases of the heart, and so on. Apothecary science specializes in the preparation, distribution, and study of the effects of drugs and other medications. Departments of Public Health focus on communal well-being. Psychiatrists combine knowledge of medicine and training in dealing with problems of the emotions or the psyche. Sometimes the various medical subdivisions may unite in dealing with some particular health issue, such as AIDS (acquired immune deficiency syndrome); at other times they seem to pursue their individual interests.

Medical science has also welcomed the genius of electronic experts and engineers who design equipment to meet specific needs of certain ailments. Tiny pacemakers regulate heartbeat. Heart and lung machines control breathing and monitor the heart. Kidneys are flushed using dialysis equipment. X-rays and other scanning gear provide pictures of internal organs, including everything from blocked intestines to blocked blood vessels. Brain scans provide cranial imagery. Modern medical diagnosis and treatment have moved a long way from the primitive knowledge possessed by our ancestors. The future gives promise of more detailed information, derived from the study of our human genetic structure.

The importance of cleanliness in treating disease is a relatively recent discovery; therefore, most patients are treated in the antiseptic environment of hospitals. There, dietitians provide balanced meals prepared in sanitary kitchens. Nurses in fresh white uniforms attend immediate needs and monitor electronic devices. Doctors are on call. The latest equipment is at hand.

Despite the best efforts of modern medical science, patients still die. Some diseases resist treatment. When an illness is terminal and there is no known cure, patients, in desperation, may turn from traditional medicine, which has failed them, to a variety of magical, occult, and faith cures. The employment of these nonmedical treatments is spurred by fear of death and related feelings of impotence and helplessness. The dying person and his or her family and friends entertain the desperate hope that miraculous relief may be found.

The Roots of Faith Healing

Hopes for miraculous cures are not new; they are rooted in the remote past. Our ancient ancestors had no way of knowing the true causes of illnesses and diseases. Germs and viruses and so forth were still unknown. To explain diseases and disasters, they conjured up a world of unseen powers and spirits and attributed to them the ailments and misfortunes that plagued humans. The invisible bacteria of today were to them shadowy evil and destructive powers. When one was ill, the place to go for healing was to the temple and to the holy healer. Shamans or priests associated with shrines and sacred places were specialists in divine-human relationships. Primitive medicine and religion were intertwined. Priests were the medical experts. The temple was the source of information about disease and medical treatment.

Healing in Ancient Egypt

Ancient Egyptians assumed that a disease might have a number of causes. It could represent a punishment from the gods. It could be caused by some malevolent dead person. It might result from evil spirits sent by enemies to prey upon a victim. If an illness was believed to be engendered by the gods, petitions, acts of reconciliation, including gifts or offerings, and the use of magical formulae might be employed to pacify the divine powers and effect healing. Demonic forces could be thwarted by magic. Appeals to the deceased, including threats to cut off tomb offerings, might appease the angry dead and bring relief to a suffering family member.

Certain Egyptian gods were associated with healing and their priests played important roles in bringing the powers of these deities to bear on human illness. Ptah, the creator god worshipped at Memphis, was also the healer of his creation. The ibis-headed Thoth, the god of wisdom and the divine healer of the gods, could be asked for help by humans. Isis, the great mother-goddess, could also be appealed to.

The power of these mythical Egyptian figures was supplemented by the healing ability of one human, who was deified after his death: the wise Imhotep, the architect who designed the Sakkara pyramid tomb and who was renowned as a healer. Imhotep provided healing for his ailing devotees through incubation rites. A man or his wife who had been unable to produce a child, or in particular a male child, would sleep in the temple. Through a dream the god would promise to grant their petition, often prescribing the use of certain rituals or medications.

Of course, incubation rites were not limited to Egypt; they were known throughout the ancient world. A similar practice is reported in the fourteenth-century B.C.E. Canaanite story of Aqht, who desired a son and heir and who was promised one as he slept in a holy place. Revelation came through dreams. Much later, when the cult of Aesclepius, the Greek healer, came into being, his shrines included sleeping quarters (*abaton*) for incubation rites. Like Jesus, Aesclepius was said to have had a divine father, Apollo, and a human mother, the princess Coronis. Like Jesus and Imhotep, Aesclepius was deified. In view of the long history of incubatory rites, it is not surprising to find that when Christians began to build shrines and churches, sick and ailing persons would sleep in them in the hope of being healed or to experience a revelatory dream. The practice was forbidden by the Canons of Hippolytus during the early third century.

Egyptian physicians possessed an intimate, sophisticated knowledge of the body, perhaps because of the practice of mummification. This custom involved incising the cadaver in the groin. Internal organs were removed, cleansed, and stored in four canopic jars, each of which was under the divine protection of one of the sons of the god Horus. Often the brain was removed by inserting a hook through the nostrils. The heart was left in the body because the Egyptians, like the Hebrews, believed it, not the brain, to be the center of thought and reason (cf. Pss. 10:6, 15:2, etc.).

The Egyptians recognized the heart as a pump whose action affected all parts of the body through what were called "channels" and which we today call veins or arteries. The Edwin Smith Papyri imply that dissections were not uncommon.

A painting in the eighteenth dynasty tomb of Userhat, the scribe (1567– 1308 B.C.E.), portrays the use of leeches to draw blood. Medicinal chests were carried by Egyptian royalty when they travelled abroad. Numerous medical instruments have been found. The stele at Kom Ombo, which is frequently pictured in medical textbooks, illustrates surgical instruments. Exactly which group of priests may have used such instruments is open to debate. Sekhmet, the lioness-headed goddess, was associated with healing. Perhaps her priests were the surgeons who employed such medical tools. On the other hand, it has been suggested that priests of Sekhmet, like priests of other Egyptian deities, served primarily as intermediaries between the goddess and her petitioners. Alternatively, it has been suggested that the surgeons may have been associated with the cult of Thoth.

Practices of healing and intercession combined magic with the use of medicinal drugs. An extensive pharmacopeia existed, but in the Papyrus Ebers prescriptions are interspersed with incantations. Some of the prescriptions contain rather ordinary and familiar materials. For example, berries of the castor oil tree taken with beer was a prescribed remedy for constipation. Other remedies included substances which we would find revolting or disgusting. For example, to remove skin incrustations or scabs, poultices made from certain berries plus human excrement and cat and dog dung were employed. The medications were used accompanied by magical incantations.

Healing in Mesopotamia

Ancient Mesopotamians believed demonic powers caused disease, and therefore magic was regularly employed to relieve the sufferer. Appeals to the great and powerful gods were often made through one's personal deity. Some ailments were diagnosed as punishments for some mistake or failure or action which had offended or angered a god or goddess. Woe betide the person who was not sure exactly which deity was upset! A particularly moving prayer addressed to any god was found in the library of King Ashurbanipal of Assyria (668–633 B.C.E.). It is truly a "to whom it may concern" appeal. The petitioner cries out:

> May the god whom I either know or do not know be at peace with me.
> May the goddess whom I either now or do not know be at peace with me.

He admits that he is guilty of evils that he cannot specify, for his sins are many. He begs for mercy and forgiveness, wondering "How long, O my goddess whom I either know or do not know, will it be before your heart will be at peace?" He goes on to state:

> Man is stupid; he knows nothing. Humankind, everyone who lives—what does he know? He doesn't even know whether he is committing sin or doing good.

One can only empathize with the petitioner in his sorry state. His plight manifests the sort of problems that often arises where there is a belief in spiritual powers and it is assumed that these powers have some direct influence on human life and health.

Although prayer and petition were part of the rituals associated with healing in Mesopotamia, magic was also employed. Certain religious functionaries were associated with rites designed to bring healing. There was also a class of healers whose professional practices were much closer to those we associate with modern medical science, although these individuals might also employ magic.

Medicinal texts from the third millennium B.C.E. in Sumer reflect the use of medicines made from mineral, herbal, and animal sources. In *History Begins at Sumer,* S. N. Kramer (1959) points out that although one particular pharmacopeia did not include the usual appeal to charms, prayers, and magic to control demonic powers, such Mesopotamian religious material is well known from other texts. Diagnostic texts and surgical instruments have been found in excavations, suggesting a high degree of medical sophistication.

Healing in the Bible

As one might expect, the healing concepts of the authors of the Bible harmonize with notions prevalent in surrounding cultures at their times. Jews and Christians possessed no deeper or more profound insight into the causes and cures of illness than their neighbors.

Healing in the Jewish Scriptures

Because the Hebrew Scriptures were composed during the thousand-year period beginning with the building of the Solomonic temple and ending with the Maccabean revolt (approximately the tenth to second centuries B.C.E.), any brief discussion of a subject over this time span will, of necessity, be a generalization. It seems wisest, therefore, not to attempt a chronological analysis of the textual material, but rather to treat it as an integral unit, based on the completed text as it existed during the early years of the Common Era.

Just how effective ancient Jewish medicinal practices were in healing broken bodies and curing diseases is debatable. Nor can we know exactly how much medical wisdom developed by the great centers of culture was used and accepted in Israel. Skulls found by J. L. Starkey during the 1936–1938 excavation of the site of Lachish give clear evidence of trepanning, which consists of making an opening in the skull, to relieve pressure on the brain (Tufnell 1953, p. 84). Of course, the explanation given for the operation in ancient times was to permit the escape of demons. The tool used in the Lachish trepanning was not a drill or chisel but a saw. Despite the crudeness of the operation, there is evidence that the patient survived for a time, since the edges of the opening indicated some bone growth. Whether the surgeon was a Judean or an Assyrian cannot be determined, for the excavation level was from the period of attack and occupation by the forces of King Sennacherib of Assyria, toward the close of the seventh century B.C.E. It is generally assumed that Hebrew medical knowledge lagged behind and borrowed from that of its powerful neighbors, although there is no clear evidence that this assumption is accurate.

Jewish food laws as set forth in Lev. 11 and Deut. 14 are sometimes cited as evidence of divinely revealed health codes, suggesting that the Jews had superior or more developed health and nutritional patterns. The notion has no basis in fact. The Jews were neither healthier nor unhealthier than their neighbors. Their food laws are to be classified under religious taboos, which included everything from matters based on primitive notions about human sexuality and conditions that rendered a person taboo, including the emission of semen to the menstrual discharge, as set forth in Lev. 15, to the taboo on wearing flax and wool at the same time (Deut. 22:11). Some taboos reflect opposition to other religions, for what was sacred to one god could for that very reason become taboo to another. For example, the pork taboo may be related to the Canaanite habit of sacrificing pigs to their gods, as witnessed by the discovery of numerous pig bones during the excavation of Canaanite sacred altars. Or the pork taboo may have been borrowed from the Egyptians. Herodotus, the fifth century B.C.E. Greek historian, noted that the Egyptians eschewed pork. It has been suggested that health issues may lie behind the taboo. However, the Egyptians also refused to use beans as food. Actually, there is nothing particularly health-threatening in pig flesh if it is properly cooked. Modern orthodox Jews keep kosher or observe food laws for religious reasons. Orthodox Jews are no healthier than any other religious group.

Some food prohibitions are curious. For example, the law prohibiting boiling "a kid in its mother's milk" (Exod. 23:19, 34:26; Deut. 14:21) probably came about as a reaction against a Canaanite fertility cult rite (Gordon 1961, p. 186). This ruling affects present-day Jewish food customs. Milk and meat cannot be served on the same table, and separate vessels are used for cooking and separate dishes are used for serving milk and meat. However, when Yahweh visited Abraham in the guise of a human sojourner, Abraham served milk and meat:

> He took curds and milk and the calf he had prepared and set it before them, and waited on them himself under the tree while they ate. (Gen. 18:8)

Perhaps, as one student suggested, it was Abraham and Sarah's cooking that caused Yahweh to prohibit the mixture! In any case, because of this archaic law, kosher Jews cannot enjoy such delicious meals as beef stroganoff, veal scallopine, veal with soubise sauce, and so on.

Some present-day kosher practices are characterized by magic based on biblical folklore. For example, kosher butchers remove the sciatic nerve from meat. Why? Because when Jacob wrestled with Elohim, his sciatic nerve was injured, and from that moment on he limped (Gen. 32:22–32):

> That's why to this day the children of Israel don't eat the sciatic nerve that runs through the hollow of the thigh, because the hollow of Jacob's thigh was struck on the sciatic nerve. (Gen. 32:33)

The leap from the sciatic nerve injury in a human to removing that sinew in an animal reflects sympathetic magic and perhaps a magical form of preventive medicine. To consume the sciatic nerve of an animal that will be used as food would endanger the eater. Anyone who has suffered the pain caused by a muscle spasm gripping the ischial nerve can sympathize with the desire to avoid such injury. But there is no connection, logical or real, between eating the ischial muscle of an animal and pain from an injured nerve in the eater. Magical thinking in the Bible becomes a practice of preventive magic in the present day.

Some plants were believed to have magical powers. The mandrake, which in Hebrew is called *dudaim,* meaning "lust plants," is usually identified with *Mandragora officinarum,* a plant that is similar to our potato but with bulbous roots that often look something like a human form (Driver 1948, p. 275). In the ancient world it was believed to have aphrodisiac powers. Rachel, Jacob's wife was barren, while her maid, her sister Leah, who was also Jacob's wife, and Leah's maid all bore children for Jacob. When Leah came into possession of some mandrakes, Rachel bargained for them. Apparently the plants were effective, for Rachel became pregnant (Gen. 30:1–24). Some found the odor of the plant pleasant (Song of Sol. 7:13).

Josephus, who wrote during the first century C.E., recounted Jewish folklore associated with the mandrake (*Wars of the Jews,* VII. vi. 3). He wrote that there was danger in digging the low-growing plant in that it could slip from one's hands. It will yield itself if a woman's urine or if blood is poured over it, but then it must be carried with the root hanging down. One could dig a furrow around it, tie the plant to a dog, and let the dog pull it out, although the dog would die instantly. He claimed the mandrake was useful for curing sick persons whose illness stemmed from demonic possession.

The Jewish custom of circumcision of the male has often been treated as a health measure. The custom was widely practiced in the ancient world. For example, a relief from the Sixth Dynasty (2350–2000 B.C.E.) tomb of Ankh-ma-Hor at Saqqara depicts the circumcision of two pubescent boys, and figures in other reliefs show that males were circumcised (Larue 1989, p. 4). Ammonites, Edomites, and Moabites circumcised (Jer. 9:25); Assyrians, Babylonians, and Philistines did not. Herodotus, who visited Egypt in the fifth century B.C.E., wrote that Egyptians practiced circumcision "for the sake of cleanliness" (II, 37), and claimed that other peoples, including the Jews, borrowed the custom from Egypt (II, 104).

Whatever the origins of Jewish circumcision, the practice had nothing to do with health. The earliest reference—from a folktale concerning Moses— was included in the tenth century B.C.E. temple literature:

> Then it happened, at a stopping place along the way, that Yahweh met him [Moses] and tried to kill him. Then Zipporah [Moses' Midianite wife] took a piece of flint, cut off her son's foreskin and touched his [Moses'] feet [genitals] with it, saying "You are my blood-bridegroom." So he [Yahweh] let him [Moses] alone. At that time she said "blood-bridegroom" in reference to circumcision. (Exod. 4:24–26)

Her act was apotropaic; it protected Moses from Yahweh's demonic intent. The term "blood-bridegroom" may reflect the custom of circumcising just prior to marriage, signifying that as the bride would lose her hymen, testified by bloody wedding night sheets (Deut. 22:13–19), so the removal of the prepuce would be the groom's parallel loss. Just how the Hebrew term for father-in-law, which translates as "circumciser," relates to the custom is not known.

In the sixth century B.C.E., Jewish religious fiction produced a different tradition that tied circumcision to a religious contract, a convenant made between Yahweh and Abraham. The seal of the covenant was the mark of circumcision (Gen. 17:10–12). Thus, what may have begun as an ethnic tradition became a divinely ordained legal requirement and the particular mark of a Jew. The performance of circumcision had nothing to do with cleanliness or health.

Throughout the Jewish Scriptures, Yahweh alone is recognized as the cause of illness and disease. The one possible exception is in the Book of Job, where Satan, one of the sons of God, is commissioned to wreak havoc on Job's health, but even here, Satan acted as an emissary of Yahweh (Job 2). Speeches attributed to Yahweh affirm Yahweh's responsibility for illness. When Moses protested his ability to be a spokesman for Yahweh to Pharaoh, Yahweh responded:

> Who has made man's mouth? Who makes him dumb or deaf or able to see or blind? Is it not I, Yahweh? (Exod. 4:11)

Most afflictions mentioned in the Old Testament relate to Israel as a nation and they result from apostasy, backsliding, and neglect of ritual commandments. If the covenant relationship was broken, if Israel sinned, Yahweh threatened outbreaks of "consumption and fever that waste the eyes and cause life to pine away" as well as plagues and pestilence (Lev. 26:16, 21, 26). Among the severe punishments promised in Deuteronomy were "boils of Egypt . . . . tumors [groin swellings] and scurvy and the itch for which you cannot find a cure," or "boils . . . from the sole of your foot to the crown of your head" (Deut. 28:27, 35). The relationship between disobedience or sin and sickness was clearly established by the writers of the Jewish Scriptures. After the Hebrews escaped from Egypt they were warned by Yahweh:

> If you will truly listen to the voice of Yahweh, your Elohim, and do what is acceptable in his sight, and obey his commands and keep all of his statutes, I will not afflict you with the diseases that I brought on the Egyptians, for I, Yahweh, am your healer. (Exod. 15:26)

The prayer put in the mouth of King Solomon at the commemoration of the temple by the author of 2 Chronicles noted that the punishment of the nation was due to Yahweh's anger:

> If they [the nation] sin against you—for there is no man who does not sin—and you are angry with them and you turn them over to an enemy so that they are taken captive to a distant or near country. . . . (6:36)

Healing and restoration came through Yahweh. The so-called "Song of Moses" in the Book of Deuteronomy has Yahweh say:

> I kill and I make alive,
> I wound and I heal,
> and there is no one who can deliver from my hand.
> (32:39)

In other words, Yahweh alone was the source of sickness and disaster; Yahweh alone could heal and rescue.

Yahweh used diseases, plagues, and all manner of illnesses as weapons against those who thwarted his divine intentions (1 Sam. 5:6–6:12) or challenged his authority (2 Sam. 24:10–15) or deserted him (2 Chron. 21:14–15) or violated his will. The health problems of important persons or hero figures were attributed to Yahweh. Miriam questioned Moses' unique relationship with Yahweh and was stricken with leprosy. She was subsequently cured by Moses' prayer (Lev. 12). King David misused his power, had Uriah the Hittite murdered, and produced a child out of wedlock with Bathsheba, the murdered man's wife. Yahweh killed the infant as punishment (2 Sam. 12:1–23). An angry Yahweh afflicted the apostate ruler, King Jehoram of Judah, with a severe abdominal illness that resulted in death (2 Chron. 21:15–19). The list could be extended.

Anyone who was in any way physically deformed or infirm or disfigured was believed to have been afflicted by Yahweh, either because of the afflicted person's own behavior or because of the misbehavior of some ancestor (Deut. 5:9). Such persons could not approach the sacred altar, but were cultic outcasts (Lev. 21:18–23). Thus, it is not surprising to find that medicine and religion were closely related. Healers were associated with the cult. If a person exhibited the symptoms of what is called "leprosy" in the Bible, but which was probably psoriasis, the natural and normal thing to do was to go to the temple and ask the priest to authenticate the ailment and prescribe treatment. The temple was thus the counterpart of the modern city hall, and the priest was functioning as what today would be the Department of Health.

The Bible provides some of the guidelines by which the priest was to distinguish between leprosy and a skin eruption that was due to some other infection. In certain cases the prescribed response of the priest was to quarantine the afflicted person for observation (Lev. 13). In others a magical procedure was followed.

Once leprosy was determined, the afflicted person became an outcast—a ritual outcast because the priest pronounced him to be "unclean," and a social outcast because he was separated from the community:

> The leper who has the affliction must wear torn clothing, let the hair
> of his head hang loose, cover his upper lip and cry out, "Unclean. Unclean."
> So long as he has the disease, he is unclean. He must live alone in a
> dwelling outside the camp. (Lev. 13:45)

Even his garments were considered leprous and subject to destruction by fire. The priest was the health official who made the decisions. He was also the person who signified when the person was to be considered cured or cleansed of leprosy and therefore admissible back into the community and to participation in Hebrew cultic rites.

Having been pronounced cured, the person was subject to ritual cleansing, which involved the use of two living birds, cedarwood, scarlet cloth, and hyssop. One bird was killed in an earthenware vessel over running water. The other materials and the living bird were dipped in the blood of the dead bird. The patient was sprinkled with blood seven times. The blood-splattered living bird was freed. Next the patient had to wash his clothes, shave off all bodily hair, and bathe. After a brief period of semiquarantine, the person was ready for the final ritual that would make him acceptable to Yahweh. He brought three lambs, grain, flour, and oil as guilt and wave offerings to Yahweh. As one might expect, a portion of the offering was retained as personal property by the performing priest "because it is especially holy" (Lev. 14:13).

One lamb was slaughtered as a guilt offering. Some of the lamb's blood was smeared on the right ear lobe, the right thumb, and the right great toe of the patient. Next the priest sprinkled some of the oil seven times "before Yahweh" and dabbed oil on the patient's right ear lobe, right thumb, and right great toe, before rubbing his oily hand on the man's shaved head. Finally, the priest made atonement for the person's sins (Lev. 14:1–20). The cleansed person was now acceptable for participation in cultic and communal ceremonies.

The ritual was elaborate. It involved mysterious performances by the priest or shaman that had a significance beyond mere health protection. Leprosy and any sickness were interpreted as punishment from Yahweh; hence, cleansing had religious importance. The procedures of ritual purification were priestly inventions and were designed, at least in part, to be financially rewarding to the officiant, and in part to be mysterious and to mystify the patient and the community. Back of the rituals lay belief in magic.

Priestly inspection had determined that the person was no longer infected. Only cultic uncleanness remained. The running water, blood, and oil were the magical cleansing elements. Sevenfold sprinkling signified complete cleansing. The bloodied bird that was freed perhaps symbolized the carrying away of contamination. Dabbing blood on the ear, thumb, and big toe, using only the right side of the body, indicated a head-to-toe consecration. The left side was considered unclean or less worthy in many cultures. Indeed, in some Arab villages, it is considered an insult if one waves to another using the left hand. The left hand is used by males in urinating; the right hand for eating and greeting. These present-day cultural patterns help clarify the notions lying behind the ancient rite.

The magical power of prayer was believed to bring healing. King Abimelech of Gerar was cured through Abraham's prayer. Yahweh had condemned the king to death because he had attempted to copulate with Sarah, Abraham's ninety-year-old wife, whom Abraham had deceitfully presented as his sister (Gen. 20). Abraham's prayer had an extra magical effect. Yahweh had "closed all the wombs of Abimelech's household." Now, miraculously, because of Abraham's prayer the queen and all the female slaves became fertile! (20:17-18). Hannah's "barrenness" was removed and she bore a son in response to her prayer and Eli's blessing (1 Sam. 1:9-20).

Prayer might be accompanied by some medical treatment. After King Hezekiah prayed for deliverance from what appeared to be a terminal illness, the prophet Isaiah placed a fig poultice on the king's ulcerous boil, thereby combining primitive medicine and prayer (2 Kings 20:1-11). The king recovered.

Some healing was purely magical. Naaman, commander of the Syrian army, was a leper. He came to the prophet Elisha, expecting Elisha to call on the name of Yahweh, wave his hand, and effect a cure. Apparently, this type of healing rite was known in the ancient world. Pronouncing the name of the god conjured up the power of the god, whether in prayer or in ritual healing. Elisha told Naaman to immerse himself seven times in the Jordan river. The indignant commander responded, as a modern scientist might, that water is water, and one river has no more power than another. When he performed the immersions, however, he was healed.

Elisha's dishonest servant Gehazi, who sought material reward for the healing, was cursed by Elisha and became leprous (2 Kings 5).

The tale is replete with magic. The sevenfold immersion reflects the sacred nature of the number seven as symbolic of completion or perfection. One might ask why a single ritual bath might not suffice or why six dippings or five would not be effective? The answer lies in the supernatural potency attributed to numbers by the ancient Hebrews and their neighbors in Egypt and Mesopotamia. Sevenfold immersion gave the action the numerical significance of complete healing and restoration to perfect health.

There is no evidence that the Jordan river, like the Ganges in India, was believed to have healing power. Hundreds of years after the time of Elisha, John the Baptizer performed his baptismal cleansings in the Jordan. But both John and Elisha appear to have chosen the Jordan because this small stream is the only river in Palestine. Of course, until recent times Christian pilgrims have hallowed the spot on the Jordan where Jesus was supposed to be baptized. When John Lloyd Stephens (1970) visited the area early in the nineteenth century he noted that "year after year, thousands of pilgrims throw themselves into the river with the blind belief that, by bathing in its waters, they wash away their sins" (p. 398). Modern Christian visitors also appear to associate some sort of magic power with the waters of the Jordan, for they bring back vials of Jordan water to be added to baptismal fonts in their local churches.

The power of the curse pronounced by a holy man is demonstrated in the fate of Gehazi. The spoken word was believed to carry the psychic force of the person who uttered it. The curse or blessing of a father or a holy man was stronger than that of some ordinary person. Thus, the curse uttered by an Elijah (2 Kings 2:24) or an Elisha (2 Kings 6:16) was particularly powerful. Curses and blessing also gained in power if they were associated with some holy place. Complaints voiced before the altar of the temple could bring the power of Yahweh into play (1 Kings 8:31). The Book of Deuteronomy contains the execration formulas of the curses to be made by the levitical priesthood (Deut. 27:14-26). The concept of the power of the spoken word runs like an unbroken thread through the Jewish Scriptures from the creation myth in Gen. 1 to the announcement of the fulfillment of the prophetic word in 2 Chronicles (the last book in the Jewish version) or the prophetic oracles in Malachi (the last book in the Protestant version) or Nicanor's invocation in the last chapter of 2 Maccabees (the final book in the Roman Catholic version).

Two stories deal with the resuscitation of dead children. In the first, the child of a widow who befriended Elijah during a famine died. The relationship between sin and suffering or death is made clear when she accuses the prophet of exposing her sin that led to the death of her son. Elijah asked Yahweh, "have you brought disaster to this widow with who I am residing by causing the death of her son?" Then Elijah "stretched himself upon the child three times and cried to Yahweh, 'O Yahweh, permit this child's life breath to come back into him.' " The ritual and the power of the prophetic incantatory request were effective. The child revived (1 Kings 17:17-23).

It has been suggested that perhaps the child was not really dead but was in a coma or a state of suspended animation. That idea is not present in the account. In the story, the child is dead, presumably by an act of Yahweh. When the prophet lay upon the child's body he indulged in a form of contact magic which was well known in Babylon and Canaan. The life strength or health of Elijah was transferred to the child. The triple performance once again reflects the notion that numbers had magical significance. The number three represented beginning, middle, and end, and hence completion or success.

In the second story, which is clearly a variant of the first, Elisha, a disciple of Elijah, is the hero. The child of a family that had befriended the prophet died. Elisha was summoned. Elisha responded by sending a servant ahead with his staff, ordering the man to place the staff on the child's face. It was believed that the staff carried the owner's power. The rite failed. Elisha arrived, prayed over the child, and

Then he went up and lay upon the child, putting his mouth upon his mouth, his eyes upon his eyes, and his hands upon his hands. And as he stretched himself upon him, the flesh of the child became warm. Then he arose and paced back and forth in the house, and went and stretched himself upon him. The child sneezed seven times and opened his eyes. (2 Kings 4:18-36)

Once again, contact magic is employed and here the details are specific (mouth to mouth, eyes to eyes, etc). The sneezing seven times symbolized the complete restoration of the breath of life or the reanimation of the body. Just as Yahweh had animated the mud-formed body of Adam by breathing life breath into his nostrils in the creation story (Gen. 2:7), so Elisha animated the dead child. No special significance can be given to the prophet's pacing through the house.

There are other references to magical healing. Relics or the bones of a holy man like Elisha could miraculously revive a dead man (2 Kings 13:2). Hebrews bitten by serpents during the Exodus wanderings were magically restored through a bronze serpent that had been cast by Moses

(Num. 21:9) This account is treated in detail in the chapter on the Cult of the Serpent.

Healing might also result from magical transference of an ailment to some object, usually an object modeling the malady. The Philistines, having been afflicted with tumors by Yahweh, returned the sacred ark which they had captured in battle together with golden models of tumors and rats by which they hoped to remove the plague (1 Sam. 5–6). The modeling of the tumors involved sympathetic magic. As the golden tumors left the Philistine territory, so would the actual tumors be removed.

The Book of Tobit is included in Roman Catholic and Eastern Orthodox Bibles but is placed in the Apocrypha by Protestants and Jews. It includes two accounts of magical rescues through the aid of the angel Raphael.

Two problems are presented. Tobit, a righteous Jew, was blinded when bird droppings got into his eyes. In far away Ecbatana in Media, Sarah, the daughter of Gabael, a man to whom the now impoverished Tobit had loaned money, was having her own problems. She had been married seven times, and each time on the wedding night a demon named Asmodeus killed the husband before the marriage was consummated sexually. Local gossips suggested that Sarah had strangled each man. Tobit sent his son Tobias to collect the money from Gabael, and Yahweh sent the angel Raphael, who became incarnate and took the name Brother Azarius, to accompany Tobias.

The two sojourners caught a fish and saved the liver, the gall, and the heart. When they arrived at Ecbatana, there was no problem about the recovery of the money. Tobias fell in love with Sarah. The marriage contract was signed, and the young couple retired to the wedding chamber for the night. Upon the advice of Brother Azarius, Tobias placed the fish's liver and heart upon the incense coals in the bridal room. The horrible smell drove the demon away to Egypt, where the angel bound him forever. Tobias and his bride journeyed to the home of Tobit and there, as advised by his angelic guide, Tobias put the fish's gall in his father's eyes. Tobit rubbed his eyes, the white film scaled off, and he could see.

The expulsion of the demon is folkloric magic (see chapter on Satanism). One can only imagine the aromatic atmosphere of the room in which the young couple were to make love! The removal of the scales from Tobit's eyes may be a combination of magic (the healing power of fish gall), religion (the angelic guidance), and a medical practice known as "couching." Couching involves pressing the lens of the eye down and back into the lower vitreous cavity. In other words, the film covering Tobit's eyes was removed and sight was restored by couching. The practice was known throughout the ancient world. It was referred to in the Hammurabi Code; it was used by the Hindu surgeon Susruta about 600 B.C.E., and it is mentioned by the Roman writer/physician Celsus around 30 C.E.

The Tobit story does not relate the unfortunate happenings of Tobit or Sarah to sin or to any ritual violation. Tobit is described as a pious Jew who took his religious responsibilities seriously. As a Jewish captive in Nineveh, he ate only kosher food, practiced charity, and buried dead Jews who would otherwise have been left to rot. Because of contact with a corpse, he had been rendered ceremonially unclean. The Torah states: "Whoever touches a corpse shall be ritually unclean for seven days" (Num. 19:11). To avoid contaminating others, Tobit slept outdoors beside a wall, and it was then that the bird droppings fell into his eyes. His misfortune was accidental and was not related to any personal misdeeds or violations of Jewish law. Similarly, Sarah is presented as a righteous woman and as a proper Jewish daughter. When tempted to hang herself because of harassment from one of her father's maidservants, she refrained because her act might have brought reproach on her father. She was a victim of the malevolence of a supernatural power. She had done nothing to deserve her treatment.

The Book of Job is a forthright refutation of the theological doctrine of the relationship between sin and suffering. The author of the book carefully set the stage. Job is portrayed as a righteous man. This is affirmed by Yahweh, Satan, and the author. He did nothing to offend Yahweh. He broke no religious rules. He had been faithful in observing cultic rites. His terrible afflictions were caused not by sin but by a cruel wager between Yahweh and Yahweh's son, Satan.

Yahweh had boasted of Job's loyalty and righteousness. Satan suggested that the pious behavior could be explained by the blessings and rewards with which God had favored Job. In other words, Job was pious because piety paid off in material goods. Yahweh decided to put Job to the test. Would this righteous man curse the deity when he lost all his goods and when his health was impaired? Job's material wealth and his family, with the exception of his wife, were wiped out. His body was afflicted with hideous sores. No sin or violation of the divine will was involved, and Job did not curse Yahweh.

Three friends came to console him. Their insights or counsel or wisdom reflected standard Hebrew religious concepts: Job's suffering was due to sin. His children deserved to die. Job probably deserved even more severe punishment. Throughout their harassing dialogue, Job insisted that he had done nothing to deserve punishment and asked only that his God let him know what was back of these tragic events. He did not curse God. He only requested an explanation so that he might understand divine justice.

The conclusion of the story provided Job with little reassurance and no understanding. God announced that the counselors were wrong. Job was not being punished for his sins (indeed, how could he be, inasmuch as he was righteous?). Job never learned why he suffered. The cruel and unethical wager that resulted in brutal treatment by his God remained a divine secret (to Job at least; it was revealed, of course, to the readers of the story). Wealth and health were restored to Job and he acquired a new family.

The story constitutes a rejection by some Hebrew writer of accepted theological teachings concerning the relationship between sin and suffering. Through Job, the author projected his belief that humans cannot know what goes on in the mind of God, and any attempt to find out why terrible things happen to decent people would receive no answer from on high. When Job sought answers, his God bullied him into silence and submission by a barrage of irrelevant questions that avoided the issue of divine justice. Job's dilemma is reminiscent of the Babylonian worshipper who could not even know which god or goddess he had offended, much less what sins he may have committed. Neither could Job know what lay behind his terrible suffering.

There are few references to physicians in the Old Testament. The Hebrew word for physician is *rapha* or *raphah,* which refers to the act of sewing or mending. Perhaps the physician was one who sewed up wounds. The term is not always used with approbation. King Asa of Judah was afflicted with some disease that affected his feet. The Chronicler noted that he sought aid from physicians rather than from Yahweh. Consequently, he was not healed and died (2 Chron. 16:11–13). On the other hand, Jeremiah's lament over Judah reflects the healing power of the physicians. He asked

> Is there no balm in Gilead?
> Is there no physician there?
> Why then has the health of the daughter of my people
> not been restored?
>
> (8:22)

Jeremiah makes other references to balm (46:11, 51:8). This particular substance has been identified as oil derived from the shrub delile. It was believed to have medicinal value. The physicians are recognized as healers by the prophet, and apparently one of their treatments included the use of balm.

Jesus, son of Sirach, the second-century B.C.E. teacher, advised that the physician should be honored:

> Reward the physician with the honor due to him according to your need
> .   of him for the Lord created him.
> Healing comes from the Most High, and he will receive a gift from the
>   king.
> A physician's head is honored according to his skill and he is admired
>   in the presence of great men.
> From the earth, the Lord created medicines and an intelligent man will
>   not despise them.
>
> (Ben Sirach 38:1-4)

The wise teacher did not question the source of illness nor of the healing. He gave recognition to the importance of medications and the physician. He recommended that a sick person purge himself of sin, make a rich offering, including incense and "fine flour," and consult a doctor. The section ends with the comment: "If a man sins in the eyes of his Maker, may he fall under the care of the doctor" (38:15). Unlike the author of Job, Jesus, son of Sirach, had not really moved beyond the association of suffering or illness with sin.

Healing in the Christian Scriptures

Modern Christian faith healers look to Jesus as their model. In Christian Scriptures, Jesus is portrayed as teacher, preacher, healer, and wonderworker. His miracles are labelled "signs" (*semeia*) or "works" (*erga*) or "powers" (*dunameis*) but never mere "wonders" (*tepata*). In every instance the term "wonders" always appears together with the word "signs," suggesting that there was a purpose in back of what Jesus did that went beyond a simple display of power, and that served to establish the divine identity ascribed to him by Christian writers.

A careful reading of the Gospels reveals the importance of Jesus' healing ministry. Wherever he went he is reported to have restored physical and mental health to those sick in body and mind. More than forty acts of healing are recorded, and if one counts duplications or parallel accounts there are more than seventy references to Jesus as healer. In some instances he cured an individual; in others large numbers of people were healed.

Because Jesus was a Jew and Christianity had its origins in Judaism, it is important to note that during the historical period when Jesus' ministry took place and the Christian Scriptures came into being, Jewish religion was in flux. Beliefs in demons and Satanism, in exorcism and spells, which in earlier times may have had some following mainly among the general populace in Israel, were now current in powerful religious circles. Christian writings reflect these notions.

In New Testament thought, sickness could be attributed to demons, it could be interpreted as a punishment for sin, or it could represent an arbitrary act of God. Similar concepts were prevalent throughout the Mediterranean world. The Greeks believed that the gods sent sickness and diseases but not necessarily as punishment for sin. In both Greek and Jewish circles, the time was ripe for deities that reached out to touch and heal the pains and misfortunes of humankind. Thus it was that the cult of Aesclepius drew multitudes to its healing shrines, just as Jesus, according to the Gospels, drew crowds.

New Testament writers were not objective reporters; they were creative authors who wrote with a purpose. For example, the reader is informed that Jesus' mighty works and wonders and signs attested to the fact that God was working through him (Acts 2:22). When the writer of Mark notes that the demonic powers that infested the ill recognized Jesus, he was, in reality, informing his readers that Jesus was "the Holy One of God" (Mark 1:23–24). The pattern is more subtle in the Gospel of John. In the pericope of the healing of a man born blind, Jesus is identified first as "the man named Jesus," then as a prophet, then as one who must be "from God," and finally is addressed as "Lord" (John 9).

Form critics have made us aware that biblical writers employed known literary structures. For example, the brief account of the healing of Simon's mother-in-law in Mark 1:30–33 has three parts. The first is the situation: Jesus learns of the fever-stricken woman. Second is the action: Jesus takes her hand and heals her. Third is the proof: she waits on the men. It is clear from the structured literary pattern that the stories are presented by accomplished writers, not by eyewitnesses who, in reporting, would not follow such a pattern.

Some healing accounts reflect the influence of Old Testament healing stories. In the story of Jesus' revitalizing the dead son of a widow in the town of Nain, the writer of the Gospel of Luke reflects the tale of Elijah reviving the dead son of the widow of Zarephath that was discussed earlier (Luke 7:11–15; cf. 1 Kings 17:17–24):

As he [Jesus] approached the city gate, a dead man was being carried out. He was the only son of his widowed mother. . . . When the Lord saw her he had compassion for her and said, "Don't cry." As he approached the bier and touched it, the bearers halted. Then he said, "Young man, I tell you get up." Then the dead man sat up and began to talk. And he [Jesus] returned him to his mother. Everyone was awestruck. Then they praised God by saying, "A great prophet has risen among us" and "God has visited his people."

The echo of the Elijah story is clear. Elijah and Jesus both raise sons of widowed mothers, one through sympathetic magic and an incantation, the other by command.

The Gospel of Luke reports the healing of a woman who for eighteen years had been afflicted by a crippling spirit (*pneuma*) that bent her double. Jesus healed her by placing his hands on her and saying, "Woman, you are freed from your infirmity" (Luke 13:11–13). In another instance, Jesus healed a young man who suffered from aphasia and epilepsy attributed to possession by a spirit (*pneuma*). Jesus' disciples had not been able to expel the spirit. Jesus said, "Spirit of dumbness and deafness, I command you to come out of him and trouble him no longer." As a result, the boy was convulsed and entered into a death-like trance, which Jesus brought him out of (Mark 9:17–27). Some spirits were labelled "unclean," which has cultic or ritualistic overtones and at the same time implies demonic possession. These, too, were expelled by Jesus (Mark 1:23–26). Illness was attributed to evil spirits and part of Jesus' healing ministry was the expulsion of these spirits.

The New Testament Gospel writers recognized the role of physicians. For example, Jesus could be made to remark: "It is not the healthy who need a physician, it is those who are sick" (Matt. 9:12). A woman with a vaginal blood flow had expended all her money over a period of twelve years on unsuccessful treatment by physicians. She was instantly cured by touching Jesus' tunic (Mark 5:25–34). In the letter to the Colossians it is noted that Luke, a Christian writer, was a physician (Col. 4:14).

Medical treatment of wounds is suggested in the parable of the good Samaritan who treated the wounds of the man who had been beaten by robbers with oil and wine (Luke 10:25–37). When Jesus was crucified, his captors offered him a soporific mixture of wine and myrrh as a palliative to ease the pain (Mark 15:23).

Jesus, the supreme healer for Christians, healed not by medicines or treatment but in the name of God, by his own Christian power, and by command. Some healing, wherein he fulfilled Christian interpretation of biblical prophecy, was designed to authenticate his role as messiah. For example, the writer of the Gospel of Matthew commented:

he drove out the spirits with a word and healed all who were sick. This was done to fulfill the prophecy of Isaiah: "He took our infirmities and bore our diseases." (8:16–17)

Some of Jesus' cures revealed compassion. Two blind men, learning that Jesus was passing by, called upon him for healing. "Jesus, in pity, touched their eyes, and immediately they received their eyesight and followed him" (Matt. 20:34).

Many healings occurred immediately; a few were delayed. Ten lepers were healed only after they left Jesus and as they went to show themselves to the priests, which they had been instructed to do (Luke 17:12–14). Some persons were healed by the spoken word: some by touch. The leper who knelt before Jesus and said, "Sir, if you want to, you can cleanse me," was immediately healed when Jesus touched him and said, "I want to. Be clean." Even Jesus' clothes had curative power, as demonstrated in the healing of the hemorrhaging woman.

It is reported that Jesus healed all manner of diseases. Some of his cures were what we, today, would call exorcisms. Simply by saying "go," he cast out devils or demons from a wild man who lived in cave tombs (Matt. 8:28–33, see also 15:22–28; Mark 1:23–27; Luke 8:2; etc.). It has been suggested that some of the mentally ill Jesus cured may have been persons afflicted by hysterical dumbness or blindness (Matt 9:32, 12:22). At Jesus' command, lame and paralyzed persons suddenly walked. On one occasion he restored a withered hand (Matt. 12:9–13 and parallels); on others he stopped a hemorrhage (Matt. 9:20–22), cured blindness (John 9; Mark 10:46–52; Matt. 9:27–30), banished fevers (Matt. 8:14–15; John 4:47–53), and cured edema (Luke 14:1–4). Perhaps the most dramatic acts were the restoration of the ear of a high priest's slave that was sliced off by one of Jesus' zealous disciples (Luke 22:50–51) and the raising of the dead (Matt. 9:18–25; Luke 7:11–15), including Lazarus, who had been entombed in a cave for four days (John 11:17–44). Some of Jesus' cures have been explained in terms of psychosomatic healing, or by arguing that the dead individual was really in a coma. For the Gospel writers, the miracles were testimony to Jesus' supernatural power and to his messiahship.

To heal a blind man in Bethsaida, Jesus spit in the man's eyes and laid hands on him (Mark 8:22–25). At Jericho, a blind man was healed by word of command: "Go on your way, your faith had healed you" (Mark 10:46–52). In a third instance, Jesus mingled spittle and clay, rubbed the mixture on the blind man's eyes, and commanded him to rinse his eyes at the pool of Siloam to regain sight (John 9:6–8). A deaf man with a speech impediment was healed when Jesus put his fingers in the man's ears, and spat and put the spit on the man's tongue, saying, "Be opened" (Mark 7:32–35). The use of spittle was an act of magic. The spit of a holy man or healer was an extension of the person. Just as the laying on of hands conveyed power, so did the spit have transforming power.

Jesus was able to heal in absentia. A centurion's servant was healed without Jesus' seeing the man (Matthew 8:5–13). He could also heal non-believers. A Canaanite woman who was not a Jew and did not believe in the Torah asked help for her demon–possessed daughter. Jesus healed the daughter without seeing her and without demanding faith from the mother (Matt. 15:21–28).

The widespread correlation between sin and suffering in Judaism and early Christianity is reflected in the question asked by Jesus' disciples concerning a man born blind:

"Rabbi, who has sinned, this man or his parents, since he was born blind?" Jesus answered, "Neither he nor his parents have sinned, but that God's work should be revealed in him." (John 9:2–3)

Jesus then healed the man. The reference to parental sin causing the blindness is based on the Torah teaching that the sins of the father could be punished in the children up to the third and fourth generations (Deut. 5:9). A child born blind could attribute the blindness to the sinful behavior of an ancestor, or perhaps even explain the malady on the basis of human sinfulness traceable back to Adam and Eve, but hardly to something a newborn might have done. The question may sound ridiculous, but it echoes Jewish and Christian thought of the first century C.E. that sin and suffering are interrelated.

It is not surprising that forgiveness of sin was often part of Jesus' healing work. In the case of a bed-bound paralytic, before Jesus commanded the man "Get up, pick up your bed and go home," he said, "Cheer up, son, your sins are forgiven" (Matt. 9:2–7).

Christians also discovered a relationship between Jesus' death and human sin. In the minds of his Roman captors, Jesus' suffering and death were proper punishment for his troublesome behavior. He had been tried and condemned as a criminal in a Roman court of law. He was punished and put to death together with two other condemned criminals. Christian theology interpreted his tortuous demise differently. His death was punishment for sin—not his own, but that of the world. Yahweh's justice called for punishment for disobedience. Humans disobeyed the divine law. Jesus took upon himself the punishment due to human sinners. Human guilt was magically transferred and placed on the shoulders of a single person. For the early Christians, the death of their leader was interpreted as an act of God. Jesus' death was removed from the category of criminal punishment and now assumed a Promethean nobility as an act of self-sacrifice for the redemption of humankind. At the same time, the Jewish notion of the relationship of sin to suffering was maintained and would become a central facet of Christian dogma.

The scapegoat concept that was used to explain why Jesus as Son of God died, had its roots in Jewish practice. On the Day of Atonement (*Yom Kippur*), the high priest of the Jewish temple in a confessional ceremony magically transferred the sins of the people on to the head of a goat known as the goat for Azazel (Lev. 16:20–22). The goat was then led out of the city into the wilderness where it perished. Azazel was a desert demon. Later, in the intertestamental Book of Enoch, Azazel appears as the leader of rebel angels that seduce humans. Some biblical scholars relate the term "azazel" to an Arabic word (*'azza*) meaning "rugged," so that the goat for Azazel could refer to a goat that was to die in some rugged, clifflike spot in the desert. Most scholars accept the demonic interpretation. But through this magical rite the nation was purged. Accumulated evils, transferred to the head of the goat, were sent into the wilderness where the demonic power known as Azazel received them.

In Christian theology, Jesus is the scapegoat, the sinbearer. As the Jewish national sin was purged with the death of the goat, so Christian sin is removed through Jesus' death. The ritual of transference of sin for Christians does not include the laying on of hands, but rather the simple acceptance in faith that the magical displacement occurs and the believer automatically is purified and made acceptable to the deity.

Some suffering was attributed to demons or to Satan, who in the current theology had assumed the role of the anti-God or devil. The Apostle Paul suffered from some affliction which he called "a thorn in the flesh, a messenger of Satan, to harass me and to keep me from being too proud." He explained that although he had begged for divine healing three times, it was denied him. He had an explanation for the denial. He claimed that Jesus had told him, "My grace is enough for you. My power is perfected in weakness" (2 Cor. 12:7–9). Just how Paul got the message from Jesus, who was dead long before Paul's conversion, is not explained. Perhaps Paul had other hallucinations comparable to his conversion experience; perhaps he just "felt" the message, or the thought came to him in the same way that some modern believers claim to get messages from Jesus or God.

Jesus was not always successful as a healer. In his home town of Nazareth he was unable to work miracles (Mark 6:5–6). The failure was explained as a lack of faith among the townspeople. Despite the lack of faith, he did lay hands on a few people and heal them. However, as we have seen, other healing efforts were successful despite lack of faith.

There is absolutely no way to verify the healing miracles attributed

to Jesus in the Christian Scriptures. Perhaps Jesus used couching to remove scales from a blind man's eye, but of this we cannot be sure. What
is lacking in the New Testament accounts of Jesus' healing ministry is what
is lacking in all anecdotal accounts of healing, both ancient and modern—
documented diagnoses by competent authorities. A patient or a narrator
can make any sort of claim without challenge. Nor are there any follow-
up studies to determine whether or not after the excitement of the moment
the ailments returned. Some cures can be related to psychogenic ailments
or to varying degrees of hypochondriasis that originate in the mind. Other
claims of healing must be categorized as religious fiction designed to exalt
Jesus' reputation, and here one would include the story of the instantaneous
healing of the severed ear. For many Christians to doubt biblical teachings
is simply unthinkable, and believers are encouraged to accept the incredu-
lous as fact.

Healing in the Apostolic Age

The early church characterized Jesus as one who "went about doing good
and healing all who were oppressed by the devil" (Acts 10:38). That is
to say, the developing church related sickness to demonic oppression. The
Gospels state that Jesus commissioned his disciples to continue his ministry
(Mark 6:7-10; Matt. 10:5-10; Luke 9:1-6), and after his death his followers healed in his name. The Book of Acts records their activities. Peter
healed a crippled man at the gate of the Jewish temple by saying, "In
the name of Jesus Christ of Nazareth, get up and walk," and by taking
his hand and pulling him to his feet. Then the bones of the man's feet
and ankles became strong and he could walk and dance (Acts 3:2-8). The
use of Jesus' name invoked the healing power of Jesus.

Healing appears to have played an important part in the work of Paul.
He refers to the "signs and wonders" he performed as he developed new
Christian groups (Rom. 15:19; 2 Cor. 12:12). When Paul and Barnabas
were in Lystra, Paul noticed in the audience a crippled man who had never
been able to walk. Sensing that the man believed he could be healed, Paul
cried out, "Get up on your feet!" The man stood up and began to walk
(Acts 14:6-10). In this setting Paul called on neither God nor Jesus. He
healed, as Jesus had done, simply by commanding the patient to obey.

Healing power was magically transferred to items associated with Paul:

And God performed extraordinary miracles through Paul so that handkerchiefs or cloths that had been in contact with his body were carried

to the sick and they were cured of their diseases and the evil spirits came
out of them. (Acts 19:11)

On the island of Malta, by laying hands on the father of Publius, the
chief magistrate, Paul healed him of dysentery and fever (Acts 28:8-9).

The use of Jesus' name in rites of baptism (Acts 8:12-13, 10:48, 19:5)
and healing implied that those who performed the ritual or caused the
healing were, so to speak, commissioned by Jesus—just as an ambassador
might speak in the name of his king. The words had back of them the
power and authority of the one in whose name they were given. The pattern occurs throughout the Bible. Hebrew prophets spoke in the name of
Yahweh. The assumption was that they were commissioned or inspired
by Yahweh. The words they spoke were not their own words but the message of the deity. In Jesus' day, it was assumed that the age of prophecy
was past. Thus, when Jesus spoke in the name of the Jewish god or as
a personal extension of the divine, his words were blasphemous to Jewish
ears. Later, his immediate followers spoke in his name. Throughout the
Book of Acts there is the presumption that these spokesmen were empowered to act and speak in Jesus' name.

Healing in the Early Church

There is some evidence that the early church continued in the healing
tradition. During the third century, Origen, the theologian, stated that the
repetition of the name of Jesus would expel demons. The Roman Catholic and Eastern Orthodox churches staked claims in the field of healing
through the use of a wondrous variety of amulets, including bones of saints,
magical cloths, bits of wood from the cross, and so on. The Protestant
reformers took a different approach.

Healing and the Protestant Reformation

The central figures in the Reformation, Calvin and Luther, believed that
physical healing by the Holy Spirit occurred in the time of the New Testament, but with the death of the apostles, the age of faith healing was over.
This tradition has continued to be part of the thinking, teaching, and practice of churches associated with these founders. Indeed, in 1962, the United
Lutheran Church appointed a committee composed of medical doctors,

clergy, and theologians to investigate some of the practices of certain faith healers. Their findings, reported in *Health/Medicine and the Faith Traditions* (Marty and Vaux 1982), charged that faith healers, seeking money and power, often exploited human desperation; that modern, proven, scientific healing methods were ignored; and that failures to heal were blamed on the sick individual's lack of faith (which they said could endanger the patient's spiritual life). The investigators did not rule out the power of prayer, but they placed more trust in scientific medicine.

The Healing Process

Healing is a normal, natural process. When the body is injured the physical system responds to the injury and a healing process begins. If a person suffers a cut, the body protein known as anti-hemophilic-globulin or Factor VIII initiates blood clotting, which seals the wound and stops the bleeding—unless, of course, the person is that one in 10,000 males who may have inherited hemophilia. The rate of healing varies from individual to individual. Some people bruise and heal quickly, others carry bruises for long periods of time.

Some illnesses, including some forms of cancer, go into sudden remission for reasons that are not completely understood by medical science. Some ailments simply go away and the person is healed. The processes, despite the fact that they are still under study, are accepted as completely normal. Why they happen to some persons and not to others is not known. Nor is there any real understanding of why some persons heal more rapidly than others.

Mind-Body Relationships

A relationship between the mind and the body, between thought and feeling, is known to exist. By means of this relationship, a person can be distracted from the pain of an injury or can focus on the pain. For example, a carload of young people were involved in an auto accident. The car slipped off a wet, oily road and rolled into a ditch. All were shaken up but no one seemed to be seriously injured beyond a few bruises and scratches. The driver, who felt personally responsible, busied himself helping others out of the overturned car. He limped and explained that he thought he had twisted his ankle. Later, a hospital x-ray revealed that the ankle had been shattered and the bone splintered. How could the young man walk and put weight on that foot? His doctor explained: "He was in shock.

He was distracted. He focussed on his friends, not his foot." This was a severe case, but many similar experiences with less traumatic injuries have been reported.

A young boy playing soccer falls and bruises his leg. He rubs the spot and goes on with the game. The girl who is riding her bike with her friends falls and scrapes her elbow. She rubs the spot, assures her friends that "It is nothing," and goes on with the cycling adventure. Later, the boy and the girl might be surprised to discover the extent of their injuries—a huge bruise and an extensive abrasion. At the moment of injury other matters were more important, so that a hurt that in other circumstances might have produced tears or cries for attention and sympathy is dismissed as unimportant. The mind and the body were united in concentrating on something other than the bruise or the scrape. The healing process of the body began immediately. The heart pumped a bit faster, the blood circulated more quickly, and the emphasis was on positive rather than negative activities.

One of the more popular recent medical approaches is known as "wholistic" or "holistic" medicine, which recognizes that some diseases of the body may be induced or enhanced by mental attitudes. The notion is not new. It is an extension of the psychosomatic concept. We are, as persons, combinations of mind, body, and psyche or spirit. Illness in one dimension affects the well-being of the whole. Successful treatment, therefore, involves a recognition of the relational aspects of the mind-body-psyche and includes psychological and in some instances "spiritual" healing. For example, a social worker seeks to help a woman who is unable to walk. The physician in charge can discern no medical reasons for the woman's incapacity. The social worker discovers that the woman has been recently bereaved. Her spouse had taken care of her for the forty years of their marriage. She never learned to drive a car, balance a checkbook, or deal with financial or business problems. She felt helpless and incapacitated when her husband died. She became immobilized. She believed she could not move. Her ailment was not physical, it was mental or psychological. Healing involved the reorientation of the woman's thinking, some reeducation, the raising of her self-esteem, and the woman's discovery of her ability to look after herself.

Medical practitioners are familiar with the placebo ("I shall please") effect. An individual with severe back pains is thoroughly examined and no physical reason for the aches can be found. The doctor may prescribe pills that he or she assures the patient will eliminate the pain. The medication works despite the fact that the tablets are sugar or salt pills.

Joel Kovel, in a discussion of "Directive Therapy," recorded a case in which a direct countersuggestion produced "healing." He wrote:

A physician I knew, weary and disgusted with the endless work of a New Year's Eve in the hospital emergency room, was confronted by an obviously hysterical woman who had come in shrieking, "I'm blind! I can't see!" Drawing himself up to his full height, he pointed an imperious finger and in his deepest and most convincing voice solemnly intoned, "You are not blind! You can see!" Whereupon—you guessed it—the woman ecstatically cried, "I can see! I can see!" and rushed back out into the night. A complete cure, purely directive. (Kovel 1976, p. 208)

Obviously the woman suffered from hysterical blindness. She was not medically blind. She believed she was blind, and the mind convinced the body that this was so. The countersuggestion reversed the conviction, and the body responded. It has been suggested that not only were some of the cures attributed to Jesus related to possible cases of hysterical illness, but that many of the present-day faith cures are, too.

The effectiveness of the placebo treatment rests on the physician's awareness that every imaginative anticipation of feeling tends to transform itself into reality. Therefore, a countersuggestion may remove the fear of illness and the sensation of pain. No one is really sure what takes place, but certainly some forms of human ailment respond rapidly to suggestion. It is suspected that the mind reacts with a chemical release of endogenous opiate painblockers such as enkephalins for transient analgesic effect or endorphins for longer lasting analgesia.

Clearly, some kinds of human ailments respond rapidly to suggestion. Mesmer's healing tub therapy, Charcot's work, and Josef Breuer's studies exhibited the relationship of mind and body, as these men helped patients suffering from hysterical paralysis, blindness, deafness, and convulsive attacks. Modern medicine recognizes the relationship of stress to heart problems and other physical ailments. As stress is relieved, the patient's health improves.

A small percentage of individuals respond favorably to hypnotic suggestion. Another, larger group, are minimally susceptible. Some medical institutions have introduced hypnotherapy into their medical programs. They have learned that the healing process can be enhanced.

Some find relief through acupuncture. They are told that life energy (called *chi*) flows along a system of twelve invisible channels or meridians along which are located trigger points related to body organs and extremities. Injury or pain weakens the energy flow along the affected meridian. The acupuncturist stimulates that meridian's trigger points by using needles or electricity or touch. Patients feel relieved simply because they are encouraged to believe they are being helped. In other words, there is communication between the brain and the body. Only peripheral and not very convincing research exists to indicate that acupuncture has any healing effect outside of its psychosomatic dimensions. For example, Dr. Joseph Helms of the Kaiser Permanente Medical Center in Oakland, California, conducted a one-year study of the use of acupuncture with women suffering from dysmenorrhea. One group was treated with acupuncture, with twelve needles placed in accepted positions. A second group was treated with needles improperly located. A third group consisted of women who made additional visits to the doctor's office, and a fourth group constituted a control group. Helms reported that ten of the eleven women in the first group experienced immediate relief from pain and were able to cut in half the amount of pain medication they usually required. After acupuncture was terminated, for forty percent of these women the benefits continued for up to nine months. Women in the second group reported less painful menstrual periods, but the relief was of shorter duration after treatments stopped.

Studies conducted at the University of Texas, Galveston, concerning the relationship between illness and stress resulting from bereavement or other causes have provided some evidence of the way the brain interacts with the immune system. Therefore, any suggestion by a powerful person, such as Jesus was, to the effect that healing is now taking place, may trigger bodily responses that overcome psychosomatic ailments, some of which may have long histories. One yields control of the self, so to speak, to a trusted person who is believed to have healing power, so that the psychological pain, which is being expressed physiologically, is relieved and healing occurs.

Modern medicine has also become interested in meditation as an aid to healing. The general interest in meditation in recent years has derived from the Far East, particularly from practices associated with yoga. Now, through the use of modern biofeedback equipment, some patients learn to control heartbeat, breathing, and physical tension. In a stress-ridden age with stress-related illnesses, the results can make positive contributions to better health. Of course, inasmuch as stress may be job-related or result from unhappiness in personal relationships, the biofeedback techniques can offer only release from physical tension. Psychotherapy may be needed to enable a person to discover ways to change relational patterns or to seek new employment as a way to alter the stress-producing factors.

Wholistic treatment attempts to fuse medical and psychological and perhaps also social factors (in that we all need the warmth and caring of friends). It honors the totality of our humanity and recognizes that surgery and medication can be augmented by mental health and feelings of spiritual well-being.

Those engaged in healing professions tell us that it is much easier to

THE MYSTERIOUS POWER OF FAITH HEALING   143

treat patients whose attitude towards life is positive than to deal with someone whose focus is negative. A cooperative, cheerful personality seems to induce healing, possibly by a willingness to cooperate without complaint with the medical staff, perhaps because positive attitudes enhance the body's healing powers. In *Anatomy of an Illness*, Norman Cousins (1979) described in detail his battle with a crippling disease by using, among other things, the weapons of laughter and joy. Physical impairment can be exacerbated by worries about family and financial problems.

What limits may be placed on mind-body healing? Do the Christian Science practitioners truly heal? The Church of Christ, Scientist, was started by Mary Baker Eddy, who claimed to have been miraculously saved from a life-threatening illness. Her teachings focussed on the immortal reality of the spirit and the mortal "error" which is matter. Humans, made in the image and likeness of God, are spirit. Evil, disease, sickness, and even death are temporary and unreal or illusory. The true or real human is not the "mortal" being but is the divine reflection of God. The world of the senses is unreal. Healing is explained metaphysically, religiously, and biblically. The teachings of the group are health-oriented, but there is a steadfast denial of medical and pharmaceutical practices, of many public health measures, and of scientific research into knowledge about human well-being. The Bible, the source book for the faith, is interpreted metaphysically.

If one attends a Christian Science service, it is impossible not to be impressed by the testimonies of those who claim to have been healed through the ministry of Christian Science practitioners. If one attends a number of these services, one discovers that there is a repetitiousness about the testimonies that can become boring. The same healings are repeated over and over again. Are the healings genuine? There can be no doubt that the psychosomatic effects discussed above function for Christian Science. On the other hand, serious charges including manslaughter and child abuse were leveled against the church in California in 1986. The case involved three families whose children died of meningitis in 1984. The parents did not seek medical help but relied upon the power of prayer by accredited Christian Science practitioners to heal this deadly illness. The prayers failed. The parents were charged with failure to provide effective treatment, thereby endangering the well-being of their children.

Rita Swan's fifteen-month-old son died of meningitis in 1977 after treatment by Christian Science practitioners in Detroit, Michigan. She claimed that the healers receive two weeks' training and that no limits are placed on what illnesses they may treat. It is important to recognize that in Christian Science some medical treatment is accepted. Eyeglasses can be fitted, teeth can be filled, broken bones can be set, painkillers can be injected by licensed medical persons. Most members of the 2,200 churches in the United States do not consult doctors. The church operates sanitaria which can receive Medicare payments. In forty-eight states church members are given exemptions from immunization requirements. In some states the children of Christian Science families are exempted from studying health sciences in school.

How an adult may choose to treat his or her own illnesses and diseases may be a personal matter insofar as the ailments are not communicable. But how parents choose to treat the illnesses of their children may be viewed in a different light. Child abuse laws call for the protection of a child's well-being. Whenever a child's health is threatened, it is the duty of the state to take action to protect that child until the child reaches a mature enough age to make personal decisions. The faith stance of the parents should be able to be overridden.

The Unity School of Christianity, which also believes in spiritual healing, published a book by Frances W. Foulks titled *Effectual Prayer* (1959). The writer states:

> The spiritual "remedies" outlined here have been given to the writer in answer to a call on the omniscient Mind for the highest help available for others in their time of need, in cleansing, renewing and making them harmonious according to the perfect pattern.

She indicates that these divine responses to her call, the remedies she received, are in harmony with the healing manifested in Jesus' life when he brought about cures. She suggests that her readers "Take the prayer that fits your need. Repeat it over and over until it is fixed in your conscious mind." She promises to anyone who follows her instruction, that:

> As he looks away from every error appearance, from pain and ache and disease, to the perfect Christ body within, bone of His bone, flesh of His flesh, the very life and substance of His being, he will find purity and perfection manifesting itself in his body temple, and he will become a new creature in Christ Jesus, every whit whole.

She provides spiritual remedies for adenoids, anemia, appendicitis, boils, broken and diseased bones, cancer, drug habits, epilepsy, gallstones, hemorrhoids, insanity, malaria, pneumonia, tumors, and venereal diseases, among other debilities.

Her healing method employs the technique of distraction. One focuses on other things than pain, which is perceived as some kind of imperfection. She also believes in the magical power of faith based on her personal revelations. One may applaud the writer's hope and good intentions and appreciate the depth of her convictions, but one can only shudder to think what might happen to persons suffering from any of the above ailments should they attempt this mode of becoming "every whit whole" and ignore the benefits and help to be found in modern scientific medicine.

The Healing Touch

Jesus, we are told, was able to heal simply by touching. Peter's mother-in-law had a fever that left her when Jesus touched her hand (Matt. 8:15). Indeed, she was so completely cured that she was able to get up and serve Jesus! It is not surprising to find that the relationship between touch and healing has had a long history within Christianity. The magic of touch was attributed to monarchs. In the seventeenth century the Anglican church provided opportunity for healing by the royal touch:

> At a special religious service conducted by leading Anglican clergy the monarch laid his hands upon each member of the long queue of sufferers. The patients approached one by one and knelt before the monarch, who lightly touched them on the face, while a chaplain read aloud a verse from St. Mark: "They shall lay hands on the sick and they shall recover." They then retired and came forward again so that the King might hang around their necks a gold coin strung from a white silk ribbon. (Thomas 1971, p. 188)

The coin was subsequently worn as an amulet.

Many modern religious healers employ touching in their ministry. Some television evangelists thump victims on the head with their open palm with such force that the person staggers or falls backward. Others employ a gentle touch.

Medical personnel are acutely aware of the significance of touch. Irene Burnside (1981) informs us that nurses employ two kinds of touch in dealing with patients: task-oriented touching and affective touching. Task-oriented touching is used in taking blood pressure or giving back rubs, and so on. Affective touching expresses caring, concern, affection, control, and of course must always be done appropriately. The positive therapeutic benefits that result from appropriate affective touching have been commented upon by Helen Colton in *The Gift of Touch* (1983).

The temperature of extremities varies in individuals. There are some who seem always to have cool hands; others seem to have hot or warm hands. A person with a fever may find the touch of another's hand on the forehead to have a cooling effect, simply because the fever sufferer's temperature is above normal. Some persons who have been touched by faith healers remark on the heat that seems to come from the healer's hands. The heat may simply indicate that the individual has warm hands, or the heat may have been deliberately induced by clenching the fists hard before making contact, or by holding the hands against the body before touching, or by using a secreted heating device to produce mechanical heat. For some, the extremely warm hands of the faith healer suggest a hidden source of power. In actuality, warm hands have no more healing power than cool hands.

What is most important in the use of touch in healing is the power of affective touching. Two factors are involved. First, many who come to healing services find themselves among the untouchables. By reason of their illness, or because of some physical deformity, or because they are not physically attractive, they are seldom touched. They long for physical contact. Now, as they come forward, the healer touches them, thus assuring them that they are not socially contaminated. Second, the touch is made authoritatively. The healer not only pronounces a magical incantation ("Be healed!") but presents himself or herself as an appointed representative of Jesus ("in the name of Jesus!") with the power to convey divine healing. The patient is assured that something magical is taking place. The person does feel better—for the moment. Someone has touched him or her in the name of the divine. Someone has said that God cares. It is a magical moment and even when the pain returns and though the ailment remains, the person will insist that "something happened." Such is the power in the gift of touch.

Modern Faith Healing

Truly, truly, I tell you, he who believes in me will also do the works that I am doing; and he will do greater works, because I am going to the Father. Whatever you ask in my name, I will do, so that the Father may be glorified in the son. If you ask anything in my name, I will do it. (Jesus, in John 14:12–14)

Christian faith healing rests on the assumption that those who perform the acts are following in the footsteps of Jesus. If Jesus could do it, then they, in Jesus' name, can also heal. If Jesus could heal by touch, then by calling on Jesus' name and power, they, too, can heal by touch. If Jesus' garment and cloths touched by Paul could convey healing power, then the bits of cloth supposedly blessed by the healer in Jesus' name can convey the same healing power. If Jesus could heal those he never saw and who were distant from him, then the modern faith healer, too, using radio and television and calling on the sacred name, can heal at a distance.

Most religious healing programs are associated with evangelical, charismatic, or fundamentalist churches. However, some so-called mainline Protestant churches have also become involved in this kind of ministry. Episcopal and Methodist churches, for example, have sponsored spiritual renewal programs that often include faith healing. Miraculous cures have been reported in connection with these programs.

Faith healers have operated in local Roman Catholic churches. It could be argued that belief in divine healing has had a long tradition in Roman Catholicism. Pilgrimages have been made for many years to the shrines at Lourdes and Fatima (discussed below). Traditional Catholics also engage in sacramental healing rites such as the "blessing of throats" at the Feast of St. Blaise in the fall of the year before the flu season begins.

The curative claims of the faith healers exceed by far the normal healing processes of nature. Healers claim that they invoke external, spiritual powers associated with God, with Jesus as divine healer, or with the Holy Spirit. The supernatural power heals immediately and is not to be associated simply with an increased rate of healing which might be confused with natural healing. These male and female religious healers claim to be in the tradition of the New Testament. They are doing what Jesus did. They invoke the name of Jesus. They call upon the Holy Spirit. Sometimes they babble strange sounds as they lay hands on the head of a patient. Sometimes they push so hard that the person topples back into the arms of waiting henchmen. They argue that mainline churches have forsaken an important part of the Christian spiritual heritage, and they act to fill this void.

The claims of miraculous healing made by some Christian television faith healers stagger the imagination. One television evangelist, W. V. Grant, has claimed to be able to lengthen a leg that is shorter than its mate, to replace missing spinal vertebrae, and to cure arthritis, cancer, and a multitude of other ailments.

Sometimes tales of healings are published by naive reporters. The Rev. Francis McNutt in his book *Healing* records, uncritically, the testimony of three American Indians he encountered at Blue Cloud Abbey in Marvin, South Dakota. They informed him that two of them had cavities in their teeth that were magically repaired with gold and silver fillings at a healing service in Minneapolis. These claims could easily have been checked, but, like so many other unsophisticated reporters who accept any anecdotal report as fact, Father McNutt simply included the story without comment in the epilogue in his book. One might have hoped that Father McNutt would have better developed his critical thinking skills, or at least have been aware that reports of wondrous, healing miracles require authentication. Without critical appraisal, rumors of healing circulate unchallenged.

When critical examination of an alleged miraculous healing produces evidence that healing did not occur, the healers are unanimous in announcing the critical claims are invalid. William A. Nolen, a medical doctor, wrote *Healing: A Doctor in Search of a Miracle* (1974). He examined the assertions made by believers in Kathryn Kuhlman, a faith healer whose radiant personality and wondrous cures were shown nationwide on television. Miss Kuhlman spoke of "documented" cases of cures of "gallstones, cancer, arthritis, everything," and explained that the cures were not her work but were occasioned by the Holy Spirit.

Nolan found no evidence of miraculous cure. He discovered that, despite clear evidence that Miss Kuhlman's and perhaps the patient's claims of cure were unfounded, both demanded from him a "blind faith" that obscured the reality of no-cure. In some cases, Dr. Nolan found, a patient's spirits were lifted and they felt better about themselves, but they were not healed. The doctor discovered that Miss Kuhlman was unable to distinguish between "psychogenic and organic diseases." This led her to protect her belief in herself and her ability to conjure up the power of the Holy Spirit by the defensive coping mechanism of denial. If the patient was not healed, the blame for failure could not be attributed to Miss Kuhlman, and certainly no true believer would deny the power of the Holy Spirit to effect cures. The problem had to be with the patient, whose faith was insufficient. Hence, someone suffering with terminal cancer had, added to the burden of the disease, the new malignancy of insufficient faith.

Recent investigation into claims by television evangelists of miraculous healing have reached conclusions similar to those of Dr. Nolan. The Committee for the Scientific Examination of Religion developed a subcommittee under the leadership of James (The Amazing) Randi, an internationally known conjurer, and Joseph Barnhart, Professor of Philosophy, North Texas State University. Randi brought to the investigation skill in detecting slight-of-hand procedures plus a well-honed expertise in investigation. For example, W. V. Grant's boasts of leg-lengthening were, in Randi's terms, explainable as a "Boy Scout camp trick." Time and again, on television, Randi has exposed the deception. All that is involved is a clever, hard to detect, repositioning of the legs, which are not in any way changed in length.

Time and again, committee members found that the individuals who were supposed to be healed, were not healed. Men and women who were brought to the front of the auditoriums in wheelchairs from which, after exorcism of demonic powers, they were commanded to stand up and walk, were found to have entered the auditorium on their own two feet. The wheelchairs had been provided by the evangelist's organization. Previously, the patient had never been in a wheelchair and their getting out of the chair and walking did not constitute a cure but a carefully orchestrated hoax. Nor were the victims given a chance to protest. Indeed, to do so before a believing audience would have been most embarrassing for them. The healer cleverly involved the patient in a conspiracy of deception.

The atmosphere of such healing meetings is a combination of circus or carnival and psychodrama. At the front is the professional huckster, rousing the audience with claims of the magical power of his cure-all— in this case the Jesus cure. He may be assisted by a band of robed songsters, accompanied by musical instruments, who pour out moving, sentimental hymns that seem to affirm the huckster's powers. At times the huckster joins in the singing and, using a microphone, lets his or her voice dominate. Television cameras focus on his or her face to capture the emotions and depict the look of rapture produced by the song, the music, the setting.

Dynamic energy is generated within the auditorium. The camera focuses on teary-eyed faces twisted with emotion. The healer calls for "amens" and "hallelujahs" and cries of "blessed Jesus" from his audience. Hypnotically, they respond, deepening their involvement in the drama. The performance reaches its climax as the sick and ailing are wheeled forward or are called from the audience to be healed. Exultant cries of "hallelujah" follow each healing. The healer never fails. His power cannot be challenged —indeed who would dare challenge so great a crowd of witnesses? And the money pours in as collection after collection is taken. Nor is there any need for proper auditing and accounting for, after all, this is church business.

We may wonder why the crowds come. In the first place, it is a good show. There is a great amount of action and involvement with singing and crying out. There is emotional purging. For those who live ordinary, everyday lives there is the opportunity to break free from human bondage and make contact with the divine. And there is a happy ending, for the sick are healed and may even live happily ever afterward. In the dramatic setting of the faith healing arena, during the healing performance, people experience feelings of emotional exultation and release from cares and worries and fears. Even those actually suffering from cancer or diabetes or other such ailments might feel better for a few moments as they are distracted from their pain by the performance. The strength of their faith is such that the results appear to conform to their expectations and to their imaginings. These people expect to be healed and their convictions and their hopes may obscure temporarily the reality of their affliction, whether it be cancer, arthritis, heart condition, or whatever. Because they imagine themselves to be healed they act, for a short time, as if they are healed. Unfortunately for them, the moment passes, reality returns, the disease or the affliction remains. The evangelist, knowing this, may warn that if the healing is incomplete, if the pain returns, if the affliction remains, it is because the patient's faith is inadequate and Satan, the great opposer to magical faith healing, is at work reversing the effect.

Programs shown on television are carefully edited. Millions of viewers are able to witness "evidence" of the televangelist's healing powers. Viewers are asked over and over again to contribute to the support of the healing ministry. But there is no way they can evaluate the genuineness of what they are watching.

On one occasion, members of televangelist Rev. Peter Popoff's audience were told to throw away their medications and rely upon "Dr. Jesus" to heal them. Randi and his associates gathered the discarded medications, which included such life-sustaining drugs as oral insulin, digitalis, nitroglycerin tablets, and so forth. Because the evangelists never bothered to follow up on the health of these trusting believers (nor could the investigating committee do this), one can only imagine what may have happened to some before they renewed their prescriptions and returned to their doctors. One can only wonder at the cruel insensitivity of these fake healers. How greedy they must be for the dollars they beg from their congregations and listeners.

Because numerous exhortations for financial support to continue and extend the "healing ministry" were made on each televised program, and because within the auditoriums each audience was solicited numerous times for financial "gifts," the annual income from such programs amounts to hundreds of millions of dollars. As a result, the modern healers, unlike the Jesus they claim to represent, live in luxury. What cannot be ascertained is the amount of damage done to those who follow the instructions given by these irresponsible faith healers.

New Age Healing

Belief in magical healing is worldwide. Shamans in every country pose as healers. The sick and ailing come, hoping for a miraculous cure. Each cult and each culture has its own format, its own incantations, its own magical formulae, its own rituals. Each age produces its own variations on ancient patterns, borrowing ideas from various sources and combining them in new arrangements.

In our Western world, religious healing has generally been associated with Judeo-Christian religions, but influences from other cults and cultures are interwoven. A healing emphasis of New Age thought has recently become popular. New Age healing is derived from the counter-culture of the 1960s, combined with Far Eastern—including Chinese, Japanese, and East Indian—healing traditions, as well as those of American Indian folk medicine. What is startling is that, despite the fact that there is no valid proof or evidence of the effectiveness of so-called New Age healing practices, the New Age groups have attracted the support of some physicians with medical degrees.

The recognition of the psychosomatic nature of human illness has opened doors to exploitation, particularly of those who are suffering from such ailments as presently incurable cancer or AIDS. In the desperate search for anything that will cure or delay the final outcome of the disease, sufferers pursue any promise of help, whether or not it seems reasonable or logical. Individuals with M.D. degrees may inform their potential patients that "AIDS is the result of multiple factors such as poor nutrition and lifestyle imbalances, which weaken the immune system." The protective clause is the reference to lifestyle, which is in accord with our knowledge that AIDS is transmitted through certain sexual and intravenous practices (some as innocent as blood transfusions). However, the healing emphasis in such claims is on nutrition. It is not surprising that those who emphasize diet as the key to the control of AIDS include in their therapy their own preparations of vitamins, minerals, and herbs, plus acupuncture, all of which are offered for a price at their clinics.

Metaphysical and occult groups have also moved into the health field. Lazaris, the spiritual being who it is supposed to channel his messages through channeler Jach Pursel, informs his followers that "The immune system corresponds to your level of self-confidence" (Lazaris 1987). He recommends confidence, humility, trust, and courage as the keys to building one's immune system, plus "immune-balancing chemicals and diets and exercise regimes." Lazaris rejects the theological pronouncements of certain fundamentalist groups that AIDS is divine punishment of homosexuals. He denies the notion of "immune deficiency diseases" as "God's punishment, or as the outgrowth of the ugliness of the Human Condition, or as a hocus-pocus evilness." With this, most nonfundamentalists would agree. Beyond this point, the wisdom provided by Lazaris and other channeled spirits consists of simplistic, dangerous, and insensitive responses to one of the most serious worldwide epidemics in recent history.

Some American Indians have attempted to move into New Age metaphysical healing. They claim to have talked with tribal elders and to have learned ancient American Indian ways of healing. They appeal to our present awareness that in many primitive cultures shamans possess knowledge of plants and herbs that have curative powers. This knowledge, derived from centuries of experimentation, has been handed down from generation to generation. Indeed, some of our modern remedies employ ancient plant cures. For example, quinine (Cinchona pubescens), which was native to South America, has been widely used to treat malaria. The plant foxglove (Digitalis pupurea), which is native to western Europe, is the source of the drug digitalis that is used in the treatment of heart disorders. Tea made from willow tree bark contains aspirin-like substances that relieve various aches and pains. Investigative reporter Nick B. Williams Jr. (1988) indicated that it has been estimated that three-quarters of plant-derived compounds used in medications were derived from research into folktales or tribal lore concerning the healing powers of certain plants. Though many tales proved to be worthless, our pre-modern-medicine forebears were deeply involved in naturopathic healing. However, the fact that modern researchers have found helpful medications through the study of shamanic medicine does not give sanction to some of the rather simplistic remedies associated with American Indian lore. One would be foolish indeed to substitute willow-bark tea for modern analgesics.

On the other hand, there is clear evidence that some folk medicines are hazardous. Maura Dolan (1989) has reported that Azarcon, a brilliant orange powder used in the manufacture of paint, is ingested in an herbal tea in Mexico to treat indigestion. Azarcon is ninety percent lead and has resulted in lead poisoning. Other lead-based Mexican folk remedies known as Greta, Liga, Maria Luisa, Alarcon, Coral, and Rueda have resulted in encephalopathy in children, which can cause mental retardation. The Asian folk remedy called Pay-loo-ah, plus Ghasard, Bali Goli, and Kandu, also contain lead. Arab kohl, used in eye cosmetics and for treatment of skin infections and diarrhea and as a tooth powder, is also lead-based. These dangerous substances are sometimes sold in herbal stores and by herbal practitioners.

It must be admitted that some Indian cures are innocent enough and reflect much of what may be found in "pop psychology" and in traditional religious rites. For example, troubled individuals are told to dig a hole in the earth and to speak their troubles into that hole to Mother Earth, cover it and leave, knowing that their problems are buried in Mother Earth, the healer. In "Laughing Winds," Gregory, a licensed California marriage, family, and child counselor, wrote (1989):

> When daily life is overwhelming, when in a state of confusion or emotional or mental pain is too much to bear; lay down on the earth, be it sand, grass or soil, nude or clothed, wrapped in blankets or on a beach towel. Face down, all chakras against the earth, legs and arms comfortably spread eagle, opening to her. Give way, speaking out loud in your mind, "Sacred Grandmother, for thousands of years your grand children have received shelter, clothing and nurturing from you. I join them in honoring you. I ask that you help me. I give my pain away to you. I give my worries so I may be clear and strong. I release my anger and tears. (With power of voice and command) I give them away."

Chakras are the seven so-called energy centers from the crown of the head to the groin.

The treatment is like that given by a radio psychologist who told a troubled listener to express in writing the anger stemming from a failed personal relationship and to take the paper and burn it in the fireplace or tear it into small bits and flush it down the toilet. In some Jewish communities, the Rosh Hashanah new year rites include a ceremony called Tashlich. Members of a Beverly Hills, California, synagogue gather at the water's edge of the Pacific Ocean and symbolically cast their sins into the waters in order to begin the new year cleansed of sin. For centuries, Roman Catholics have gone to the confessionals, recited their sins to listening priests, been assigned acts of penance, in the assurance that the rite, seriously and honestly carried through, would bring divine forgiveness, purification, and release from the burden of guilt. In other words, the radio therapist, the Indian healer, the Jewish congregation, and the Roman Catholic believer employ means to give expression to whatever it is that burdens the individual, and then to magically release destructive, troublesome, emotions, guilt-feelings, or memories. Having symbolically eradicated the burdensome feelings, the individual is supposed to be able to leave troublesome events in the past and move on to new adventures in life. New Age healers, like positive-thinking rabbis, ministers, or priests, might comment on the importance of focussing on emotionally beneficial and rewarding actions or thoughts.

Probably there is no lasting harm in any of these techniques—except if the exorcism does not work and now the patient is also burdened with worry about personal failure with the technique. However, when the Indian healer expresses belief in the power of Indian herbal medicines to cure terrible ailments like cancer or AIDS, he or she is urging his or her readers or listeners to use untested, primitive folk-medicine. As with other New Age medical therapy, there is absolutely no scientific evidence to support claims of miraculous healing with untested, unproven cures.

Some New Age healers claim that they can detect auras that emanate from or surround the bodies of individuals. Certain colors are more healthful than others. Some refer to claims made by those who experiment with Kirlian photography. The technique, which is named after its Russian inventors, Semyon and Valentia Kirlian, involves placing one's hand on a photographic plate. Twenty-five thousand low-amperage volts go through the plate. The result is a darkened hand image with color corona at the finger tips. This colorful imagery is supposed to result from the body's natural bioelectricity. Differences in coronas are supposed to reveal healthy or sick people. Healthy people have bright, sharp coronas; sick people show blurry or indistinct images.

The idea is that if one surrounds oneself with positive healing colors that are consonant with good health, then one's aura or Kirlian image will change. Often diet and vitamin pills are associated with the healing program. The aura notion parallels New Testament descriptions of Jesus at the so-called "transfiguration" (Matt. 17:2; Mark 9:3; Luke 9:29), the angelic figures at Jesus' tomb (Matt. 28:3; Luke 24:4), or the reports by Christians who claim to have had visions of Jesus or Mary. These divine persons are often described as possessing light auras.

Healing Centers

Places of healing are usually associated with some sort of revelatory experience by which a god or goddess or some occult power has been manifested. The reputation of the locale is expanded by tales of wondrous cures, and in modern times by advertisements or "news reports" that tend to be uncritical examples of "objective reporting" in which the investigator simply relates what he or she has been told by the attendants at the shrine or by those who have faith in the healing powers of the place. Questions about authenticity are not asked; thus, news reports tend to become advertisements rather than in-depth investigations. Of course, some faith centers produce their own propaganda, a practice that has had a long history.

An account of propaganda for a healing shrine has come from ancient Egypt. The "Bentresh Stele," found at Karnak near the temple of the god Amon, is what the late John A. W. Wilson (1950) has politely labelled "a pious forgery," and which, in modern parlance, might be called a "scam." Its purpose was to lure pilgrims whose gifts and contributions would enhance the temple treasury. The text was composed during the third or fourth centuries B.C.E. But the tale is set in the reign of Ramses II in the thirteenth century B.C.E.

According to the story, the younger sister of Ramses II's Hittite wife Nefru-Re was ill, possessed by evil spirits. The husband of the ailing woman sent a substantial gift to Ramses II. Consequently, the statue of the god Khonsu of Thebes, the divine son in the Theban triad (Amon, Mut, Khonsu), was sent to the ailing woman. The evil spirits causing the illness were expelled and the woman was healed. As this tale circulated, it could only add to the luster of Khonsu, the healer, and encourage gift-bearing pilgrims to come to the shrine for magical cures.

Healing centers are mentioned in the Christian Scriptures. The water in the Sheep Gate pool in Jerusalem was believed to have magical healing powers when the waters "were troubled" or stirred because of some spiritual power. Those fortunate enough to get into the pool when the waters rippled might be healed. Jesus healed a man who had been ill for thirty-eight years. The unfortunate fellow had never been able to get into the pool at the right time. Jesus ordered him to pick up his pallet and walk (John 5:1–9).

Almost from the beginning of the Christian era, legends concerning wondrous cures at Christian holy places have abounded. Often the healing was attributed to the power of some artifact or relic associated with some holy person or Christian saint. After all, if handkerchiefs and cloths that touched the body of the Apostle Paul could produce magical healing, why shouldn't artifacts associated with other holy individuals such as saints or popes, who were called "holy father," have special power? Many European churches claim to possess such sacred relics—bones or other objects—preserved in containers or encased in silver or gold. Miraculous cures associated with these relics are claimed. On display in the churches are crutches, canes, and other paraphernalia said to have been discarded by the healed patrons of the shrine. These symbols of human ailments are similar to the terra-cotta models of human body parts which were offered to the god Aesclepius, and in modern times are found by archaeologists in excavations of temples to Aesclepius. Over the centuries, pilgrims have donated liberally to particular churches or cathedrals or shrines, and of course local businesses benefited simultaneously. Some of these sites continue to exploit visitors and encourage the sick, the maimed, and the ailing to come in the hope of receiving a miraculous cure.

Bits and pieces of sacred relics may be widely distributed. For example, thousands of fragments of "the true cross" on which Jesus was crucified are enshrined in Roman Catholic churches throughout the world. These bits of wood (which appear to be pine) are all supposed to have come from the cross discovered during the fourth century by the pious and credulous Helena, mother of King Constantine. According to the legend, three crosses were found at the site of the present Church of the Holy Sepulchre in Jerusalem. To determine the identity of the cross of Jesus, they were brought, one at a time, into the presence of a mortally ill woman. The true cross brought about instant miraculous healing. Who was responsible for breaking the true cross into a multitude of pieces is not known. Indeed, one might wonder at the daring of a person who would perform such a sacrilege. Presently, naive Roman Catholics are encouraged to believe that the fragment of wood enshrined in their particular church is part of this wondrous cross.

Critical scholars reject the Helena story as pious fiction. Some suggest that the so-called cross fragments are nothing more than bits of wood found in the vicinity of the Church of the Holy Sepulchre. If this theory has any validity, the wood fragments might just as well have come from the shrine of the goddess Venus which Hadrian built on the site and which was destroyed to make room for the Christian church.

It should be noted, that it is not only non-Catholics who dismiss the authenticity of the fragments; many Roman Catholic scholars question the authenticity of these fragments as parts of the cross of Jesus. But what is known to the scholars is not always shared with the laity, perhaps because raising doubt in one area of faith might occasion distrust in another.

Lourdes

Perhaps the most famous present-day healing center is associated with the cult of the mother goddess, Mary, at Lourdes, France. On February 11, 1858, Bernadette Soubiros, an illiterate fourteen-year-old miller's daughter, announced that she had seen an apparition in a cliff grotto near the Gave River. She said she had seen a beautiful lady dressed in a white robe with a blue sash. She would claim to have seventeen more visions of this lady during the next few months. The vision identified itself as "The Immaculate Conception" (which the young girl did not understand) and ordered a chapel to be built on the bluff above a point where the vision had caused a spring of water to bubble up. The chapel became a massive basilica. The grotto and the spring have become the central Roman Catholic healing shrine, hosting over four million pilgrims a year, many of whom are seriously ill. The sick, the dying, the crippled, the injured, the deformed, the retarded, the blind, the deaf, the dumb, line up to enter the grotto, to touch its stone walls, to be bathed in the chilling waters, and to take water from the sacred spring. Since 1970 no cures have been accepted as miraculous, despite the fact that hundreds of pilgrims claim unregistered, unauthenticated healings. The fact that crowds continue to come despite the multitudinous failures should serve to remind us that "one apparent cure will efface the memory of a hundred failures" (Thomas 1971, p. 193).

To protect against unfounded claims of miraculous healing, the Roman Catholic Church has set up a protocol for investigating cures. First, the illness must be registered with the Medical Bureau of Lourdes, where doctors must determine whether or not the illness is truly life-threatening. That is to say, they are not willing to classify the natural healing of a broken limb as miraculous. Then the recovery from the life-threatening illness must be complete and permanent. The medical authorities also need to know if the patient was receiving medical treatment that could account for the cure, since modern medical treatment reverses many illnesses that at one time would have been thought of as terminal or fatal. If a sudden reversal occurs and the patient claims to be healed, and if the Medical Bureau states, as they have only fifty-seven times since 1947, that the cure was a medical mystery, the case is then turned over to religious authorities. The bishop of the locale from whence the patient came may convene an ecclesiastical tribunal to adjudge the case—a process that may take years. The religious tribunal may decide that no miracle has occurred, even though medical experts cannot explain the healing. Or the case may never be decided. It is not surprising that in the more than one-hundred-year history of the healing shrine, only sixty-four cases have been authenticated—and some of those are questionable.

With so few healings on record, why do millions of pilgrims still go to Lourdes? In desperate situations, when modern medicine appears to be unable to help, suffering persons and those who love them will seek any remedy. When parents believe that an affliction such as mental retardation may be an act of God, they may seek the help of Mary, the bride of God, the mother of Jesus, to intervene on their behalf and cause a miracle to occur (see chapter on the Cult of the Mother Goddess). Because the Bible is the textbook for Christian belief, thought, and life, because the New Testament records miraculous healings, and because Jesus is believed to be "the same yesterday and today and for ever" (Hebrews 13:8), believers reason that it is possible that a miracle might occur. Finally, the propaganda of the Roman Catholic Church, which appears in church publications, emphasizes Bernadette's hallucinatory experience but says little about the limited number of cures associated with Lourdes. On the contrary, regular masses are given at Lourdes in six languages, along with candlelight processions and great pomp and circumstance of church ritual that lends drama and glamor and expectation and hope to the setting.

Perhaps some pilgrims are given help in dealing with their illness. They have been to the sacred shrine, they have been bathed in and drunk the miraculous waters, and, in their minds, have been in physical contact with the divine and holy. They have done all they can. What remains or continues is, in religious thought, "the will of God." After the Lourdes experience, they can be resigned to what is. They must now learn to live without hope of divine intervention. Perhaps there is some healing in being compelled to face reality. On the other hand, a healing failure at Lourdes can engender a deep sense of personal failure, inasmuch as God or Mary, for reasons beyond the individual's understanding, chose not to give healing.

One can only imagine what the constant influx of tourists means to the local economy and to the 18,000 permanent residents of Lourdes who, by the way, are no healthier than residents in surrounding villages, despite their proximity to the magical waters. This small town has an international airport and 400 hotels to accommodate the pilgrims. Merchants peddle a wide variety of religious amulets, particularly images of Mary, some containing the waters of Lourdes. What wealth pours into church coffers at Lourdes can only be imagined!

The Shroud of Turin

In recent years, the so-called "Shroud of Turin" has attracted much attention in the press. The shroud is a piece of linen which has been known historically since about 1353 C.E. It is supposed to be the cloth in which Jesus' body was wrapped after it was taken down from the cross. Brown stains on the linen portray the figure of a man. This was identified as the impression made by Jesus' body. Actually, there are two images, because the single linen sheet covered both the back and the front of the body. The double image meets at the head. The brown stains are explained as the result of the mixture of aromatics that were smeared on the body prior to burial and blood from wounds. The image portrays a bearded male, approximately six feet tall, and apparently a victim of crucifixion. The image does not appear, at first glance, to be painted on the cloth. Could this be the authentic burial shroud of Jesus? If it is, and if power is conveyed through cloth that has been in contact with the body of a New Testament character, one can only imagine the potential it may possess for healing and for miracles. There can be no question of its potential for drawing patrons with their financial gifts.

Unquestionably, it is not the burial shroud of Jesus. In the first place, the shroud of Turin was not the only piece of linen that was accepted as Jesus' shroud. The holy shroud of Besancon was also said to be that cloth. The Besancon shroud was declared fraudulent and ecclesiastical authorities ordered that it be shredded into lint. The authenticity of the Turin shroud was also challenged by fourteenth-century clerics. An investigation conducted by Bishop Henri de Poitiers dismissed the shroud as a fraud after he learned the truth about its composition from the artist who painted it. Even the healing miracles associated with the shroud were found to have been staged.

It is important to note that the shroud had no history prior to the fourteenth century. The deCharny family, which owned it, refused to tell de Poitier how it came into their possession. There is no mention of the shroud in the New Testament, and certainly no reference to a cloth bearing Jesus' image.

Three of the Gospels (Matt. 27:59; Mark 15:46; Luke 23:53) state that Joseph of Armathea wrapped Jesus' body in a linen cloth (*sindon*). The Gospel of John (19:40) refers to the binding of the body in linen cloths (*othonia*). When the disciple Peter entered the tomb just after the resurrection, he found only the burial cloths (*othonia*), rolled up, and a napkin (*soudarian*) that had covered Jesus' face (John 20:6–7). It might be argued that perhaps Joseph of Armathea first wrapped Jesus in a shroud and then in the burial cloths. Should this have happened (and there is no record of any such shroud wrapping in the New Testament), the shroud would also have been in the tomb, since any burial cloth, because of contact with a dead body, would automatically be considered unclean. Moreover, one would assume, the presence of an imprinted linen sheet would have been included in the Christian Scriptures or in the records of the early church. No such recording was made, however, most probably because no such shroud existed.

Why did the shroud suddenly come into prominence in the twentieth century? On May 1, 1898, for the first time in thirty years, the shroud was placed on exhibition during a showing of the sacred art of the city of Turin. Since the fifteenth century, it had belonged to the Royal House of Savoy and had been rolled up and kept under lock and key. For special occasions it was put on display, as in 1814 at the request of King Victor Emmanuel, in 1815 at the request of Pope Pius VII, in 1822 upon the accession of Charles Felix, in 1842 at the marriage of Victor Emmanuel I, and in 1868 at the marriage of Prince Humbert. At all other times it was kept from public view.

In 1898, the shroud was photographed by Secondo Pia, and on the photographic negative, which reverses light and dark images, a positive portrait was revealed. It was at this time that an official commission was appointed to look into the authenticity of the shroud. A new discipline called "sindonology" (from *sindon,* the Greek word for "linen") came into being. Early theories about the image suggested that it may have been produced by actual body contact and may have been the result of impregnation by body sweat, oils, and funereal spices. This theory was quickly disproved. Another theory called "vaporgraphic" suggested that ammoniacal fumes from body morbidity reacting with burial spices imprinted a vapor photograph on the cloth. This theory was also discounted.

In 1978, a group of scientists formed The Shroud of Turin Research Project. Their investigation resulted in a number of controversial theories pertaining to the pollen found in the shroud, which at first was said to be uniquely Palestinian, and to the coins which were pictured on the eyes of the dead figure, which were said to be from the first century C.E. Both claims were completely discredited.

Perhaps the most unusual suggestion was the "burst of radiation" hypothesis to account for the image. The suggestion was that the corpse had emitted a burst of radiation which projected the image onto the cloth. Of course, there was absolutely no evidence to substantiate this notion. Indeed, no one is quite sure just what such a burst of radiation might entail. This notion was based on the belief that the shroud actually was associated with Jesus. Because the investigators believed in the divinity of Jesus, all sorts of magical powers could be attributed to him, including a burst of radiation. If such an event was possible, the Turin shroud would provide the only known record of it occurring.

Much earlier, on September 6, 1936, Pope Pius XI had made the following pronouncement:

> These are the images of the Divine Redeemer. We might say they are the most beautiful, most moving and dearest we can imagine. They derive directly from the object, surrounded by mystery, which—this can be safely said—it has now been established is no product of human hands. It is the Holy Shroud at Turin. We say it is surrounded by mystery because much remains unexplained about this affair, which is certainly holy as no other is. But this much can be said—it is absolutely certain that it is not the work of man. (Shepard 1970, p. 4)

Now, it would seem, the Pope spoke too soon. He was wrong. There is clear and certain evidence of man-made pigments in the colors on the shroud including iron oxide and vermillion, which are artists' colors known and used in the fourteenth century. Joe Nickell (1987) has demonstrated how easily the process that produced the image can be duplicated using only materials and technology known in the fourteenth century. He has produced similar photo-negative images.

The test that most reliably established the date of the shroud is carbon 14 dating. C14 is an unstable form of radioactive carbon with an atomic weight of fourteen as compared to ordinary non-radioactive carbon that has an atomic weight of twelve. C14 is constantly being created in the upper atmosphere by the bombardment of nitrogen 14 by cosmic rays. The resultant C14 combines with oxygen to make a particular form of carbon dioxide that combines with normal carbon dioxide in fixed, definite proportions, thereby becoming a part of the earth's atmosphere. In the act of breathing, every living creature—plant or animal—absorbs some of the unstable C14 in a proportion of about one trillionth of a gram to one gram of C12. At death, the intake of C14 is, of course, halted, and the C14 already absorbed remains, but begins to diminish at a regular, measurable rate. The half-life of C14 is 5,568 years plus or minus thirty years, so that the amount of C14 in an organism at the moment of death would diminish by one-half in 5,568 years. The C12 would remain constant. Thus, by measuring the amount of C12, the original amount of C14 can be determined, and by calculating the proportion of C14 remaining, the date of death can be established.

C14 tests of the shroud linen have been conducted at the University of Arizona, Oxford University, and The Swiss Federal Institute of Technology in Zurich, with the British Museum acting as the certifying institute. The tests have demonstrated that the shroud is a forgery and has nothing to do with Jesus. Based on the tests, the shroud has been dated between 1260 and 1390 C.E. It was produced either in the late thirteenth or the fourteenth century.

Presently, the shroud rests in a silver reliquary in the Chapel of the Dukes of Savoy in an Italian cathedral at Turin. Cardinal Anastasio Ballestrero is reputed to have said that the cloth had been long "venerated" but never declared to be an authentic relic (Dart 1988). Perhaps he is correct. No "official" statement was ever made, but in view of the over-enthusiastic remarks by Pope Pius XI, it is clear that the shroud was popularly regarded as a "relic," even by the Pope. So today, it is no longer a "relic"; it is now an "icon," a sacred artifact! And it continues to attract pilgrims seeking the miraculous.

The Guadaloupe Shrine

Another cloth said to be divinely imprinted is on display in the Basilica of Our Lady of Guadaloupe in Mexico City. According to Roman Catholic tradition, the cloth was once a cloak worn by an Indian named Cuauhtlatoatzin, who was given the name Juan Diego when he was baptized by Franciscan priests.

According to one account, on the morning of December 12, 1531, the Virgin Mary is supposed to have appeared to Juan Diego, placed flowers in his cloak, and instructed him to take them to the Bishop of Mexico City as a sign of her miraculous appearance. Juan Diego followed the instructions, but when he opened his cloak before the bishop to reveal the flowers, the image of the Virgin materialized suddenly and miraculously on the cloth. As a result, the cult of the Virgin flourished throughout Latin America.

According to a second version, the Virgin appeared to Juan Diego, affectionately addressed him in Aztec as "my son," and ordered him to tell the bishop to build a sanctuary to her on the site where the Spanish had destroyed a shrine to the Aztec earth and corn goddess known as "Little Mother." When the bishop refused, the Virgin miraculously caused Castilian roses to bloom on a rocky hillside. Juan gathered them in his cloak and presented them to the bishop, and on his cloak was found the imprint of the Virgin with a brown Indian face and black hair. Thus, the Roman Catholic goddess replaced the ancient Aztec goddess, even to the extent of acquiring Aztec features.

Bishop Juan de Zumarraga left no record of this wondrous occurrence—at least none that has been found. A chronicle, written in Nahuatl, the Aztec language, but using the Latin alphabet, was supposed to have been made by Antonio Valeriano, an educated Italian who spoke Nahuatl, Latin, and Spanish. The first known publication of the Valeriano chronicle appeared in 1649, about a century after the miracle is supposed to have happened. Serious doubts have been raised about whether there ever was a Valeriano manuscript. The seventeenth-century edition is probably a pious forgery.

The cloth of the cloak is made from cactus fiber and is still in excellent condition. Infrared photographs made by Phillip S. Callahan, a researcher in the U.S. Department of Agriculture, Gainesville, Florida, demonstrate that the original painting has been altered substantially. Callahan suspects that the alterations were designed to make the painting conform to the vision described in Chapter 12 of the New Testament Book of Revelation to John.

Despite the fact that before the painting was placed under glass it was exposed to light and the smoke of candles, the colors remain bright and clear. The painting deserves study using the best research tools. It has been suggested that inasmuch as no sizing was used to make the paint adhere to the cloth, and because there is no underdrawing—both of which were common for that period—perhaps there is something miraculous about the image. The fact that the image has undergone changes indicates that more than one artist contributed to the picture.

Meanwhile, the imprint of the brown Virgin Mary on Juan Diego's cloak is displayed behind bulletproof glass. Religious festivals, promoted by the church, promote the painting's miraculous nature. The image appears everywhere in Mexico. The shrine continues to draw millions of worshippers seeking miracles of healing for body, mind, and soul, together with their money.

The Virgin of Guadaloupe is honored each December throughout the Spanish-speaking Americas. Her banners are carried in protest demonstrations, reflecting the use of her image by Father Hildago during the Mexican War of Independence in 1810. Modern festivities begin at dawn in Catholic churches where *mananitas* or songs honoring Mary are sung. After the early morning masses and breakfast, processions, which may include the use of mariachis and *matachin* dancers, follow the Marian banner through the streets before returning to the church. The local rites serve to strengthen the Guadaloupe legend and encourage those who suffer in mind and body to seek magical healing at the Guadaloupe shrine, or if that is impossible, wherever, but through Mary's healing power.

Oral Roberts's City of Faith

One of the more notorious centers of faith healing, founded by the Rev. Oral Roberts, was doomed to failure despite Roberts's claims that it was established by divine command. In the early days of his ministry, Roberts operated out of a tent that he moved from city to city. Then, in his own name, he constructed a City of Faith Medical and Research Center as part of the Oral Roberts University complex in Tulsa, Oklahoma. Within the hospital, modern medical and surgical techniques were employed, supplemented by prayer and laying on of hands. No miracles of healing occurred in this institution. Some patients recovered through the use of modern scientific medicine. But just as many patients died in the City of Faith hospital as in other hospitals.

Of course, Rev. Oral Roberts claimed divine inspiration for his healing center. He stated that he was visited by a 900-foot-tall Jesus who commanded him to build the hospital in Tulsa. (One might argue that if a postresurrection Jesus could appear to his disciples, and later appear to and speak with Paul, there is no reason why this same Jesus might not have a chat with Oral Roberts!) Roberts's healing center was, therefore, in his estimation at least, a place that came into being in response to a vision and divine command. Unfortunately for their finances, though, there was no healing spring of water or magically imprinted cloth to bring credulous pilgrims with their money to support hotels, eating establishments, and transportation companies, and to give gifts from which the center might benefit. Their patients paid regular hospital fees out of their own pockets and through insurance policies and Medicare. When the sixty-story diagnostic clinic and the thirty-story hospital ran into financial difficulties and the third building of the complex, the twenty-story research center, was unfinished, Roberts claimed he had another encounter with Jesus, who informed him that the hundreds of thousands of "prayer partners" were to each give another $240. In return Jesus promised "to bring mighty and greater breakthroughs for the cure of cancer." Roberts promised donors a set of forty-eight tapes containing his commentary on the New Testament and said that each would receive up to fourteen unique blessings, including improved health, family harmony, increased mental ability, more money, and success.

As at other healing centers, money-raising was an important part of Oral Roberts's ministry at the City of Faith. On January 4, 1987, Oral Roberts informed his television viewers that in March 1986 God had told him that he, Roberts, had to raise eight million dollars in one year to permit the University's medical students to graduate debt-free and become missionaries in Third World countries. In February 1987 Roberts announced that only $3.5 million had been raised and that if the remaining $4.5 million were not forthcoming by March 31, 1987, God would call him "home." Some television stations refused to air this heavy-handed extortionistic appeal. In an Associated Press release, Roberts is purported to have said:

> The devil came to my room just a few nights ago, and I felt those hands on my throat and he was choking the life out of me. I yelled to my wife, "Honey, come!"

His wife Evelyn came to his room. Roberts said:

> She laid her hands on me and rebuked the devil and commanded the devil to get out of my room. I began to breathe and came out of my bed strong.

The dramatic appeal paid off. The money was raised and Oral Roberts did not die. God did not call him "home."

In a nearby structure, Roberts's televangelism program dramatizes something quite different from the medical reality of the hospital. Oral's son, Richard, is master of ceremonies of a program that includes choral groups accompanied by Richard singing sugary gospel songs to a modern beat, interviews with visiting evangelists, announcements, appeals for money, sales pitches for a variety of tapes, books, etc., and over-the-air magical healing. For example, Richard will suddenly interrupt a conversation and act as if he was getting a personal message from God. He may grab his arm near the elbow and ask "Here, God?" Then move his hand further up the arm to the triceps region and ask again, "Here, God?" Now, satisfied that this is the place where God wants to concentrate healing, Roberts will announce "Someone out there has a pain in the upper arm." He may go on to define it as bursitis or rheumatism. He will then shout: "In the name of Jesus" the arm is healed. A few days later he may read a letter from someone who will claim that an ailing arm was healed. And after all, if Jesus could heal at a distance, why shouldn't Richard Roberts be able to do the same? His success (failure never seems to occur) is attributed to the magical power of the divine name "Jesus."

Clearly, Oral and Richard Roberts are more successful healers than Jesus, who, according to the Gospels, was not always successful. One wonders, also, if Jesus found it necessary to shout and scream as Roberts and other healers do.

There is absolutely no medical evidence that any healing has taken place. Indeed, one wonders why, if Richard Roberts is in such intimate contact with God, he doesn't go into the hospital, which is a short distance from the television center, and perform there. The most obvious reason is that he knows he has no real healing power. When his mother, Evelyn, Mrs. Oral Roberts, suffered from cataracts, neither son Richard nor husband Oral intervened with God on her behalf. She went into the medical hospital for treatment. She seemed to know where real healing could be found.

But the Roberts' ministry entered a decline and by the close of 1989 the divinely founded university was in troubled financial waters. The law school was sold to fellow evangelist Pat Robertson, the City of Faith medical school was defunct, hundreds of employees were fired, and Roberts had to modify his luxurious lifestyle by selling four Mercedes automobiles and three vacation homes in California to raise four million dollars (Abrams 1989). The television "healing ministry" continues, but reaches a smaller audience through fewer stations. The faith healing miracle center has failed despite the claims of divine revelations and divine guidance. The divine promises of miraculous medical breakthroughs remain unfulfilled.

Spiritual Healing in Mexico

Spiritualist healers in Mexico operate out of temples in various communities. Their healing methods combine Christian concepts and traditional Indian beliefs and practices. The Spiritualist churches see themselves as "The Children of Israel, the Chosen People, and their pantheon consists of Jehovah, Moses, Jesus Christ and the Virgin Mary" (Finkler 1985, p. 20).

The word of God comes to members through a medium in a trance "who, according to Spiritualists, is but a radio transmitter for His message." The congregation is brought into a semitrance state through ritual that may, in itself, have some therapeutic effect on the autonomic nervous system. Tactile communication between healer and patient may facilitate positive feelings, and, in combination with the patient's belief in the power of the healer, bring relief from psychologically induced illness. Herbal purges, which are seen as "cleansings," may also produce beneficial results inasmuch as the believer is convinced that negative forces that may be afflicting his or her body are expelled. Symbolic acts reinforce the notion of expulsion of demonic powers.

The results of healing services in Mexico have been studied and both successes and failures have been catalogued. It is clear that the successes are associated with psychosomatic ailments.

Spiritual Healing in the Philippines

For more than twenty years, seriously ill persons have traveled to the Philippine Islands in search of magical healing. Some suffer from terminal cancer, others from devastating diseases such as multiple sclerosis. There they are treated by practitioners who are members of the Union Spiritista Cristina de Filipinas, Inc. Travel and accommodations may have been arranged by a "Spiritual Consultant" of the Christian Travel Center in Manila. They may be given privately produced pamphlets such as "A Guide to Spiritual, Magnetic Healing & Psychic Surgery in the Philippines," by George W. Meek, or a photocopy of a fifteen-page typewritten essay by Virginia M. Tiburcio that tells the story of how Pepito M. Gamboa, by working as an assistant to healer Marcelo Jainer, learned to become a psychic healer himself.

The Meek pamphlet opens with a disclaimer warning that although "on some occasions [spiritual healers] are said to provide relief to patients who have not obtained the relief they desired from organized medicine," the healer "makes no warranties or representations of any kind regarding the degree of success which may be expected for any individual patient." A positive attitude is encouraged inasmuch as "it has been found that the patient's *attitude* toward the healing is the biggest single factor in whether or not the healing becomes *permanent*" (Meek 1973, p. 1).

Psychic surgery is defined as follows:

> By means totally unexplainable in terms of modern science, certain individuals [usually with little or no academic training] possess the ability to "operate" on the human body using only their bare hands, and remove diseased tissue, blood clots and pus. The means by which this activity is carried out and the question of what is actually going on is under serious study by many researchers. At this time it is not possible to give any definite and truly scientific statement of just what is taking place. A study of hundreds of cases indicates that often beneficial results seem to follow. Of equal significance—*there is no documented case of any patient having been harmed* by such psychic surgery. (Meek 1973, pp. 2–3)

The text continues with emphases on proper attitude, with a list of recommended readings that advocate faith healing, and with a statement on the beliefs of the healers. They believe in the Fatherhood of God, the Brotherhood of Man, the continuous existence of the individual soul, personal responsibility, communion with the spirits, the ministry of angels, compensation and retribution for earthly acts, and eternal progress open to every human soul. Obviously, the belief system harmonizes Christian and Eastern mysticism.

It is often stated that the healers seek no compensation for their work. This may be true in the sense that the healers *themselves* may make no requests for compensation, but compensations and donations are encouraged. The travel centers that arrange for patients to come to the Philippines and who plan the sightseeing trips are part of an organization that works with the organized healers. Patients stay at hotels, the arrangements for which are made by the tour planners. Obviously, the healers and their agents receive remuneration. Patients are reminded that the healers have not asked for payment, but it is suggested that donations be given in specified amounts (often $500 and up). After all, what would it cost to be cured of cancer back home?

A woman who was desperate to be healed went to the Philippines for psychic healing. She shared with me a diary she kept of her experiences. She was suffering from multiple sclerosis, cancer (she had undergone a mastectomy of one breast eighteen years earlier), and problems resulting from a caesarean and tubal ligation (twenty-seven years earlier). Here is part of what she recorded:

> Saturday morning: Marcello removed blood clots from the motor centers. No marks. Aware of spots on back. Tender to lay on.
>
> 1:30 worked on legs. Right thigh, both calves, bottom of feet. Mostly blood clots taken out. Mass with short tail from one foot. Was told to exercise every day and have a magnetic massage on Monday. Leg work is to improve circulation and balance. No visible marks. I watched closely. I could not see the opening but saw his hands were bare, the towel at some distance, and the clots were in his hands.
>
> Sunday: Did yoga exercises before breakfast. Very weak and shaky. Better an hour after eating. Went on Tagaytay tour. Had lunch and saw show at the Taal Vista Lodge. Slept 2 hours. Very stiff and staggering after leaving French restaurant. Went walking with group. Had a very difficult time with eyes and legs.
>
> Monday: Worked on both sides of the neck. Also down spine. No visible marks, however I feel where he worked. Julie took pictures. Did not see skin open but saw red marks when he took his hands away. Ran his thumbs down the spine. The bumps are cholesterol. Very painful. Worked out the lumps. Did the same on the legs. On the face. The poor circulation affects memory. Said the C-section cut a vein that helped support the stomach and intestines, causing constipation. Improving the circulation will help improve my sex life also. Said he would teach me how to clear the veins. No shower until tomorrow. Worked on my neck. It moved without pain or stiffness. However, the soreness was back at the base of the skull and neck on the left side in one hour.
>
> 1:30 p.m. Went in at center of the waist. Very deep. Felt warm blood ooze out. Large lump taken out. Cleaned both ovaries. 3 pictures taken. 2 horizontal creases about 2 inches wide over ovaries. No red, just indentations. Got sick to my stomach. Laid down. There was an indescribable feeling under the spot at my waist for about 1½ hours. Got up at four. Felt weak. Went back to bed. By 7 p.m. took all I had to get down to dinner. Very weak. After dinner my ovaries really hurt. I think the weakness is low blood sugar. I may be getting fat, but I can't let this happen again.
>
> Monday: Had magnetic massage with Mario. He said the mass taken from my middle was from the esophagus.
>
> Tuesday: Told Pepito about the blood sugar problem. He took several blood clots and several small masses out of the pancreas. He said yoga was alright. Felt the warm blood come out. He put quite a bit of blood

in the bowl with the cotton. Have hollow indentation left side below waist. Went into the right of the spine in the neck. Vertical red line. Felt the cutting but no pain. Blood clots taken out from back of head. Large double tumor taken out. Said this was for balance and circulation.

Wednesday: Went into the C-section. Took out large scar tissue. Blood clots from both legs. Vagina has twinges and small spasm. Went into buttocks, lower and outer part, also the lower spine. Removed blood clots and scar tissue.

The diary continues with accounts of removal of blood clots, tumors, dead veins, from the heart, hips, spine, stomach, head, etc. One tumor was over an inch in diameter and looked like "flat cord wound into a ball with blood dots on the side like brain clumps."

Was the patient cured? Of course not. She felt better from the massages, but nothing was changed. Did she believe that her body was burdened with the blood clots, tumors, and dead veins reported by the healers? She was skeptical and she had pictures taken by a friend, but they could discern no deception. After she was away from the psychic healing environment, she realized that the medical jargon was nonsense.

Some observers who have studied so-called psychic or spiritual healing think that the process may be dismissed too quickly. Allison and Malony (1981) wrote, "We must, in all fairness, avoid Western man's tendency toward reductionism. The compulsive need to oversimplify has often led to premature closing of profound issues. We must acknowledge the possibilities of yet-to-be-discovered truths and similar truths disguised by linguistic/religious/cultural differences" (p. 61). These authors deny the claim by James (The Amazing) Randi that legerdemain is employed in psychic surgery. On numerous occasions, Randi has demonstrated that by folding the fingers it can be made to appear that the body is being penetrated. By the use of what is called "the magician's thumb" (a device that slips over the thumb) blood and material passed off as blood clots and tumors could be made to appear to come from the body (Randi 1982, pp. 177–188). Others have analyzed the materials that the psychic healers pretended to extract from the body and have found them to include everything from chicken gut to fibrous plants. The fact that Allison and Malony were associated with Fuller Theological Seminary, where a course is taught that includes faith healing, might have affected their conclusions. The fact that some persons appear to have been healed by psychic surgeons can be explained in terms of mind-body relationships discussed above and by the fact that many illnesses heal themselves. One does not need the flim-flam of the Philippines healers to induce reversals.

Ethical Issues

There have been some tragic episodes in the recent history of faith healing. In some cases in which individuals put their trust in a religious theory or in the advertised power of some healer, they abandoned medical treatment; as a result, some patients died from illnesses that could have been successfully treated.

In May 1983, *The Chicago Tribune* carried a story about a failed faith healing. In April 1978, Dustin Gilmore, age fifteen months, came down with a flu-like disease. His parents took him to their church, where the pastor prayed for the child. This particular congregation believed that faith alone could heal any disease and that turning to scientific medicine exhibited lack of faith in God's healing power. Prayers for the child continued during the following weeks, but on May 15 the child died from a form of meningitis that could have been treated.

Randy Frame (1984) wrote about the indictment of Hobart Freeman, leader of the Faith Assembly sect in Wilmot, Indiana. Freeman claimed that he had received the "baptism of the Holy Spirit" in 1966 and subsequently had spent no money on medicine or medical care. He taught that medicines were evil and Satanic and that those who went to doctors invited demonic possession. He believed that if one's faith was genuine, God was obligated to heal every illness. If symptoms of an ailment or injury persisted, it was because of deception by the devil.

It is not surprising to find that the birth-death rate among female members of the Faith Assembly was reported to be one-hundred times greater than that of women in general in the State of Indiana. Freeman's indictment resulted from the death of fifteen-year-old Pamela Menne, who died of chronic kidney failure, a condition that the coroner stated could have been treated medically.

There are numerous similar accounts. One can only wonder how many stories have been withheld because of fear of disrupting faith patterns or of being accused of betraying a belief system. Moreover, one wonders how effective the hands-off-religion legal principle—enhanced by the 1974 order to states by the now-defunct U.S. Department of Health, Education and Welfare (HEW) to exempt faith healing sects from child neglect prosecution—has been in protecting and thus encouraging faith healing.

Faith healing as practiced by exploitive televangelists constitutes a fundamental denial of one of the basic tenets of the faith they claim to represent—the ethic of love. These men and women treat those who come to them in pain and need as subjects to be victimized. They practice deceit, they dishonestly seek only one thing—money. They must know what any investigator can demonstrate: that healing simply does not take place. They manifest no concern for human pain, for human suffering, for human need. An aware or critical observer can only be nauseated by the performances and by such exploitation of human pain and suffering.

The bilking of hundreds of thousands of viewers out of millions of dollars constitutes a further ethical issue. People in dire financial straits give because they are promised magical financial rewards for their "seed money." They give televangelists money they themselves and their families need for food, medication, to pay overdue bills, and so on. Consequently, they are further impoverished. The Christian call to care for those in need, based on the teaching in Matt. 25:31-46, is ignored and violated.

What is equally unethical in this age of modern science is the continuing emphasis on religious magic which encourages individuals to remain in ignorance of, or to reject, the finest medical knowledge that humans have developed.The use of logical thinking is discouraged and believers are taught to rely on blind, uncritical faith to heal their illnesses. The denial of human rationality is a rejection of one of the qualities that defines the human species. Noncritical thinking is encouraged throughout Christendom. Once the Bible is accepted as a divine or authoritative book, its nonscientific contents condition believers to accept on faith or at least as "perhaps possible" that which common sense would ordinarily reject. When biblical dogma is mingled with "the power of positive thinking," then "possibility thinking" encourages trust in questionable healing methods.

Once again, the supernaturalism of the Bible merges with the occult notions of New Age magic. The result is a negation of the highest ethical principles evolved by humans, including the ethic of love and of responsible human interaction and behavior.

References

Abrams, Garry, "Ebbing Empire," *The Los Angeles Times,* October 20, 1989.

Adams, Junius, "Psychic Healing: Does it Really Work?" *Cosmopolitan,* March 1984, pp. 244ff.

Allison, Stephen H., and Newton Malony, "Filipino Psychic Surgery: Myth, Magic, or Miracle," *Journal of Religion and Health,* Vol. 20, No. 1, 1981, pp. 48–62.

Badgley, Laurence E., M.D., "Immune Enhancement Through Natural Therapies," *L.A. Resources for Healing, Growth and Natural Therapies,* Fall 1987, p. 3.

Bailes, Frederick, *Hidden Power for Human Problems.* Englewood Cliffs, N.J.: Prentice-Hall, 1957.

Borgen, Peder, "Miracles of Healing in the New Testament," *Studia Theologica,* 35, 1981, pp. 91–106.

Brand, Paul, and Philip Yancy, "A Surgeon's View of Divine Healing," *Christianity Today,* November 25, 1983, pp. 14–21.

Bryan, Cyril P., *Ancient Egyptian Medicine; The Papyrus Ebers.* Chicago: Ares, 1974.

Burnside, Irene Mortenson, "The Therapeutic Use of Touch," in *Nursing and the Aged,* edited by Burnside. New York: McGraw-Hill, 1976, 1981, pp. 504–518.

Champollion, Jacques, *The World of the Egyptians.* Geneve: Minerva, 1971.

Clapp, Rodney, "Faith Healing: A Look at What's Happening," *Christianity Today,* December 16, 1983, pp. 12–17.

Colton, Helen, *The Gift of Touch.* New York: Seaview/Putnam, 1983.

Cousins, Norman, *Anatomy of an Illness.* New York: Norton, 1979.

Dart, John, "Scientists Confident That Shroud of Turin Tests Are Conclusive," *The Los Angeles Times,* October 15, 1988.

del Guercio, Gino, "More Doctors Use Hypnosis to Counteract Pain, Disease," *The Los Angeles Times,* December 10, 1984.

de Saint-Pierre, Michel, *Bernadette and Lourdes.* New York: Doubleday Image Books, 1955.

Dobbin, Muriel, "When a State Takes Aim at Faith Healing," *U.S. News and World Report,* March 24, 1986, p. 22.

Dolan, Maura, "Folk Remedies Often Turn Out to be Prescriptions for Danger," *The Los Angeles Times,* July 10, 1989.

Driver, S. R., *The Book of Genesis.* London: Metheun & Co., 1948.

Farah, Charles, Jr., "A Critical Analysis; The 'Roots and Fruits' of Faith-Formula Theology," *Pneuma,* Vol. 3, 1981, pp. 3–21.

Feigenbaum, Aryeh, "Early History of Cataract and the Ancient Operation for Cataract," *American Journal of Opthamology,* 1960, pp. 305–325.

Finkler, Kaja, *Spiritualist Healers in Mexico,* New York: Praeger, 1985.

Foulks, Frances W., *Effectual Prayer,* Missouri: Unity School of Christianity, 1959.

Frame, Randy, "Indiana Grand Jury Indicts A Faith-Healing Preacher," *Christianity Today,* Nov. 1984, pp. 38–39.

Furniss, George M., "Healing Prayer and Pastoral Care," *The Journal of Pastoral Care,* 1984, Vol. XXXXVIII, pp. 107–119.

Gillette, Robert, "Exotic Ways to Learn Doubted by U.S. Study," *The Los Angeles Times,* December 4, 1987.

Gordon, Cyrus, "Canaanite Mythology," in *Mythologies of the Ancient World,* edited by S. N. Kramer. Chicago: Quadrangle Books Inc., 1961, pp. 183–218.

Grad, Bernard R., "Healing and Dying," *The Journal of Pastoral Counseling,* 1980, Vol. XV, pp. 50–54.

Gregory, Ina "Laughing Winds," "The Giveaway," *Orange County Resources for Healing, Growth and Transformation,* La Mesa, Calif.: Spring 1989.

Guignebert, Charles, *Ancient, Medieval and Modern Christianity.* New York: University Books, 1961.

Haferd, Laura, "Arthritis Cured at her services, says Preacher at Catholic Church," *Akron Beacon Journal,* April 30, 1986.

Hasel, Gerhard F., "Health and Healing in the Old Testament," *Andrews University Seminary Studies,* Vol. 21, 1983, pp. 191–202.

Hurry, J. B., *Imhotep, The Egyptian God of Medicine,* Chicago: Aries Publishers, 1978. Reprint of Oxford, 1926 edition.

Hurwood, Bernhardt J., "Healing and Believing," *Health,* June 1984.

Kelsey, Morton T., *Healing and Christianity in Ancient Thought and Modern Times.* New York: Harper and Row, 1973.

Kirby, Daniel B., *Surgery of Cataract,* Philadelphia: J. B. Lippincott, 1959, pp. 24–30.

Kovel, Joel, *A Complete Guide to Therapy.* New York: Pantheon Books, 1976.

Kramer, Samuel Noah, *History Begins at Sumer.* New York: Anchor Books, 1959.

Larue, Gerald A., "Religious Traditions and Circumcision," *The Truthseeker,* July/August 1989, pp. 4–8.

Latourette, Kenneth Scott, *The First Five Centuries.* New York: Harper and Bros., 1937.

Lazaris, Channeled by Jach Pursel, "Building Body's Immune System Begins With Personal Self-Confidence," *Los Angeles, Resources for Healing, Growth and Transitions,* Fall 1987, pp. 26–27.

The Los Angeles Times, "Money Furor Sent Him to 'Hell and Back', Roberts Says," February 21, 1987.

MacNutt, Francis, *Healing.* New York: Bantam Books, 1974.

Marty, Martin E., and Kenneth L. Vaux, eds., *Health/Medicine and the Faith Traditions.* Philadelphia: Fortress Press, 1982.

Mayhue, Richard, *Divine Healing Today.* Chicago: The Moody Bible Institute, 1983.

Meek, George W., *"A Guide to Spiritual, Magnetic Healing & Psychic Surgery in the Philippines,"* pamphlet, 1973.

Moore, Robert L., "Contemporary Psychotherapy as Ritual Process: An Initial Reconnaissance," *Zygon,* Vol. 18, 1983, pp. 283–294.

Nickell, Joe, *Inquest on the Shroud of Turin,* Buffalo, N.Y.: Prometheus Books, 1983, 1987.

Nolen, William A., *Healing: A Doctor in Search of a Miracle.* New York: Random House, 1974.

Olson, Stanley N., "Interpreting the Miracles of Healing for Preaching," *Word and World,* Vol. II, No. 4, 1982, pp. 353–360.

Pilch, John J., "Biblical Leprosy and Body Symbolism," *Biblical Theology Bulletin,* 1981, Vol. XI, pp. 108–113.

Randi, James, *Flim-Flam.* Buffalo, N.Y.: Prometheus Books, 1982.

———, *The Faith Healers,* Buffalo, N.Y.: Prometheus Books, 1987.

Shepard, Leslie, "New Forward," In Paul Vignon, *The Shroud of Christ.* New York: University Books, 1970.

Simundson, Daniel J., "Health and Healing in the Bible," *Word and World,* Vol. II, No. 4., 1982, pp. 330–339.

Snyder, Charles, "Aurelius Cornelius Celsus on Cataracts," *Archives of Opthamology,* January 1964, pp. 144–146.

Stephens, John Lloyd, *Incidents of Travel in Egypt, Arabia Petraea and the Holy Land.* Norman: University of Oklahoma Press, 1970 (reprint of 1837 edition).

Streiker, Lowell D., "Ultrafundamentalist Sects and Child-Abuse," *Free Inquiry,* 1984, pp. 10–16.

Struthers, Susan, "New Light Thrown on Old Shroud," *Industrial Chemical News,* December 1981.

Swan, Rita, "Christian Science, Faith Healing and the Law," *Free Inquiry,* Spring, 1984, pp. 4–9.

Thomas, Keith, *Religion and the Decline of Magic.* New York: Charles Scribner's Sons, 1971.

Thorwald, Jurgen, *Science and the Secrets of Early Medicine.* London: Thames and Hudson, 1962.

Timburcio, Virginia M., "Pepito Gamboa," pamphlet, 1982.

Time, "A New Shrine for the Brown Virgin," December 20, 1976.

Tufnell, Olga, *Lachish III: The Iron Age.* London: Oxford University Press, 1953.

Twomey, Steve, "The Making of a Miracle," *The Buffalo News,* September 28, 1987.

Tyndall, Katie, "Acupuncture Relief," *Insight,* February 23, 1987, p. 65.

Vignon, Paul, *The Shroud of Christ.* New York: University Books, 1970.

Walker, Williston, *A History of the Christian Church.* New York: Scribners, 1959.

Williams, Nick B., Jr., "Rain Forests and Its Medical Secrets Shrinking Fast," *The Los Angeles Times,* April 11, 1988.

Wilson, John A., "The Legend of the Possessed Princess," in James B. Pritchard, editor, *Ancient Near Eastern Texts Relating to the Old Testament.* Princeton, N.J.: Princeton University Press, 1950, pp. 29–31.

YaDeau, Richard E., "Healing," *Word and World,* Vol. II, No. 4, 1982, pp. 317–321.

The Cult of the Mother Goddess

> . . . born of the Virgin Mary.
> The Apostles Creed

According to Christian theology, Jesus was both human and divine. He had a human mother and, most of his contemporaries assumed, a human father. However, his followers, members of what was to become the Jesus cult, were to claim that Joseph, the carpenter, was not his real father but that Jesus was divinely conceived. Obviously, there was a conflict between these theories. For example, according to the Gospel of John, when Jesus was talking to Jews near the Sea of Galilee, his claim to be the "son of God" provoked the comment:

> Isn't this Jesus, the son of Joseph, whose father and mother we know. How can he now claim "I have come down from heaven?" (6:42)

Of course, the idea of divine impregnation was not new. For centuries the Egyptians had accepted the notion that certain persons could be the son of a god and at the same time have a human father and mother. They believed that a god borrowed a human body, usually that of the husband, to conceive a child. Thus it was that when Imhotep was elevated to divine status, he was said to be the son of the Memphite god Ptah, even though the identity of his human father and mother was known. The pharaohs, too, who were accepted as incarnate divinities, had human parents and were born in the normal way.

Jewish Scripture contained the myth of the sons of Elohim copulating with earth women (Gen. 6:1–4). In Graeco-Roman myth, Hercules,

Perseus, and Alexander the Great were said to be the product of the union of Zeus with human females. Aesclepius, Pythagoras, Plato, and Augustus were the results of Apollo's sexual adventures with women. The claim that Mary, a virgin, was impregnated by the Holy Spirit was in compliance with legendary birth stories of hero figures common to New Testament times.

The Jesus story is different. The Gospel accounts display a pattern of continual reinterpretation by which the explanations of his divinization undergo change and development. In Mark, the earliest gospel, which was probably completed around 70 C.E., there is no mention of a miraculous birth. Jesus was proclaimed Son of God at his baptism. The announcement came from heaven. And only Jesus heard the heavenly proclamation of divine adoption: "You are my beloved son, I am well pleased with you" (1:10–11).

The same scene is described in Luke, written some years later, probably around 85 C.E.. Some early manuscripts of Luke contain an additional phrase, "Today, I have begotten you," underscoring the adoption notion of the Markan account. In Matthew, also composed about 85 C.E., the pronouncement was public, not private: "This is my beloved son, with whom I am well pleased." It is clear that the notion of adoption at the moment of baptism underwent change. However, for Matthew and Luke, Jesus did not assume sonship or divinity when he was baptized; he was divine from birth.

Matthew's account states that Mary was engaged or promised to Joseph. Before the marriage was consummated she was found to be pregnant out of wedlock. Through a dream Joseph learned that Mary's pregnancy was "of the Holy Spirit" (1:21). The Lukan account expanded this idea and introduced a sexual motif. In Luke, Mary was confronted by an angel who told her that the Holy Spirit would "come upon" her, and "the power of the Most High" would "overshadow" her and she would be divinely impregnated (1:35). In the Gospel of John, composed about 90 C.E., there are no references to divine-human intercourse or impregnation: Jesus was God incarnate, a manifestation in human flesh of the eternal deity. "He was in the beginning with God" (1:2). John's gospel assumed that Jesus entered the world by means of a human birth (John 2:1).

The progression in interpretation is clear. In Mark, Jesus was divine because he was "adopted" by God at the moment of baptism. In Matthew and Luke, Jesus was divine because of the miraculous impregnation of Mary by the Holy Spirit. In John, Jesus was presented as preexisting, one with God, and therefore divine from all eternity.

Mary is important because she bore the Christian savior. New Testament information about Mary is sparse. The traditions, the folklore, the popular mythology that became part of the church dogma emerged during the second century C.E. and later.

Mary's Virginity

Because Christian theology presented Jesus as having a divine father, the mother who bore him had to be a divinely approved individual. To conform to the accepted patterns for mothers of heroes in the Graeco-Roman world, she had to be a virgin, untouched by a human mate; otherwise the child could be said to be the product of intercourse with a human. Indeed, Jewish brides had to be virgins (Deut. 22:13–21). To bear a legitimate child in Jewish society the woman had to be married.

The New Testament writers stated that Mary was a virgin, that she was engaged when the Holy Spirit impregnated her, and that Joseph, the man to whom she was promised, accepted the pregnancy as being of divine origin. He married her and raised the bastard son, Jesus, as his own. If the narrative contains any factual data, it testifies to Joseph's naivete (assuming that he actually believed the tale of divine impregnation), and to his compassion in his response to Mary's difficult situation. How many of Joseph's Jewish neighbors would have accepted Mary's story of impregnation by the Holy Spirit can be imagined!

Did the mother of the divine Messiah, the mate of the deity, ultimately become the sexual partner of a human? Did Mary and her husband Joseph engage in sexual intercourse after Jesus' birth? Apparently their neighbors were unaware of mythical birth traditions and assumed she and Joseph engaged in normal marital relationships. When Jesus taught in his own community the people were surprised at his authoritative stance and said,

> Isn't this the carpenter, Mary's son, and the brother of James and Joses and Judas and Simon, and aren't his sisters here with us? (Mark 6:3)

The Gospel of Matthew phrases the questioning a bit differently,

> Isn't this the carpenter's son? Isn't his mother called Mary? Aren't his brothers James and Joseph and Simon and Judas? (Matt. 13:55–56)

It has been suggested that the Markan comment, which emphasizes the mother rather than the father, contains a slurring reference to Jesus' legitimacy. This emphasis was changed in Matthew's gospel. Nevertheless, in both gospels, it is clear that local Jews were familiar with Jesus' father, Joseph, the carpenter (whose trade Jesus followed), and with his mother, brothers, and sisters. We note that one child bore the father Joseph's name. The New Testament contains other references to Jesus' family members (Acts 1:14; 1 Cor. 9:5; Gal. 1:19)

The Christian church wrestled with the problem of Mary's relations with Joseph. The Greek terms for brothers (*adelphoi*) and sisters (*adelphai*) refer to persons who are born from the same womb. These children were Jesus' brothers and sisters—or in early Christian theological definition, his half brothers and half sisters, inasmuch as Joseph was not supposed to be Jesus' father. Today, most liberal scholars accept Jesus' brothers and sisters as products of the sexual union of Mary and Joseph. There are those who continue to insist upon Mary's perpetual virginity. The efforts to preserve Mary's virginity have a long history.

During the second century, a Christian document known as the Protevangelium or the Gospel of James came into being and was widely circulated. In it Joseph is described as an old man with grown children. Mary is presented as a twelve-year-old girl who has reached puberty. Throughout this gospel, it is made clear that Joseph had no sexual contact with Mary. This notion was widely accepted in the early church, even though there is absolutely no New Testament basis for the notion. It is current today in popular Roman Catholic thought.

To preserve the uniqueness of Jesus' birth, the Roman Catholic church has suggested that Jesus' brothers and sisters are products of a previous marriage between Joseph and some unknown woman. They accept the second-century notion that Joseph was quite old when he married Mary and that he and Mary never copulated. They argue that the Matthean passage that states that Joseph "knew her not [i.e., had no sexual intercourse] until she had borne a son" (1:25) does not imply that they had conjugal relations after Jesus' birth. Perhaps some Roman Catholic theologians entertained the erroneous belief, as some uninformed persons still do, that men lose sexual desire and potency after a certain age (for a refutation see my *Sex and the Bible*), and assumed that Joseph was too old to perform sexually! The reference in Luke 2:7 to Jesus as Mary's "firstborn" is dismissed as a Semiticism that does not imply subsequent births. Such are the efforts made to keep Mary's spiritual intercourse the single impregnating event of her life and to deny conjugal relations with her husband Joseph.

The title "Virgin" is important to the Marian cult. The term is introduced in the Gospel of Matthew:

All this happened in order to fulfill what the Lord had declared by the prophet, Behold, a virgin will conceive and bear a son, and he shall be called Emmanuel [which means "god is with us"]. (Matt. 1:22)

The prophet to whom Matthew referred is Isaiah, but, as we shall see, the eighth-century B.C.E. prophet's statement reads differently in the Hebrew. Moreover, the Hebrew prophet was not concerned with an event that was to take place some seven hundred years later; he was a man of his own time and spoke about his own time.

This was the situation during the eighth century B.C.E. Assyria was the dominant Near Eastern power. Small kingdoms like Syria and Israel (the northern Hebrew kingdom) paid tribute to keep Assyrian armies from invading. Judah (the southern Hebrew kingdom) was ruled by King Ahaz, a man who, in Isaiah's writings, appears weak and vacillating. In 735 B.C.E., the kings of Israel and Syria were convinced that the time was ripe to throw off the Assyrian yoke. They insisted that King Ahaz join their rebellion, and threatened to invade Judah should Ahaz fail to comply with their wishes. Ahaz was terrified and decided to appeal to Assyria for help. The prophet Isaiah, who appears to have had good political insight, advised against an alliance with Assyria. He believed that Assyrian forces would soon overrun the two northern kingdoms (he turned out to be right). Still Ahaz wavered. Isaiah became impatient. He referred to an unidentified young woman (perhaps, as some have suggested, his wife) and said,

Behold, a young woman (*almah*) is pregnant and will bear a son and will call his name Immanuel. . . . And before the child knows how to refuse the evil and choose the good, the land before whose two kings you are in dread will be deserted. (Isa. 7:14,16)

The word *almah* refers to a young woman old enough to bear a child, or in other words, to a girl who has reached puberty. It does not mean "virgin," nor does it indicate whether the woman is or is not a virgin. The Hebrew word for virgin is *bethulah*. In the context in which Isaiah was speaking, the term "virgin" would have had no particular significance. The notion of a virgin birth would have been irrelevant. As we consider the historical situation in which Isaiah's conversation took place, it is clear that he was dealing with a current problem, not with some far-off future event. Indeed, Isaiah and Ahaz could not have cared less about what might happen seven hundred years later!

Matthew sought to prove to Jewish readers of his gospel that Jesus had fulfilled Jewish Scriptures. That is why he frequently commented that something occurred to fulfill what he interpreted as a biblical prediction. He did not quote from the Hebrew Scriptures but from a Greek translation of Isaiah's work. The Jews who translated the Book of Isaiah to Greek for the Septuagint version, for some reason, had chosen the Greek word *parthenos*, which does mean "virgin," to translate *almah* of Isaiah 7:14. There was a perfectly suitable Greek counterpart to *almah*, namely the Greek word *neanis*, which represents exactly what Isaiah said. Why *parthenos* was used has never been satisfactorily explained. In any event, the Matthean passage is based on a mistranslation of Isaiah 7:14. Matthew used the passage to introduce the notion of a virgin birth.

How could Mary be proven to be a perpetual "virgin," which implies an intact hymen? Would not the hymen be torn during the birth process? Again, that remarkable Christian writing, the Protevangelium, preserved in the Apocryphal New Testament, testifies to the permanency of Mary's hymen even after Jesus' birth. The setting is the birth cave in Bethlehem. Mary was about to give birth and Joseph, in panic, left her to seek a midwife. When he found one and they returned to the cave, it was overshadowed by a "bright cloud." As the cloud slowly dissipated, the infant apprared "and it went and took the breast of its mother Mary" (James 1953, p. 46).

As the midwife left the cave, she met Salome and told her that a virgin had given birth. Salome was a skeptic and desired to examine Mary to determine whether or not the hymen was intact. It was indeed intact! But Salome's hand, that had been inserted into the vagina, was affected: "my hand falleth away from me in fire." The hand was miraculously and instantly restored when, at the advice of an angel who suddenly appeared, Salome held the infant Jesus. Salome was told to keep the whole matter secret. In such a manner did the early church seek to affirm the perpetual virginity of Mary.

The basis for this pious fiction is twofold. First, if the postresurrection Jesus could pass through closed doors without opening them (John 20:19–29), then it was quite reasonable to believe that the prenascent Jesus could pass through the vaginal canal without rupturing the hymen. Second, the story is modeled on the account of the doubting Thomas, who would not believe in Jesus' resurrection until he had thrust his finger into the wounds of the risen Christ (John 20:24–28). So the doubting Salome would not believe until she had thrust her fingers into Mary's vagina.

Not everyone in the early church accepted the tale of the unbroken hymen. Tertullian, a third-century Christian apologist who mocked the Greek mythologies and theologies, rejected the notion that Mary's hymen remained intact. He accepted the brothers and sisters of Jesus mentioned in the gospels as children of Mary and Joseph, born after Jesus. But there were other theological problems to be confronted.

The Case for the Sinless Mary

Early Christians believed in original sin, which resulted from the disobedience to Yahweh by Adam and Eve in the Garden of Eden. This mythical account of primeval noncompliance assumed monstrous proportions in Christian theology. Because of a transgression by Adam and Eve, all humans were tainted in the eyes of God. How could a tainted woman, stained with original sin, be a fit vessel for the birth of the Christ? Would she not transmit the stain of original sin to her son Jesus? The Protevangelium provided answers to these questions.

Mary was no ordinary child. Her mother Anna, like Hannah in the Jewish Scriptures, was barren (1 Sam. 1). Like Hannah, Anna prayed and was rewarded with pregnancy, and like Hannah she promised to give the child as "a gift unto the Lord my God." When Mary was six months old, Anna lifted her to her feet and made the infant stand. Mary took seven steps. Anna promised that the child's feet would not touch the ground again until she was taken to the temple. Mary's bedroom was converted into a sanctuary where Jewish laws of cleanliness were ritually observed. At the age of three she was taken to the temple, where she served until she was twelve. Then, through fear that should she menstruate and thus pollute the temple, she was given to Joseph in marriage.

The wondrous birth of Mary was not in itself enough to remove from her all taint of original sin. This was accomplished on December 8, 1954, by Pope Pius IX. In his papal bull *Infallabilis Deus* he stated:

> the doctrine which holds that the Most Blessed Virgin Mary at the first moment of her conception was, by singular grace and privilege of the Omnipotent God, in virtue of the merits of Jesus Christ, Savior of the human race, preserved from all stain of original sin, is revealed by God and thereto to be firmly and resolutely believed by all the faithful.

Thus, at last, Mary was officially declared free of original sin, and thereby acclaimed a suitable mother for Jesus and worthy of the title "Holy Mary, mother of God" recited by the faithful in the rosary.

Mary, Mother of God

The term *theotokos* (mother or bearer of God) became popular after the Council of Ephesus in 432 C.E.. A debate among theologians concerning the nature of Jesus as the Christ was in progress. The Nestorians mocked the term, but their opposition transformed it into a rallying cry. Politics were involved and the Nestorians fell out of favor with the rulers, after which the reference to Mary as "Mother of God" became part of Christian vocabulary.

Only one more step was necessary for the cult of Mary to be fully established. She had to become part of the heavenly hierarchy. There were biblical references to others who had been given miraculous entry into the abode of the gods. For example, concerning Enoch, who lived for 365 years, it was written "Enoch walked with Elohim, and he was not, for Elohim took him" (Gen. 5:24). Jewish savants assumed that the text meant he was translated into heaven. During the two centuries preceding the Common Era, a number of Jewish writers contributed to what has come to be known as "The Book of Enoch." This important pseudepigraphic writing, which reflects Jewish theological perspectives on everything from messiahship to ideas about the afterlife, was reputed to be the record of a vision, a revealed scripture, from the hand of Enoch. It is quoted as a scriptural source by the author of Jude in the New Testament (14).

Jude also refers to a tradition that the body of Moses was taken into heaven (9). This first-century C.E. notion is partially preserved in the pseudepigraphical work "The Assumption of Moses." The prophet Elijah was supposed to have ascended to heaven in a whirlwind (2 Kings 2:11). Of course, Jesus ascended physically into heaven. Thus, there were precedents for Mary's translation.

Traditions of the ascension of Mary began early in Christianity. By the fourth century C.E., tales about the assumption of Mary were being circulated. In *The Apocryphal New Testament*, M. R. James (1953) published material from Coptic, Arabic, Greek, Latin, and Syriac texts. These materials vary in details, but all agree on the admission of Mary into heaven after her death. For example, in "Transitus Mariae," written by Pseudo-Melito, Jesus resurrected Mary's dead body and transported it to heaven. In "The Falling Asleep of Mary," by Pseudo-John the Evangelist, only Mary's soul was taken to heaven. Her body was carried away by angels to be preserved with the bodies of other saints in a terrestrial paradise until the time of the general resurrection. Despite the fact that these fifth-century texts were condemned by Pope Gelasius I at the end of that century, they continued to circulate. During the Middle Ages, the "Transitus

Mariae" story became accepted, and in 1950 Mary's bodily assumption was proclaimed by papal decree. Thus, Mary became the heavenly Mother of God.

Some Catholic reasoning concerning the assumption of Mary evinces sugary, sentimental qualities. Jean Guitton in *The Virgin Mary* (1952) wrote:

> The Assumption may reasonably be deduced from the notion of divine motherhood: if the Virgin is the mother of Jesus Christ, he himself once glorified in body could not but have glorified, in some mysterious manner, the body of his own mother also, from whom alone his own body was derived. The Lawgiver, who made the giving of due honor to parents one of the conditions of eternal salvation, could not have allowed his mother's body to see corruption. (p. 147)

Of course, what underlies these contentions is nothing more than pious reading of idealistic ought-to-be notions into New Testament persons and events. Moreover, if Jesus was so concerned about honoring parents, it seems that Joseph, his earthly father who raised him, was accorded no special honors!

Through the assumption, Mary became part of the heavenly hierarchy. As mother of the savior and Queen of Heaven, seated at the right hand of Jesus, she has become, in Roman Catholic thinking, a heavenly power to whom petitions and prayers can be directed. Versions of a popular medieval tale suggest that Mary may admit to the heavenly kingdom some souls that could not be admitted through regular channels where they would be judged (more harshly) by Jesus. The tale tells of a vision in which a certain Catholic Brother saw two ladders reaching into Heaven. Jesus was at the top of the red ladder. Some of those who attempted to climb this ladder fell back time and again. At the top of the white ladder was Mary, who with outstretched hand, enabled all those who came to her to enter Heaven.

Pious imaginings, similar to that quoted above concerning the assumption, circulate with regard to Mary's role as redemptress. It is suggested that those who pray to Mary have a strong advocate, for what son could refuse the requests of a mother. Jean Guitton in *The Virgin Mary* asked:

> Who could refuse a mother? Who would condemn those she supports? These are the hopes in which the Catholic conscience is content to rest. (p. 143)

As mediator, Mary's role contradicts the New Testament teaching attributed to Jesus, who said "No one comes to the Father, except by me" (John 14:6). Mary's role as a heavenly advocate is rejected by Protestants.

The Status of Mary

So it was that the Jewish girl from the village of Nazareth became the archetype of the eternally pure, undefiled virgin. Despite the fact that she bore a child, she remained the eternal virgin. She stands in stark contrast to other wives and mothers, who in Christian tradition must inherit the punishment curse inflicted on Eve by Yahweh. As the eternal virgin, Mary's sexual nature is devalued. She is the mother who conceives without intercourse—at least without human intercourse. She is the virgin who bears and remains a virgin. Thus, the developing church successfully removed Mary from any semblance of normality as a woman. She stands in stark contrast to the first biblical woman, Eve, who represents, in Jewish Scripture, the normal woman, desiring, and perhaps initiating, intimate sexual relations with her mate. To the church, Eve became the symbol of the fall from grace, the evil woman, and Mary was elevated to the bride of God, the perfect female. In this manner the cult of Mary was born.

Pre-Marian Goddesses

Of course, there were female deities who preceded Mary and who existed in competition with her. In fact, it has long been recognized that the Marian cult borrowed much of its early emphasis from the cult of the Egyptian goddess Isis. E. A. Wallis Budge, the famous Egyptologist, published a two-volume work titled *The Gods of the Egyptians* (1904). In the second volume he stated,

> Among the various peoples by whom Isis is venerated must be mentioned those of Syria, who identified her with certain of their local goddesses, and it is clear that the early Christians bestowed some of her attributes upon the Virgin Mary. There is little doubt that in her character of the loving and protecting mother she appealed strongly to the imagination of all the Eastern peoples among whom her cult came, and that the pictures and sculptures wherein she is represented in the act of suckling her child Horus formed the foundation for the Christian figures of the Madonna and Child. Several of the incidents of the wanderings of the Virgin with

the Child in Egypt as recorded in the Apocryphal Gospels reflect scenes in the life of Isis as described in the texts found on the Metternich Stele, and many of the attributes of Isis, the God-mother, the mother of Horus, and of Neith, the goddess of Sais, are identical with those of Mary, the Mother of Christ. The writers of the Apocryphal Gospels intended to pay additional honour to Mary the Virgin by ascribing to her the attributes which up to the time of the advent of Christianity they had regarded as the peculiar property of Isis and Neith and the other great indigenous goddesses, and if the parallels between the mythological history of Isis and Horus and the history of Mary and the Child be considered, it is difficult to see how they could possibly avoid perceiving in the teaching of Christianity reflections of the best and most spiritual doctrines of the Egyptian religion. The doctrine of parthenogenesis was well known in Egypt in connection with the goddess Neith of Sais centuries before the birth of Christ; and the belief in the conception of Horus by Isis through the power given her by Thoth, the Intelligence or Mind of the God of the universe, and in the resurrection of the body and of everlasting life, is coeval with the beginnings of history in Egypt. We may note too in passing the probability that many of the heresies of the early Christian Church in Egypt were caused by the survival of ideas and beliefs connected with the old native gods which the converts to Christianity wished to adapt to their new creed. Be this, however, as it may, the knowledge of the ancient Egyptian religion which we now possess fully justifies the assertion that the rapid growth and progress of Christianity in Egypt were due mainly to the fact that the new religion, which was preached there by Saint Mark and his immediate followers, in all its essentials so closely resembled that which was the outcome of the worship of Osiris, Isis and Horus that popular opposition was entirely disarmed. In certain places in the south of Egypt, e.g., Philae, the worship of Osiris and Isis maintained its own until the beginning of the fifth century of our era, though this was in reality due to the support of the Nubians, but, speaking generally, at this period in all other parts of Egypt Mary the Virgin and Christ had taken the places of Isis and Horus, and the "God-mother," or "mother of the god," was no longer Isis, but Mary whom the Monophysites called *theotokos.* (pp. 220–221)

Mary replaced other goddesses as the Christian cult spread. Kenneth Scott Latourette (1937) noted:

The cult of the Virgin Diana may have contributed to the worship of the Virgin Mary and more than a coincidence may be seen in the facts that one of the earliest churches in honour of Mary rose at Ephesus on the site of the famous temple of Diana, and that in the same city in 431 a synod was held which first officially designated Mary the Mother of God. In some places in Italy the ancient Lares are said to have been replaced by the Virgin, or the saints, or figures of the child Jesus. Presumably under such circumstances something of the functions assigned to the old were transferred to their successors. In Sicily the Virgin is said to have taken possession of all the sanctuaries of Ceres and Venus, and the pagan rites associated with them are reported to have been perpetuated in part in honour of the Mother of Christ. At Naples lamps burning before the image of the Virgin are said to have replaced those before the family gods. At Naples, too, the popular cult of the Madonna is conjectured to have proceeded from that of Vesta and Ceres. (p. 320)

Of course, goddess worship has had a long history. Paleolithic figurines, often called "venus" statuettes, portray the feminine form with sexual organs, exaggerated breasts, and often a corpulency that suggests pregnancy. Perhaps these carved figures were associated with magico-religious rites associated with childbirth. Certain cave paintings of women with pendulous breasts together with male images seem to picture a dance that some have suggested may represent a cultic rite associated with fertility and birth. If these speculations (and they can only be speculations) are accurate, these may be the earliest known artifacts of the mother-goddess cult.

From the Neolithic period, when humans progressed from food gathering to food production, a large number of mother-goddess figurines have been found. For example, at Mosul, about ten miles north of ancient Nineveh, at Tell Arpichiyah, a large quantity of headless female figurines were found. Some are modeled in the round, others were flat. All had pendulous breasts, prominent navels, slender waists, and highly developed hips. Most are represented in the squatting position, suggestive of childbirth, and some would appear to be symbols of pregnancy. Some of the flattened models appear to have been worn as amulets. It is surmised that these amulets were designed to promote fruitfulness and to provide magical aid in childbirth. Other figurines were found at Tepe Gawra and Warka (Erech), some holding their breasts, some with eyes painted in black, some with sexual features prominently marked, some fiddle-shaped, and some with large breasts.

During the Iron Age in Israel two types of goddess figurines were common. The first was the so-called *dea nutrix*, the nursing mother. She is a pillar figurine with prominent breasts that she appears to be offering. There are no other sexual features. The other type of image, found as plaques, is assumed to be a representation of the goddess Astarte or perhaps Anat. She is slender and holds her small breasts. Her sexual features are clearly delineated. Two aspects of femininity are thus represented: the maternal figure and the sexual partner. It should be noted that the goddess Anat is called a "virgin " in the Canaanite texts, but the term is used rather loosely inasmuch as she copulates with the god Ba'al.

When textual material is found, the goddesses have names and personalities. They were called Ninhursag or Ninmah or Nanshe or Bau or Nunbarshegunu or Ninlil or Inanna, etc., among the ancient Sumerians; Tiamat or Gula or Ereshkigal or Sarpanitum or Ishtar, etc., in Babylonia; Astarte or Anat or Asherah in ancient Canaan; and, as we have seen, Isis or Neith or Sekmet or Hathor or Nekhebet or Nephthys or Wadjet or Heket or Bast, etc., in Egypt. They personified the many facets of the human female—love, seduction, loyalty, betrayal, pregnancy and birth, anger, fury, revenge, forgiveness, compassion, inventiveness, industry, and so on. They were feeling divinities who expressed the passion of a woman for her lover, the tenderness of a mother for her child, the stability of a homemaker, the independence of the unattached, the reliability of the committed. The language they shared with their lovers echoed passion and desire, and they provided role models for lovers in the areas where they were worshipped. Sometimes mythic dramas presented dimensions of interaction that prepared the audience for the many aspects of femininity. Human emotions and feelings and characteristics were projected into these divine beings to teach people who knew the myths and watched the cultic dramatizations what was normal and natural, expected and acceptable in human relationships. Some female divinities were responsible for specific aspects of nature, including life, fertility, birth, death, and so on. The ancient Near Eastern world and the Mediterranean world were well prepared for the advent of the cult of Mary.

Within Greek culture and religion, which were prominent in Palestine and the Mediterranean world at the time of Jesus' birth, various aspects of the mother-goddess found expression. Artemis was the huntress, Aphrodite was the love goddess, Hera was the mother-wife, and Athena was the virgin warrior. Athena (the term is a title meaning "the Athenian one"), whose central shrine was the Parthenon ("virgin temple") in Athens, was said to have been born from the head of Zeus. This birth is believed to reflect the resentment felt in the Greek patriarchal society regarding the one significiant function possessed exclusively by women—childbearing. Some Greek physiological theory proposed that the child was complete in the male seed and that the mother was like the earth in which seed was sown. Athena eschewed marriage and was famous as the companion of warriors, in whom she inspired courage and heroism. Unlike the Christian virgin, she remained unmarried and did not bear a child.

The Cult of Mary

The cult of Mary is rooted in Christian Scripture. After her divine impregnation, Mary visited her cousin Elizabeth. Elizabeth was also pregnant and her foetus became agitated when Mary appeared. It was on this occasion that Mary uttered the words that have become known as the "Magnificat" (from the opening word of the Latin translation). Luke's account is patterned on the story of Hannah in 1 Samuel 2, and Mary's words echo Hannah's. Mary says:

> My soul magnifies the Lord,
> and my spirit rejoices in God my Savior,
> for he has regarded the low status of his handmaiden.
> For behold, henceforth all
> generations will call me blessed . . .
>
> Luke 1:46–48

It would appear that by the time Luke was written (possibly about 85 C.E.) that the status of Mary as mother of Jesus was already being developed, at least to the point of earning her the designation "blessed." As I have noted previously, the fictional history of Mary served only to further enhance her status. Her power as an influence in the lives of believers is expressed in the Ave Maria, which is recited over and over and over again by believers using the rosary as a devotional tool:

Ave Maria,	Hail Mary
gratia plena, Dominus tecum.	full of grace, the Lord is with thee.
Benedicta tu in mulieribus	Blessed art thou amongst women
et benedictus fructus	and bleseed is the fruit
ventris tui, Jesus.	of thy womb, Jesus.
Sancta Maria, mater Dei,	Holy Mary, mother of God,
ora pro nobis peccatoribus	pray for us sinners
nunc et hora mortis nostrae.	now and at the hour of our death.
Amen.	Amen.

The "blessed" Mary, dead and transported to the realm of the divine, is asked to pray for her followers, because she is believed to have especial influence with Jesus and with God.

The Marian cult was given recognition in 1987 when Pope John Paul II issued a 115-page encyclical titled "Redemptoris Mater" (The Mother of the Redeemer). The purpose of the authoritative papal letter was to mark the Marian Year, which was to run from June 7, 1987, to August

15, 1988. Mary was described as "our common mother" and devotion to her, it was noted, "takes on special importance to women and their status." The Pope believes that by studying the example of Mary, women can discover "the secret of living their femininity with dignity and of achieving their own true advance." Of course, this statement omitted to mention that there is little if any hope for the admission of Roman Catholic women to the priesthood. The Pope stated that he was moved to declare the Marian year as he contemplated "the prospect of the year 2000, now drawing near, in which the Bimillennium Jubilee of the birth of Jesus Christ at the same time directs our gaze toward his mother."

As a virgin wife, Mary can never be a model for the complete wife—the warm, sexual, intimate woman. She is the madonna, elevated on a pedestal, pure, untouchable, austere. One cannot imagine Joseph caressing her body, fondling her breasts, or engaging in sexual intercourse with this distant, untouchable female. The disasters that this image has wrought for many marriages have been discussed by therapists under the theme of the "madonna-whore" syndrome (see my *Sex and the Bible*).

It is through the role of the mother-goddess that Mary has been given power within Christianity. As the mother of the ascended Christ, who, according to the creed "sits at the right hand of God, the father almighty, from when he shall judge the living and the dead," she is believed to have parental influence with her judgmental son. But it is as the understanding, caring, loving mother-goddess that Mary makes her greatest appeal.

There is a deep need in those who have experienced loss, who feel lonely, isolated, misunderstood, and unappreciated, for a mother figure to whom they can turn—a loving goddess who has herself experienced loss and known sorrow. Mary watched her infant son grow to manhood, gain notoriety, confront criminal prosecution, and ultimately suffer physical abuse and death. She represents the mother who can understand our pain, our losses, and our tears because she experienced all of these herself. God is aloof and far away. Jesus is a man and despite the compassion he is supposed to have expressed as a first-century figure in Palestine, he cannot be compared to an idealized mother figure. As E. Wallis Budge noted, the model for the role of Mary was Isis. Isis had experienced loss and sorrow in the murder of her husband. She had borne the infant Horus and knew parental love. She was the compassionate mother figure. Just as the ancient Egyptians and others in the Mediterranean world worshipped Isis as the compassionate, caring mother-goddess, so do modern Roman Catholics worship and pray to Mary.

Apparitions and Cult Centers

The gods and goddesses of the ancient world had their cult centers, and centers were soon established for the Marian cult. In some instances, her worshippers simply took over shrines and sacred places associated with other goddesses. As one might expect, there are sacred places associated with Mary in Palestine. For example, in Nazareth the place where Mary was told she was to bear the divine savior is commemorated in The Basilica of the Annunciation. The site in Ain Karim where she visited her cousin Elizabeth after she became pregnant is honored in The Church of the Visitation. Of course, in Bethlehem, the place where Mary gave birth is marked in The Basilica of the Nativity. Finally, in Jerusalem, on Mount Zion, there is a shrine known as The Church of the Dormition, where Mary died, or as it is usually said "fell asleep."

Some sacred sites were places where a revelation of Mary had supposedly taken place. Lawrence Cunningham in *Mother of God* (1982) has noted that:

> The great Marian shrines and pilgrimage sites were focused centers of this manifestation of power. Even the great Roman basilica of St. Mary Major, rebuilt to honor the *Theotokos* doctrine of the Council of Ephesus in the fifth century, is connected with legend. Pope Liberius, the story goes, built the original church on the Esquiline Hill in the fourth century because of a snowfall there in the month of August, which covered the exact site for the building and was interpreted as a sign from Mary herself. By the Middle Ages, imposing Marian sanctuaries, sites of her miraculous intervention multiplied in Europe as the medieval love for pilgrimage (and miracle) increased. Among the more celebrated pilgrimage goals associated with the Virgin founded in the Middle Ages include: Einsiedeln in Switzerland (ninth century), Our Lady of Walsingham in England (eleventh century), Mariazell in Austria (twelfth century), Our Lady of the Pillar in Saragossa, Spain (thirteenth century), Our Lady of Czestochowa in Poland (fourteenth century), and the House of the Virgin at Loreto in Italy (fourteenth century. (p. 68)

Of course, there have been continuing claims that Mary has manifested herself in visions or in other ways. Since 1930 more than 200 alleged apparitions of Mary have been reported. None of them have been accepted as authentic. Some are clearly illusions caused by distortions in lighting, illusory shadow effects, and so on. For example, a 1931 sighting of Mary's shadow on a wall was caused by reflected light from across the street. In May 1987, believers in Wilkes-Barre, Pennsylvania, gathered before a wall of a house which depicted a human shape under an arc of light. It was decided that the image was that of Mary. Others suggested that the image was caused by a reflection of a five-inch-tall figurine in the window of a house across the street. When the figurine was moved, the shadow of the Virgin moved, too. Some of the claims of revelation are purely in the mind or eye of the beholder. The desire to believe creates the necessary image.

Other visions can be classified as hallucinatory because only the seer perceives anything. In 1950, Anna Van Hoof, of Necedah, Wisconsin, announced that she had had seven visions of Mary. Over 100,000 people turned out to watch her talk to an apparition that was visible only to her. In May 1987, a forty-six-year-old woman in Willesden, England, reported a series of visitations by the Virgin Mary. Sofia Richmond (aka Sister Marie Gabriel) had been a devout, pious follower of the mystical way of Roman Catholic saints since age eleven. Her claims have received support from the local clergy. In 1981, a Roman Catholic bishop blessed a rock and dedicated it to the Virgin Mary in the African village of Ndonko in Cameroun. During the next fifteen months, twenty miraculous healings were reported. In 1987, in Pleasant Grove, Texas, the Reyna family discerned an image of the Virgin in the black and grey shades of the bark on the trunk of a gnarled oak tree. The sighting was publicized and drew crowds of the curious. Finally, in Cairo, Egypt, there have been repeated claims that the Virgin Mary has appeared on the roof of the Coptic Orthodox Church of St. Demiana. Numerous cures have been attributed to the apparition. In June 1986, the authenticity of the vision was confirmed by a special committee appointed by the Coptic Orthodox Patriarch Sehnudah III.

The reports seem endless. Many are quickly dispelled. For example, in May 1988, a "Mary's Hour" program in the Hollywood Bowl was sponsored by the Roman Catholic Archdiocese of Los Angeles. The service, which included hymns, prayers, and a procession behind an image of Mary, was held in connection with the papal proclamation of the Marian Year. John Dart, a religious writer for *The Los Angeles Times,* noted that

> . . . many in the crowd reported seeing a prism effect and brightness in the sky to the north. The reports by some of "another sun" or a "rainbow" or both prompted speculation about a supernatural sign.

Church authorities refused to attach any supernatural meaning to the claims. Dart contacted meteorologist Dan Bowman, director of operations of Weather Data, Inc., Wichita, Kansas. Bowman labeled the phenomenon "a sundog" and explained:

The sun passes through water droplets or ice particles high in the atmosphere or through high, thin clouds, which refract the light in such a way as to have a coloration effect. That area of the sky also looks brighter than the surrounding sky. It actually looks like the sun.

This explanation is most significant for it provides an explanation of the phenomenon reported at Fatima (see discussion below). Furthermore, it suggests that many so-called apparitions may have naturalistic explanations. Visions by individuals appear to be private hallucinations. Some reports seem to take on a validity just by virtue of continuing publicity.

Obviously, it will be impossible in this book to examine all of these hallucinatory experiences. A few of the more famous or notorious will be considered. The faith center of the Virgin of Guadaloupe is discussed in the chapter on Faith Healing.

Marian Relics and Art

During the Middle Ages relics associated with Mary began to accumulate. Milk from the Virgin's breast was to be found in some seventy locations. Hairs from Mary's head, bits of her clothing, a letter she was supposed to have written, and even her engagement ring were displayed! The inventiveness of the church in devising means to lure pilgrims and their money to shrines seemed to know no boundaries.

As Marian pietism grew, so did Marian art. As she supplanted Isis, her images borrowed themes from popular depictions of the Egyptian goddess. Isis had been portrayed with the infant Horus on her knee, so now Mary was pictured with baby Jesus on her lap. But this was only the beginning. She was Queen of Heaven and the art depicted her in this role —crowned and standing alone, not in the company of her divine son. Despite ecclesiastical denials, she had become a goddess in her own right, having replaced the female deities of earlier ages.

Sacred Sites

Bernadette Soubirous of Lourdes, age fourteen, was an unhappy child. She had been compelled to leave a beloved aunt and a loving godmother and for a short time live with a foster family where she was not loved. She was then returned to her real parents, who were poverty-stricken. It was at this time she began to experience her visions of the Virgin Mary.

The details concerning her vision and the healing center that developed as a consequence are discussed in the chapter on Faith Healing, where the Marian revelation associated with Guadaloupe is also considered.

Fatima

It is difficult to believe that a cult center could develop on the basis of hallucinatory visions of an angelic figure and Mary reported by three deeply religious children. Fatima represents such a center. The original vision was experienced by Lucia de Jesus dos Santos, a lonely child whose older sisters had left home either to marry or to work. Her initial vision was not identified as the Virgin Mary, but it has been suggested that perhaps she was projecting her need for the attention of an older sister.

The village of Fatima is located in the center of Portugal, about seventy miles north of Lisbon. Lucia was born on March 22, 1907, in the hamlet of Ajustrel and was the youngest of seven children. She was a precocious child and learned her catechism well enough to receive her first communion at age six. Her earliest playmates were children of the hamlet, but from 1917 (when she was ten years of age) her sole companions were her cousins Jacinta (born in 1910) and Francisco (born in 1908) Marto. The in-home education of the children could be characterized as pietistic, with evening instruction in Roman Catholic religious literature. There was also regular attendance at Mass.

Apparently Lucia's visionary experiences began in 1915 when she and three other little girls saw a cloud formation that looked like a man hovering over the foliage of the village. Lucia recalled it looking "Like a cloud, whiter than snow, slightly transparent, with a human outline." The apparition appeared twice more.There was no verbal communication.

A year later, while watching the family sheep in the company of her cousins, a transparent form of a young man was manifested. He was "about fourteen or fifteen years old, whiter than snow, transparent as crystal when the sun shine through it, and of great beauty." This apparition spoke, "Fear not! I am the Angel of Peace. Pray with me!" Three times the children repeated the prayer uttered by the specter before it disappeared. Some months later the angelic figure reappeared. All three are supposed to have seen the figure, but only Lucia and Jacinta heard it speak, and only Lucia entered into conversation with it. The angel identified itself as the Guardian Angel of Portugal and commanded the children to offer up sacrifices for the sins that offended God. They were informed that "the hearts of Jesus and Mary" had "designs of mercy" for them. The third angelic appearance involved the three children in a sacral communion rite in which the angel held a chalice in one hand and the "host" (the bread wafer symbolic of Jesus' body) over it. Blood dripped from the wafer into the chalice and the contents of the cup were given to Jacinta and Francisco to drink; Lucia got the wafer. The children were commanded to make reparation for the crimes of mankind.

It was not until May 1917 that Marian apparitions began. The "beautiful lady" appeared near midday in a flash of blinding light hovering over a holmoak (*Quercus coccifera*), a small evergreen about three feet high. Lucia has described the apparition as "a Lady all dressed in white. She was more brilliant than the sun, and radiated a light more clear and intense than crystal glass filled with water, when the rays of the sun shine through it."

The children were asked if they wished to offer themselves "to God to endure all the sufferings that He may choose to send you, as an act of reparation for the sins by which He is offended and as a supplication for the conversion of sinners?" (Konder 1976, p. 67) The children agreed to offer themselves. They were told to say the rosary daily to bring about the end of the war.

The story of the encounters with the visionary Mary continues, marked with accounts of the children's pious sacrifices of food and energy in response to their commissions. Jacinta and Francisco died in childhood. Lucia joined the sisters of the Convent of Pontevedra, and later, in 1948, transferred to the Discalced Carmelites. As a consequence of the visionary experience, a huge shrine honoring Our Lady of Fatima, together with a convent, a retreat center, and a hospital were located on the site of the apparitions.

Lucia's "reminiscences" are supposed to reflect the actual messages of the apparition. Lucia revealed two of three "secrets" imparted to her by the vision. The first was a vision of Hell:

> Our Lady showed us a great sea of fire which seemed to be under the earth. Plunged in this fire were demons and souls in human form, like transparent burning embers, all blackened or burnished bronze, floating about in the conflagration, now raised into the air by flames that issued from within themselves together with great clouds of smoke, now falling back on every side like sparks in a huge fire, without weight or equilibrium, and amid shrieks and groans of pain and despair, which horrified us and made us tremble with fear. The demons could be distinguished by their terrifying and repellent likeness to frightful and unknown animals, all black and transparent. (Kondor, p. 108)

The second secret was concerned with the salvation of sinners from this terrible fate. The children were told that "God wishes to establish devotion to my Immaculate Heart." Indeed, to prevent divine punishment by means of "war, famine, persecution of the Church and of the Holy Father," ritual prayers for the consecration of Russia to the Immaculate Heart of Mary were to be said. The promise was that if Russia was converted there would be peace. The third secret has not been revealed. It is sealed and in the hands of the Pope.

Of course the claims of the children were investigated by church and other authorities. Multitudes gathered and still gather at the place of the apparitions. Wealth has flowed into the community. Miraculous healings are supposed to have occurred. And there were other "spiritual" manifestations.

On October 13, 1917, the apparition identified itself to the children as the Lady of the Rosary. The children alone saw the vision. The crowd of thousands that had gathered during the night and early morning at the wondrous holmoak were told to close their eyes and recite the rosary. After the vision had informed the children that the war would soon end, Lucia notes, "Then, opening her hands, she made them reflect on the sun, and as she ascended, the reflection of her own light continued to be projected on the sun itself." At this moment Lucia cried out "There she goes! There she goes!" causing the crowd to look at the sun. The sun appeared to be glowing with shifting colors, appearing to some as a silver disc. Then the sun seemed to dance and appeared at one point to be falling on the people. Then, as the people cried out in terror, the sun moved back into orbit. This event is accepted by Roman Catholic writers on the matter as a "miracle."

Of course there are other, more logical explanations of what took place. In the first place, everyone did not see the sun dancing. The sky on that day was overcast. Many of us have witnessed the thinning of clouds when the sun appears as a silver disc. Dust in the air can give sunlight a variety of hues. As for the sun dancing, one can only ask for confirmation at solar observatories. Of course, there was absolutely no evidence of such an event. Mass hallucinations are not unknown and it would appear that this is what occurred at Fatima.

The ease with which a natural phenomenon can become a miraculous sign is reflected in the spectacular display of the aurora borealis in 1938. For Lucia it was a Heaven-sent sign that God was going to punish the world for its sins. For astronomers and for nonprofessionals familiar with the marvelous shifting lights of the aurora borealis, it was a spectacular but perfectly natural phenomenon. Lucia had difficulty with this naturalistic explanation. She wrote,

> I don't know for certain, but I think if they investigated the matter, they would discover that, in the form in which it appeared, it could not possibly have been an aurora borealis. Be that as it may, God made use of this to make me understand that His justice was about to strike the guilty nations. (De Marchi, p. 203)

The pious believer discovers what he or she wants in natural phenomena, interprets these observations as he or she wishes, and will accept no other explanation.

The visionary calls for sacrifice reflect Roman Catholic teaching. Accounts of the children's attempts to meet the harsh demands reflect the spiritual indifference of religious leaders to human well-being, the glorification of self-mortification, and the idealization of martyrdom associated with some aspects of Christianity. When the three youngsters inflicted suffering on themselves in the name of their faith and gave away their food, they became more susceptible to hallucinations.

It seems obvious, as one reads Lucia's memoirs, that she was the key person in the visionary experiences. She seems to have envisioned the specters first and she is the one who could explain to the others the significance of what they believed they saw. She was deeply immersed in Roman Catholic teaching, and it is not hard to imagine that a lonely child, raised in a Roman Catholic village, hearing Roman Catholic teachings in the home and in the church, could be carried away into a fantasy world of communication with the divine.

As in other reported contacts with Mary, the messages are banal. There is nothing in what Lucia says that she could not have absorbed in one way or another from her religious settings. Portrayals of hellfire are standard in certain religious meetings. The honoring of Mary is and has been widely accepted in Catholicism. Lucia had role models in other visionaries. The messages from Mary appear to be products of Lucia's own mind, formulated out of what she had heard in her home, in her village, and in her church. Nevertheless, these childish hallucinations have been accepted as genuine and the faithful continue to worship at the pretentious structure that came into being because three youngsters claimed they had been talking with the Virgin Mary.

Medjugorje

In June 1981, Ivanka Ivankovic, age fifteen (born in 1966), claimed to have experienced a vision of Mary. She was with Mirjana Dragicevic, age fifteen (born in 1965), who did not see the apparition. Later, accompanied by thirteen-year-old Milka Pavlovic, the vision appeared to all three. The next day they went again to the hillside spot where the vision had appeared, accompanied by Ivan Dragicevic, age sixteen (born 1965), Vicka Ivankovic, age seventeen (born 1964), and Jakov Colo, age ten. The apparition of the young woman appeared again and motioned to the children to come to the summit of the hill, where they fell on their knees. There the apparition identified herself as the "Blessed Virgin Mary," noting that she came as "the Queen of Peace." She told the children that Thursday, June 25, 1981, was to be considered the beginning of her appearances.

Soon other wondrous phenomena were reported. For example, the Serbo-Croatian word *mir* (peace) appeared in great flame-colored letters across the night sky, terminating above the parish church. In August 1981, it is reported that the people who gathered saw the sun begin to spin and move toward them as the earth began to darken. On other occasions, during the time when the vision is supposed to appear, a huge stone cross erected on a local mountain peak is supposed to be brilliantly lighted. Indeed, this same cross is said to be spinning in rainbows of colored lights almost daily. Attempts to photograph these miraculous lighting effects have failed and the developed prints show nothing of the reported miraculous colors. It is reported that once a fire blazed between heaven and earth on the mountainside, but when the police investigated they found no evidence of burning. A partially paralyzed three-year-old deaf-mute was the first to be miraculously healed. Since then, numerous miraculous healings have been reported.

The children, and only the children, have experienced several thousand visitations by the specter. In the past, the phantasms lasted up to an hour, but in recent times have been reduced to about two minutes. The apparitions take place daily at 5:30 P.M. in a small side room of the Church of St. James. The visions are supposed to continue until each child has received "ten secrets." When this number is reached, the children no longer experience visions. Ivanka and Mirjana have received their ten messages and no longer see the apparition except on their birthdays or special occasions. Despite the fact that Mary appears to them simultaneously, each child receives a separate revelation. Each hears his or her message mentally, in the Croatian language.

The apparition is reported to begin with a brilliant light. Mary is described as a young woman, about nineteen years old, wearing a light-grey ankle-length dress with a white veil that permits one lock of black hair to be visible on the left side of her face. Her skin is olive-colored, with the rosy tint associated with country girls in the Yugoslavian highlands. Around her head is a circular crown of brilliant stars. She smiles, "glowing with holiness," and raises her hands toward heaven. Her greeting is always "Praised be the name of Jesus Christ." Her farewell is "Peace be with you." During the visitations the children appear to have entered a trance state so that they are oblivious to the presence of onlookers or to the popping of flashbulbs when photos are taken.

The publicizing of this Marian appearance has resulted in swarms of visitors, numbering hundreds of thousands, who go to Yugoslavia to participate in and worship at the site of the revelations. Information centers on the Medjugorje apparitions have been established in Prairie City, Kansas, and in London, England. Books and audio- and videotapes are offered for sale. Pilgrimages are conducted, led by Roman Catholic clergy. Medjugorje has become, in the language used in a publication of the Kansas center, "the goose that lays golden eggs" for the tourist industry in Yugoslavia.

The messages reported by the children are religiously simplistic and reflect unsophisticated laity-level Roman Catholic teaching. The emphases are on reciting the rosary, peace, reconciliation with God, the need for repentance and prayer, and so on. The Madonna warns that the world is at the brink of a great catastrophe that can only be averted through prayer, sacrifice, and penance. She is supposed to have stated, on one occasion, "Christians have forgotten that they can stop war and even natural calamities with prayer and fasting," a comment that can only be seen as encouraging magical thinking.

Vicka and Jakov claim that the Virgin transported them to heaven on All Saints Day. They failed to describe what they experienced, saying only that "It's too beautiful . . . too exciting to describe." Apparently, in her conversations, Mary had confirmed the existence of Heaven, Hell, and Purgatory. Heaven, we are informed, "is for the people who live out the Gospel."

The major question is: are these children playacting or are the experiences real? The children have been subjected to questioning by church authorities and Communist officials, and subjected to numerous psychological and psychiatric tests. The test results are inconclusive and reveal only that the children are normal, healthy, devout without being fanatical. They have not wavered in their statements over the past years. The local bishop, Pavao Zanic, is convinced that the youngsters have been manipulated by the local clergy and that the young people were victims of "collective hallucinations." Other clergy believe the appearances are authentic. The Holy See has refrained from commenting on the apparitions but has noted that the controversy between Bishop Zanic and the other clergy serves to "create confusion among believers" and hinder church investigations.

Ivanka Ivankovic's mother died shortly before the girl began to experience the apparition. At the time, when she had her visions, her father was working in another country. It is legitimate to wonder whether the hallucinatory experience of the divine mother might have been a psychological replacement for the dead mother and whether the absence of real parents in the teenager's life led her to envision a divine parent substitute.

It is possible that the six children have had hallucinatory experiences. Critical research could investigate their stories separately to check for discrepancies, etc. It would be useful to examine the visionaries' environment for models of the Virgin they describe and to understand the preaching and teaching to which they have been exposed. For example, accounts of the apparitions of Bernadette Soubirous at Lourdes and of Lucia Santos at Fatima have been published and are available in pamphlets designed for the laity and for children. In the messages they have related, the Medjugorje children seem to be simply repeating church dogma. Their words echo the messages reported from Lourdes and Fatima. At this point, it is only possible to state that the young people have reported hallucinatory experiences that they seem to believe are real. They seem to enter a trance state around 5:30 P.M. each day when the vision is supposed to appear, and they stick by their accounts of what they have experienced.

It is disappointing to learn that nothing particularly new has come out of these multitudinous encounters with Mary. The published statements are simply regurgitations of standard Roman Catholic teachings. One might conjecture that life must indeed be dull in the heavenly realm for the Madonna to expend so much time over the past years repeating religious cliches.

Lubbock, Texas

Texas's experiences of Mary appear to represent a fallout from Medjugorje. Right Rev. Monsignor Joe James, the founding pastor of St. John Neumann Roman Catholic Church in Lubbock, Texas, made two pilgrimages to Medjugorje. He returned in February 1988, convinced, according to newspaper reporter Barry Bearak, that he could feel the presence of the Virgin Mary at a Sunday evening prayer meeting. During services on the following Sunday the scent of roses was discerned in the chapel, although no flowers were present. Msgr. James declared it was like the odors he experienced on the Mount of Apparition in Medjugorje. Then the apparitions began.

Parishioner Mary Constancio believed that she could mentally discern the Virgin, who informed her that by praying three rosaries per day for six months she would see many conversions. Theresa Werner and Mike Slate reported out-of-body experiences that transported them into the heavenly presence of Jesus. Soon the crowds began to come—upwards of 15,000 on a given day, and as many as 2,000 for Monday evening prayer sessions, according to Bearak's report (1989).

On August 15, 1988, the Feast of the Assumption of Mary, thousands came for the evening mass and the courtyard of the church was crowded with people. As the sun began to set, some claimed to experience visions. One saw Mary in a Christmas card nativity setting, some saw Jesus or an eagle or a beady-eyed serpent. Some claimed the sun spun and pulsated, moving close to the earth, then retreating. Many saw nothing unusual. Some miracles were reported. Rosaries dipped in the courtyard fountain became golden. One person was cured of back pain. Someone else claimed that the legs of a child afflicted with cerebral palsy were healed.

Church authorities examined the claims. It was determined that the magical events were products of the mind. The charismatic influence of a powerful pastor, deeply affected by his pilgrimage to Yugoslavia, had affected some of his flock. The claims were not accepted. No shrine would be built.

The furor has diminished. The divinely revealed messages provided no new insights. The usual church admonitions concerning Satan and the need for prayer were given. One parishioner had a revelation of a threat to the earth by the impact of a star within two years. Theresa Werner appeared to prefer watching the television show "MacGyver" to attending the Monday rosary sessions that once provided her with contact with Mary.

In a radio-telephone conversation, a woman who claimed her silver cross had taken on a golden hue told me a jeweler told her that, while the metal was not gold, the color had permeated the whole cross. An investigator suggested that the cross was tarnished and the polished tarnished surface gave it the golden tone. My feeling was that the investigator was correct. A simple test could have been performed in ten seconds—dropping the cross in Tarnex and seeing if the color remained. The woman was adamant. She knew what she had seen, and of course a skeptic like myself could not understand.

Bayside, New York

Mary and Jesus are said to have appeared and to have given messages to Veronica Lueken at Bayside, Queens, New York. The apparitions began in 1966, when, according to Mrs. Lueken, a visionary St. Theresa began to visit her and to dictate poems and sacred writings. On April 7, 1970, the Virgin Mary visited Mrs. Lueken in her home and announced that she would appear on June 18, 1970, on the grounds of the old St. Robert Bellarmine Church in Bayside. The vision ordered that the parish clergy be told to prepare for her coming and asked that a shrine to be called "Our Lady of the Roses" be built in her honor on this site. The clergy were not persuaded, and the vigils were not held at the appointed place but in Flushing Meadow Park. Despite the publicity concerning the apparitions, and despite the messages that were purported to have been transmitted through Mrs. Lueken, the Roman Catholic church has not accepted her claims. The Diocese of Brooklyn has labeled the purported visions inauthentic and some Roman Catholic clergy have publicly called the whole thing a sham.

The divine messages from Bayside include warnings of the end of the world, including threats of a fiery comet striking the earth. Humans are urged to repent, keep the Ten Commandments, pray the rosary, read the Bible, and so on. This manifestation of Mary has informed her visitors that since Vatican Council II, the real popes have been imprisoned and the Vatican's teachings, which stress ecumenism, are the voices of the antichrist and Satanic agents. Thus, Mary has become engaged in church politics! It is not surprising to find that thousands have made pilgrimages to the locale, that miraculous healings have been reported, that literature and tapes are available for sale, and that the pilgrimages made by true believers have been recorded for television.

Bullsbrook, Perth, Australia

In 1947, Bruno Cornacchiola, a Rome taxi driver, had a vision of the Virgin Mary. Up to this moment he had been an unbeliever; now he became a devout convert. He formed an organization called "Sacri," recognized as fervently and militantly Christian. There were more visions and in one he was commissioned to construct a church at Bullsbrook. In 1978 he visited Perth, where land for the shrine had been donated to Sacri by the Lombardo family. There was no water on the land. After several dry holes were drilled, the place where water was to be found was revealed by the Virgin Mary to Mrs. Rosa Lombardo.

Today, the shrine of Our Lady of the Revelation contains a statue of Mary wearing a green rather than the traditional blue robe, because this was how she appeared in the vision to Cornacchiola in 1947. Of course, there have been miraculous healings. In 1985 a Perth woman claimed that water from the shrine was responsible for the recovery of her husband who was close to death with diabetes and a chronic kidney condition (medical specialists note that such recoveries are not infrequent). Crowds of worshippers come to the shrine with bottles and cans to collect the magical water for sick relatives and friends. To date, church authorities have not formally authenticated the apparitions nor approved the worship of Mary at this shrine.

Tears of Mary

Every so often there are reports of statues or icons of Mary that shed tears. Some are clearly hoaxes, others, kept in protective custody by church officials, cannot be examined by scientists. The claims about a weeping, moving statue in Thornton, California, were dismissed by Roman Catholic investigators, but not before pilgrims contributed enough money to repair a leaky roof on the church. The weeping Virgin statue in the Roman Catholic Church of St. John of God in Chicago that was reported in 1987 is still under investigation. Just what causes the tears, which have not been shed when investigators were present, is not known.

A weeping icon of the Virgin Mary drew thousands of visitors to St. Nicholas Albanian Orthodox Church in Chicago during 1987. Emissaries sent by the Greek Orthodox Archdiocese of North and South America to investigate the icon decided that the tears that appeared on the canvas painting glued on wood were the result of a miracle. The tears are interpreted officially as a plea from Mary that the world abandon materialism and a call for prayer and repentance. Requests by members of the scientific community to examine the icon or to chemically analyze the tears were refused.

Meanwhile, in Berkeley, California, Dr. Shawn Carlson, a physicist and a member of the Committee for the Scientific Examination of Religion, created his own weeping icon. To avoid being labeled "impious," he used the face of the Mona Lisa. Liquid tears fall from her eyes and streak down the front of the picture, just as they do in the photographs of the weeping icon in Chicago. Dr. Carlson does not claim that the Mary icons produce tears by the same process that he has created. He simply wished to show how easy it was to make a picture weep.

Cultic Celebrations

As Marian cult centers developed, so did rites and rituals associated with the virgin goddess. A Marian calendar developed. By the fifth century she had become the goddess or patron of fertility. Her festivals, associated with sowing, harvesting, and the vintage, were celebrated in mid-May at the feast of Mary's Queenship, in mid-August at the feast of the Assumption, and in March at the feast of the Annunciation. Today, festivals associated with Mary are celebrated worldwide in every month except April and June. Lawrence Cunningham has provided a variant list containing the following: January 1, the Solemnity of Mary, the Mother of God; February 2 (Candlemas Day), the Purification of Mary and the Presentation of the Child Jesus in the Temple; February 11, Our Lady of Lourdes; March 25, the Annunciation (the day of Mary's impregnation, based on Jesus' birth date being December 25); May 31, the Visitation; in May, the Immaculate Heart of Mary; July 16, Our Lady of Mount Carmel; July 26, Joachim and Anna, Mary's parents; August 5, the Dedication of the Basilica of Saint Mary Major (Our Lady of the Snows); August 15, the Assumption of the Blessed Virgin Mary into Heaven; August 22, the Queenship of Mary; September 8, the Birth of Mary; September 15, Our Lady of Sorrows; October 7, Our Lady of the Rosary; November 21, the Presentation of Mary in the Temple; and December 8, the Immaculate Conception (the date of the impregnation of Mary's mother Anna by her husband, Joachim, based on the acceptance of September 8 as Mary's birth date).

Mary's nativity festival (September 8) is based on a private revelation. The festival was established in Angers, France, after a man told St. Marilius that he had heard angels singing during the night. When he inquired of them the reason for the chorale, he was told that it was Mary's birthday.

Perhaps one should not be surprised to learn of the continuing belief in Marian appearances. The Bible records numerous similar visionary revelations and Mary herself is supposed to have had such experiences. The Marian cult has been and is characterized by magical thinking called revelations, by hallucinations that are termed visions, and by beliefs that provide the basis for the acceptance of all sorts of New Age revelations and visions. Mary's messages to the world are boring repetitions of church cliches. For some educated Roman Catholics the cult is an embarrassment. There can be little doubt that the Roman Catholic insistence on the validity of the Marian apparitions encourages the kind of thinking that in turn encourages belief in extraterrestrials. Magical thinking in the church community is no different from magical thinking in the nonchurch community.

References

Bearak, Barry, "Visions of Holiness in Lubbock," *The Los Angeles Times*, April 9, 1989.

——, " 'Miracles' Are Explained but Not Forgotten," *The Los Angeles Times*, April 10, 1989.

Budge, E. Wallis, *Egyptian Religion*. London: University Books, 1959 (originally published in 1900).

——, *The Gods of the Egyptians* (in two volumes). London: The Open Court Publishing Company, 1904; reprinted New York: Dover Publications, 1969.

Cacella, The Rev. Joseph, *The Story of Fatima*. New York: St. Anthony's Press, n.d.

Cunningham, Lawrence, *Mother of God*. San Francisco: Harper and Row, 1982.

Dart, John, "Visions of Mary: Hallucinations?" *The Los Angeles Times*, July 27, 1985.

——, "Surprises Mark Revival of Mary's Hour Bowl Service," *The Los Angeles Times*, May 21, 1988.

De Marchi, John, *Mother of Christ Crusade*. Billings, Mont.: Mother of Christ Crusade, 1947.

Devillers, Carole, "Haiti's Voodoo Pilgrimages of Spirits and Saints," *National Geographic*, March 1985, pp. 395–408.

Florida Times-Union, " 'Weeping' Icon a 'Sign', Orthodox Archbishop Says," Jacksonville, Fla., February 14, 1987.

Guitton, Jean, *The Virgin Mary*. New York: P. J. Kenedy and Sons, 1952.

Hoch-Smith, Judith, and Anita Spring, eds., *Women in Ritual and Symbolic Roles*. New York: Plenum Press, 1978.

James, M. R., *The Apocryphal New Testament*. Oxford: Clarendon Press, 1953.

Karminski, Theresa M., "Eyewitness to a Miracle" and "Are the Apparitions in Yugoslavia for Real?" *The Catholic Standard and Times*, August 24, 1983, and February 2, 1984.

Kondor, Fr. Louis, ed., *Fatima in Lucia's Own Words*. Cambridge, Mass.: Ravengate Press, 1976.

Kramer, Samuel Noah, *The Sumerians*. Chicago: University of Chicago Press, 1963.

Larue, Gerald A., "Astronomy and the Star of Bethlehem," *Free Inquiry*, Winter 1982, pp. 25–28.

Latourette, Kenneth Scott, *The First Five Centuries*. New York: Harper & Brothers, 1937.

Lichtheim, Miriam, *Ancient Egyptian Literature*. Los Angeles: University of California Press, 1975, Vol. I.

Lloyd, Seton, *The Art of the Ancient Near East*. London: Thames and Hudson, 1961.

Reuther, Rosemary Redford, *Mary—The Feminine Face of the Church*. Philadelphia: Westminster Press, 1977.

Ringgren, Helmer, *Religions of the Ancient Near East*. Philadelphia: Westminster

Press, 1973.

Saggs, H. W. F., *The Greatness That Was Babylon*. New York: Hawthorn Books, 1962.

Schanche, Don A., "Pope Urges Christian Unity in Devotion to Mary," *The Los Angeles Times,* n.d.

The Cult of the Serpent

Be wise as serpents.
Matt. 10:16

I give you power over serpents.
Luke 10:19

The serpent has various roles in the Bible. Sometimes it is recognized for just what it is, simply a snake, one of the creatures inhabiting Palestine (Amos 5:19; Rom. 3:13; et al.) Sometimes it symbolizes evil or danger. Jeremiah portrayed the Babylonian conquerors of Judah as serpents (8:17); a wisdom writer described the power of wine as "snakebite" (Prov. 23:31–32); and Jesus called the scribes and Pharisees "serpents" (Matt. 23:33). The serpent was also associated with magic and both Egyptian and Hebrew magicians (Moses and Aaron) converted their wands or staffs into snakes (Exod. 4:3; 7:9–12).

Of course, according to the oldest (tenth century B.C.E.) biblical creation myth, in the beginning, the serpent (*nahash*) was nothing more than one of the creatures formed from clay and animated by Yahweh as a possible companion for man (Gen. 2:4b–3:24). According to the story, the serpent was wiser, cleverer, more discerning than any of the creatures Yahweh had formed, including the two humans. When Eve protested against eating of the tree of moral knowledge on the grounds that Yahweh had warned "the day you eat you die," the clever serpent knew that this was nonsense and that Yahweh was lying to frighten the humans:

> You won't die. Elohim knows that when you eat of it your eyes will be opened and you will be like Elohim, knowing good and evil. (Gen. 2:4–5)

The serpent was right. The couple did not die and they, unlike other creatures, became morally aware, that is, they could make conscious choices before acting concerning good and evil. The deity acknowledged that his deceptive tactics had failed:

> Look, the man has become like one of us, knowing good and evil. Now, lest he reach out and take from the tree of life and eat and live forever . . .

This address to the heavenly court broke off in mid-sentence as the creator went into action and expelled the humans from paradise lest they should eat of the second magical tree—the tree of life—and acquire immortality, the one attribute that separated them from divinity (3:22–23).

Although to the priestly creators of the myth a snake was just a snake, perhaps the Hebrew temple priesthood attributed sagacity and a potential for critical analysis to the serpent because it had acquired mythic status in surrounding cultures. For example, in the Gilgamesh epic, a snake devoured the wondrous root, which Gilgamesh had set aside while he bathed, that made "the old man young." Thus the snake robbed humans of the potential for rejuvenation and acquired an ability to renew itself by shedding old skin for new. In Egypt the snake goddess Udjet was both a protector and fertility symbol and was represented on the red crown of upper Egypt as the Uraeus.

What seems to be a more direct source of serpentine influence comes from the Canaanites, the pre-Hebrew inhabitants of Palestine. The serpent was a prominent symbol in the Canaanite fertility cult "being specifically associated with the mother-goddess Asherah in pendant reliefs from the Late Bronze Age at Ras Shamra and on clay-moulded incense altars of the pre-Israelite period at Bethshan" (Gray 1963, p. 608).

A bronze serpent called Nehushtan was worshipped by the Israelites in the precincts of Solomon's temple in Jerusalem. To explain its presence, the temple priesthood concocted a legend which is found in Num. 21:4–9. According to this sanctuary tale, the Hebrews, having escaped from Egypt, became wanderers in the wilderness area near the kingdom of Edom. When they complained loudly about lack of food and water, Yahweh reacted in anger to their grumbling and sent "fiery serpents (*nahashim seraphim*) to bite and kill his unhappy people (Num. 21:5–6). When the people repented, Moses prayed to Yahweh and was told:

> Make a fiery serpent (*saraph*) and set it on a pole, and every one who is bitten, when he sees it, he will live. (Num. 21:8)

According to the story, Moses cast the bronze serpent and elevated it on a pole, and the magic worked:

> Then Moses cast a bronze (*nehoshet*) serpent (*nahash*) and fastened it on a pole and when a snake (*nahash*) bit a man and he looked at the bronze serpent (*nahash nehoshet*) he lived. (21:9)

Subsequently the bronze artifact became a sacred icon and one of the accouterments of the temple.

Despite the legend that justified its presence in the temple area and the rituals associated with it, the Yahwists knew the bronze serpent had a Canaanite, not a Hebrew, origin. At the close of the eighth century B.C.E., when King Hezekiah decided to purify the temple and remove all non-Hebrew elements:

> He smashed into pieces the bronze serpent Moses had made, because up to that time the people of Israel had burned incense to it. It was called Nehushtan. (2 Kings 18:4)

Obviously, temple religion was a conglomerate of Hebrew and Canaanite traditions and rituals (witness the horned altar and the bull figurines that supported the cosmic sea, etc.), and a serpent cult existed in the sacred precincts. The adoration of the snake in the Moses fiction was associated with prophylaxis and healing, so that it is legitimate to suggest that the Nehushtan cult had a similar focus, although fertility may also have been involved (Joines 1974, p. 101).

Nehushtan (the name may be a play on the Hebrew word for "bronze" or the word for "serpent") was still in the temple when the prophet Isaiah had his vocational hallucination. Isaiah's visionary experience occurred in 742 B.C.E., the year that King Uzziah died, and some forty years before Hezekiah initiated his reforms. The prophet described his experience:

> In the year that King Uzziah died, I saw the lord (*adonai*) sitting on a high, exalted throne, and the train of his robe filled the temple. Seraphim stood around him each with six wings: with one pair he covered his face, with a second pair his feet [genitals] and with one pair he flew. They kept calling to one another:
>
>> Holy, holy, holy, is Yahweh of the (heavenly) armies, the entire earth is full of his splendor
>
> The door posts shook as each called out and the house was filled with smoke. Then I said,

Woe to me. I am lost, because I am an unconsecrated man dwelling among an unconsecrated people, yet my eyes have seen the king, Yahweh of armies.

Then one of the seraphim flew to me carrying in his hand a heated stone which he had removed from the altar with tongs. He touched my mouth and said,

> When this has touched your lips
> Your guilt is purged
> Your sin is wiped away

Then I heard Adonai's voice asking, "Whom shall I send? Who will go for us?" I responded, "Here I am! Send me!" (Isa. 6:1–8)

The ritual described is a mouth purification rite similar to those performed in Egypt and Mesopotamia. The performers are priests—seraphim priests—decked out in costumes familiar to us from the priestly regalia depicted on Assyrian plaques from the same era. Their title "seraphim," connotes a connection with the seraph (fiery) snakes of the Moses legend. In the visionary experience in which Isaiah believed he actually saw the invisible Hebrew god, the seraphim priests were seen as attendants on the deity. What was most significant for the prophet was that the purging rite enabled him to become a spokesman (prophet) for the deity.

We have no information about the function of serpent priests in the Canaanite cults. Nor is there adequate information to explain the roles of the Assyrian priests in their winged costumes, some shod in bird's feet or wearing bird masks. It is clear that costumes were part of the ancient cults just as in Roman Catholicism priests wear different garb for different festivals.

Hezekiah destroyed the Nehushtan icon and apparently purged the temple of the seraphic priests. When his successor, Manasseh, came to the throne in 767, non-Hebrew symbols and worship were reintroduced. There is no information as to whether the serpent cult was reestablished.

The role of the serpent in the Garden of Eden was reinterpreted in the centuries immediately prior to the development of Christianity. Now the snake was identified as Satan. No longer was it merely a more clever creature that revealed to Eve the truth concerning the importance of the tree of moral knowledge; it became the devil himself who, disguised as a serpent, misled the woman and caused what was to be called "the fall" and the source of "original sin." This reinterpretation of the Eden myth also transformed the status of women. Eve was no longer the liberator who lifted humankind to a stage above animals and closer to the gods; now she became the gullible female who brought sin into the world and cost humans paradise. She was to symbolize the fallen woman, as opposed to Mary, the eternal virgin.

The Serpent in the Christian Scriptures

Somewhere about the middle of the first century C.E., the Apostle Paul wrote letters to the Christians in Corinth. In one he made reference to the wilderness serpents in the Moses legend (1 Cor. 10:9) and in the other to the Garden of Eden myth (2 Cor. 11:3). In the first instance he warned against "putting the Lord to the test as some of them did and were destroyed by serpents." In the second, he expressed concern that other Christian teachers might corrupt the instruction he had given to the group:

I fear that just as the serpent by his cunning deceived Eve, your thoughts may be corrupted and you will stray from sincere and single-minded devotion to Christ. (2 Cor. 11:3)

The Gospel of John utilized the healing power of the bronze serpent as an image of the healing power of the crucified Jesus. The author attributed the allusion to Jesus, who said:

As Moses lifted up the serpent in the wilderness, so must the son of man be lifted up so that whoever has faith in him may have eternal life. (John 3:14)

The crucifixion elevated Jesus on a cross, so that the elevated crucifix could be said to have replaced the elevated serpent. The Christian myth added a promise of the immortality Adam and Eve failed to acquire when they were expelled from the garden before they could eat of the tree of life.

The scriptural basis for present-day Christian serpent cults is found in two New Testament passages. The first is Luke 10:18–19. Jesus had appointed seventy persons who went, two by two, to the towns he planned to visit in much the same way that Billy Graham campaigns are preceded by his crew who line up churches, choirs, and congregations so that the evangelist, when he takes the stage, is assured a huge, symapthetic audience. When the seventy returned, filled with excitement over their conquest of demons, Jesus commented:

> I saw Satan fall like lightning from heaven. See now, I have given you the authority to tread on serpents and scorpions, and over all the power of the enemy, and nothing shall harm you.

The second passage is in the Gospel of Mark. Modern translations end this gospel at Chapter 16, verse 8. Verses 9 to 14, which appear as part of the chapter in the King James Version, in more modern versions are set in italics or otherwise separated from the main text. These verses, written in a style dfferent from the rest of the gospel, are not found in the best and most reliable ancient manuscripts. They were compiled out of material from the other gospels during the second century C.E. and appear to represent a reaction against the abrupt ending of the original writing.

In this later addition the disciples were told by the resurrected Jesus to carry the gospel to the world and were given the signs of genuine conversion:

> And these signs will accompany those who believe: in my name they will cast out demons; they will speak in new tongues, they will pick up serpents, and if they drink any deadly thing, it will not hurt them; they will lay hands on the sick and they will recover. (Mark 16:17–18)

There is no indication that drinking poison or handling poisonous reptiles to demonstrate faith became a popular pastime in the early church.

Modern Christian Serpent Cults

Since the beginning of the twentieth century snake-handling Christian groups have existed in West Virginia, Tennessee, Kentucky, and North Carolina. The Pentecostal, fundamentalist, evangelistic, Holy Roller, tongue-speaking congregations are composed of poor, mostly white members with limited formal education. The services include preaching, hillbilly-type singing, and witnessing, punctuated by ecstatic shouts—all designed to rouse the participants to a highly emotional state. At the peak of the emotional high, members plunge their hands into the box containing poisonous reptiles (rattlesnakes, copperheads, cottonmouths), pull out a snake, and fearlessly hold it and let it slither over their arms and neck before passing it to another person. If someone should be bitten, the congregation prays for healing, and although there have been some deaths, some members claim to have been bitten dozens of times and survived.

Of course, the biblical justification for this bizarre behavior is the verse in the last chapter of Mark's Gospel. In fulfillment of the entire verse, members also drink "salvation cocktails" composed of hazardous liquids, including dilutions of lye, strychnine, and battery acid. These drinks have resulted in some deaths.

Laws prohibiting snake handling have been passed in North Carolina, Virginia, Tennessee, and Kentucky. However, despite the legal restrictions and the potential for suffering and death, these people, who are familiar with poverty and suffering, feel that any suffering that results from following biblical prescriptions is unworthy of serious attention.

The superstitions associated with the Bible interpreted as the "word of God" rather than the prescriptions of ancient religious cults encourage a literalism that endangers health and well-being. Because the Scriptures promise supernatural power to overcome deadly poisons, some believers seek to prove the depth of their faith by engaging in life-endangering rituals.

References

The Calgary Herald, "Snake-handling Churches still in Soul-saving Business," March 7, 1987.

Carden, Karen W., and Robert W. Felton, *The Persecuted Prophets*. New York: A. S. Barnes, 1976.

Gray, John, *I & II Kings*. Philadelphia: The Westminster Press, 1963.

Herbert, A. S., *The Book of the Prophet Isaiah*. Cambridge: University Press, 1973.

Joines, Karen R., *Serpent Symbolism in the Old Testament*. New Jersey: Haddenfield, 1974.

Lasson, Egon, *Strange Sects and Cults*. New York: Hart Publishing Company, Inc., 1971.

Madden, Tom, "Cult Proves Faith by Taking up Serpents, *The Los Angeles Times*, June 29, 1980.

Amulets—Control Through Artifacts

Amulets are natural or man-made objects believed to have magical or supernatural power. They are supposed to be able to ward off evil, engender good fortune, health, or happiness, and enable their owners to exercise a measure of control over difficult situations. They may be used to provide protection and guidance or answers to questions.

For example, some fasten iron horseshoes over doorways to bring good luck. There is debate as to whether the horseshoe should have the prongs up to contain the magical luck as in a cup, or down to permit the luck to pour out upon those who pass through the doorway. Key rings often have dried rabbit's feet attached to charms to ensure good luck (without much attention given to the luck of the rabbits to whom the feet belonged!) Such secular amulets are outnumbered by far by religious tokens. The use of sacred amulets and objects has had a long history.

From the earliest times humans were burdened by the notion that much if not all of life was out of their control. Unseen forces, powers, demons, and deities affected their well-being and determined their destinies. In modern theological parlance, this notion is labelled "providence." It refers to the relationship of the deity to his creation and the ways in which God foresees, affects, and ordains events. The term is usually employed in the context of a loving deity who cares and provides for his creation.

The idea of controlled destiny appears also in secular thought, for example, when someone affirms the inevitability of progress or when Marxists proclaim the dialectical movement of history towards some utopia. The implication is that there is some inexorable, overwhelming power at work which renders human choices and human desires ultimately meaningless. It really doesn't matter whether the determinant force is a god or history or progress or even DNA. The pattern is fixed and humans are enmeshed within it. Moreover, what is ordained for the future is not open to human cognition. Humans may, by the use of intellect and by the study of history and the flow of events, attempt to predict the probable direction of events, but as anyone who has played the stock market will verify, one cannot be certain. Human assessments are never certain.

Certain belief systems suggest that acting solely upon one's personal judgment is a prelude to failure because the future is in the hands of the deity. For example, in the Bible obedience to laws and commandments guaranteed favorable response from Yahweh. To decide for oneself might violate divine precepts, "For my thoughts are not your thoughts, nor are your ways my ways, says Yahweh" (Isa. 5:8).

Abraham's blind trust in Yahweh "was counted as righteousness," which meant he was judged as having done the right thing (Gen. 15:6). The wise teacher, ben Sirach, assured his students that "he who trusts in Yahweh will not suffer loss" (Sirach 32:24). For Jews, the Torah contained the divine will and was the source of all wisdom. The wise followed its teachings in assurance of acceptance and blessing from Yahweh. When trouble came to Israel, it was always explained in terms of violation of divine will.

What if humans were uninformed about divine revelations? The Apostle Paul informed Gentile Christians who had not been acquainted with the Torah that some had spontaneously fulfilled the Torah and could rely on the testimony of their heart. That was to say that by following their conscience rather than their intellect, they had lived in accord with the divine law. Human incapacity to do the right thing was due to the fact that humans led their lives according to the flesh; Paul dealt with such problems in Chapter 7 of his letter to the Romans. Christian and Jewish Scriptures reflect distrust of free will and free thought and free life. The emphasis is on obedience and conformity to that which has been revealed.

Life Controls in Modern Society

There have been few changes in the above attitude in the nearly 2,000 years since the Bible was composed. Present-day notions of human destiny are influenced by biblical concepts. For the vast majority, God is in charge of human fortune and misfortune.

But if life's patterns are determined by forces outside of human control, might it be possible to sway these powers by petition or prayer, or by gifts and offerings? In human affairs, those who wield power can often be wheedled into changing a decision or persuaded to act on someone's behalf; why shouldn't supernatural powers respond similarly? Consequently, whenever a crisis or disaster strikes, believers pray to their god to intervene, to change the course of events, to save some beloved family member from inclusion among those hurt by the disaster, or to alter the outcome of the crisis situation. Sometimes some saint or martyr is asked to intervene on behalf of the petitioner, because it is believed that God, like humans, can be swayed by influential individuals (see chapter on The Cult of the the Dead). Many Christians not only believe that "prayer changes things," but that the course of destiny can be altered. Published Roman Catholic testimonials consistently give thanks to one saint or another who is believed to have interceded for a petitioner. Christians thank God that a family member has survived an accident, no matter how many others may have perished. Common expressions of this sort of thinking include: "Someone upstairs is looking after me (or him or her)," or "Thank God he (or she) is safe."

Of course, little heed is given to unanswered prayers. When petitions fail, it is argued that God had a different plan. Most religious leaders are prepared to admit that at times God says "no" to a request. When in Nazi Germany six million Jews went to their deaths crying out for help to their traditional God, it was clear to Richard Rubenstein, a Jewish rabbi, that God was dead! But belief persists despite denials.

Is Magical Power Available?

If the present and future are determined by supernatural powers, and if prayers and petitions don't always work, perhaps powerful magical instruments can be utilized to affect the shape of things to come, ward off unexpected dangers, protect against illness or accidents or violence. When this kind of thinking develops, amulets are used as tools to thwart the external powers and bring beneficial results for the possessor.

Magical Objects in the Bible

The ancient Hebrews believed in the power of certain artifacts. For example, the ark of the covenant, the boxlike structure carried by the migrating tribal groups, used as a palladium in time of war (1 Sam. 4), and finally enshrined in the temple of Solomon, was believed to represent the visible presence of Yahweh or to be the seat on which the invisible Yahweh was enthroned. It was directly addressed as the deity (Num. 10:35–36). It was perceived as possessing holy or supernatural power (holiness) so that only the priests should approach or touch it (Josh. 3–4; 2 Sam. 6:6–7). One legend records that when it was taken as a trophy of war by the Philistines it wreaked such havoc in the temple of the god Dagon that the Philistines were eager to return it to the Hebrews (1 Sam. 5). Obviously, the legend suggested, the holiness of Yahweh was more powerful than the holiness of Dagon. The Philistines placed magical amulets on the cart that conveyed the ark back to the Hebrews. Ultimately, it disappeared when the Babylonians sacked Jerusalem and the temple in the sixth century B.C.E. It was probably taken as a prize of war to Babylon. By this time, it seems to have lost its destructive powers—at least no reports of its destructive effects in Babylon have been preserved. A late legend claims that the prophet Jeremiah hid the ark in a cave on Mount Nebo (2 Macc. 2:4–5). Apparently some Jewish writer believed that the magical holiness of the ark would not permit it to be destroyed.

As every Palestinian archaeologist knows, the ancient Hebrews wore amulets. They are found with skeletal remains during the excavation of tombs. Some are tiny faience representatives of Egyptian deities, including Sekhmet, Isis, or the dwarf god Bes, who was associated with childbirth. Apparently some Hebrew women decided that although Yahweh was the national deity, it was still wise to call upon a birth expert when children were conceived and delivered.

Of course, some objects may have been worn for decoration only. Isa. 61:10 describes the bride decked out in her jewelry. Ezekiel's list of bridal gifts included bracelets, neck chains, nose rings, ear pendants, a coronet, and ornaments of gold and silver. Archaeologists have found that polished colored stones, including onyx, agate, quartz, opal, amethyst, lapis lazuli, etc., were strung as beads or mounted in brooches. Sea shells were pierced and strung together. Sometimes colored clay balls or tiny glass beads were used in necklaces. Bronze bracelets or anklets have been found on skeletons. Some items may have been tokens of friendship (Gen. 41:41f.); some were gifts to bind relationships (Gen. 24:22). There is nothing unusual or supernaturalistic in such objects.

Nevertheless, although there is no clear evidence of the attribution of magical power to ordinary jewelry, some objects had occult significance. Necklaces that included small, shaped, fragments of animal bone, decorated with circles with dots at the center, might be dismissed as nothing more than boneware utilizing a motif common throughout the ancient Near East. On the other hand, because the pattern is familiar with beads that were, and even today still are, used to ward off the evil eye, they can be considered progenitors of that superstition.

The Book of Isaiah, in a warning about what women would lose during a siege, listed the finery worn by Hebrew women:

> In that day, Yahweh will take away the frills, anklets, sun and crescent moon amulets, ear pendants, bracelets and shawls, headbands, armlets, sashes, charm-boxes and talismans, signet and nose-rings, low-cut party dresses, capes, cloaks and handbags, frilly [see-through] gowns, mantles, linen head-coverings, turbans and veils. (3:18–20)

Sun and crescent moon pendants are referred to in Judg. 8:26 as amulets worn by Midianite rulers and hung about the necks of their camels. Their purpose was to ward off evil, to protect the kings and their livestock. The inclusion of these items in Isaiah's list might indicate that they were simply employed as jewelry, but because astrological divination using the sun, moon, and stars was popular in ancient Israel, they probably had a magical significance (see chapter on Astrology).

Earrings and nose-rings were also amulets worn to protect the woman from evil influences and to signify acceptance of non-Hebrew religious beliefs. When Jacob urged his household to get rid of all tokens associated with foreign religion, among the artifacts he collected and buried beneath an oak near Shechem were earrings (Gen. 34:4). Hosea's wife, Gomer, became a follower of the Canaanite fertility god Ba'al. To Hosea, her rejection of Yahweh was tantamount to adultery. He asked that

> she put away her harlotry from before her face and her adultery from between her breasts. (2:2)

The reference was to the protective cultic nose-ring and pendants she wore symbolizing her adherence to Ba'al. The custom may be compared to the wearing of Christian crosses and Jewish stars where the decorative is combined with the religio-magical.

Colored Stones and the Presence of Yahweh

Biblical theophanies are generally described in terms of light, brightness, and rainbow colors, all images associated with the sun, the moon, and the sky. It has been suggested that the light given off by polished colored stones may have some connection with hallucinatory accounts of the appearance of Yahweh.

Ezekiel's description of his theophanic experience referred to "flashing" or "sparkling" lights and to colors like the rainbow. In his vision the vault that represented the firmament was crystalline. The throne seat was like sapphire (Ezek. 1:4–28). The god-figure in Rev. 4:3 is described in terms of jasper and carnelian. The rainbow was like an emerald, the glassy sea before the exalted throne was crystal. Jewel images are associated with theophanies, but the cultic significance of such descriptions is not clear.

Jewels, Stones, and the Cult

Cultic vestments worn by the high priest in ancient Israel were called "holy garments" (Exod. 28:2) and while they may have served an official and social purpose as an ornate uniform "for glory and for beauty," they were essential for admission into the holy of holies—the innermost precinct of the temple where the sacred icon, the ark, was kept. Only when properly attired could the high priest go where no layman could—into the very presence of Yahweh (28:30).

The garment was bejeweled. Two onyx "remembrance stones," each inscribed with six names of the twelve tribes of Israel, were affixed to the shoulders of the priestly ephod (Exod. 28:12). The inscribed names served to remind the deity that the priest standing before him represented the whole of Israel.

The priestly breastplate, which may have been added to the costume at a later date, was bordered with twelve colored gemstones, each engraved with the name of one of the twelve tribes (28:21). The stones included carnelian, topaz or peridot, emerald or carbuncle, feldspar, sapphire or lapis lazuli, jacinth, agate, amethyst, beryl or feldspar, onyx, jasper, and one other hard polished stone (not diamond, which was not cut and polished until the fifteenth century C.E.). It is impossible to determine whether or not a particular gemstone represented a particular tribe or a zodiacal sign, or whether unique esoteric qualities were associated with each type of gem.

According to Ezek. 28:13, the King of Tyre is supposed to have worn a similar set of jewels. The Ezekiel account makes reference to a Garden of Eden myth that appears to have been known and accepted in the sixth century B.C.E., but which differs from the myth in Gen. 2. Apparently, this myth was rejected when the sacred canon was completed. The Hebrew text lists only nine stones, but the Greek version names twelve. Walther Eichrodt (1966) has commented that, "This [ornamentation] probably stands for the protective powers attributed to such jewels, and is also intended to signify the special blessedness of the person thus distinguished" (p. 393).

The twelve-stone pattern appears in Rev. 21:19–21. Here the jewels are associated with the mythical new Jerusalem, which was supposed to exist, ready-made, in heaven. Most scholars associate the stones in this passage with the zodiac and suggest that zodiacal imagery was implicit in the high priest's vestments.

In a special pocket in the ephod or breastplate, the high priest carried two sacred lots known as Urim and Thummin (Exod. 28:30). These objects were employed to get yes-or-no answers from Yahweh. No description of their appearance or composition is provided. They may have been made of metal or pottery, or they could have been semiprecious stones. They have been compared to dice. They may have been objects with two faces, one dark and the other light. If both showed the same color, the answer was either Urim or Thummin, depending on the color. If one showed light and the other dark, it meant that the deity refused to answer.

The Urim and Thummin figured in a story about King Saul. As Saul led the Hebrews to battle against the Philistines, he sought divine guidance. He asked: "Should I attack the Philistines? Will you put them in Israel's hand?" Yahweh refused to respond (1 Sam. 14:37). Clearly, the deity was upset. To determine what had vexed Yahweh, Saul began an elimination process using the sacred Urim and Thummin to determine whether the fault lay with him and his son Jonathan or with the people in general. He said:

> O Yahweh, god of Israel, why have you not responded to your servant today? If the guilt lies with me or my son Jonathan, O Yahweh, god of Israel, respond Urim, and if the guilt lies in your people Israel, respond Thummin (1 Sam. 14:41, Greek text).

The sacred lots showed Urim. Unfortunately, that is all the information provided about the use of the oracle objects.

Of course, there are other biblical references to the search for divine guidance, but no information concerning methodology is provided. For example, when Joshua and the Hebrews were defeated in their primary attack on the city of Ai, it was clear that someone had offended Yahweh, prompting the deity to withdraw his power. To determine the guilty party, Joshua, like Saul, employed an elimination process. No information is given about the method employed (Josh. 7).

The Book of Deuteronomy commands the use of certain amulets: "You shall write [these orders] on the doorposts of your house and on your gates" (6:9). This requirement is still observed by many modern Jews who fasten a mezuza—a small case containing parchment with Deut. 6:4–9 and 11:13–21 inscribed—to their doorjambs. The initial purpose of the ruling was for an educational aid. Today Jews kiss their fingers and touch the phylactery as they leave their home in what is tantamount to a magical gesture invoking divine protection. Male orthodox Jews wear leather phylacteries on their left arms and on their foreheads during prayer as ordered by Deut. 6:8. Because these containers hold scriptural quotations they often assume amuletic quality.

Amulets were in common use throughout the Graeco-Roman world when Christianity developed; hence, it is not surprising to learn that amulets were popular in the early Christian church. Historian Kenneth Scott Latourette has written:

> . . . the pagan employment of amulets was replaced by the Christian use of relics, of portions of the Gospels, crosses, medals, and the like. Chrysostom preached against the inroads of such practices in Christian circles, including the hanging of Gospels around the necks of children. In Egypt, in which sacred charms had long been popular, the use of spells carried over into Christian times . . . in Gaul Christians employed the sign of the cross to protect their cattle against the plague. (p. 323)

According to a British Museum pamphlet *Magical Gems*, in 318 C.E., Constantine the Great passed a law expressly sanctioning "spells for preventing rain and hail from damaging harvests." At the same time "in prescribing severe punishments for those using magic to harm others he was confirming a long-standing prohibition within the Roman Empire." The museum collection includes gemstones engraved according to the prescriptions of a magician invoking the aid of a deity. Egyptian gods including Horus or Anubis or Isis were well known. By far the most commonly invoked god was IAO, whose name rendered the Greek pronunciation of the Hebrew YAHWEH. One amulet of orange jasper, from the third century C.E., represented the crucifixion, without the cross but with the inscription "Jesus M(essiah)" and two adoring figures. The Jesus figure wears a halo and magical signs are inscribed on the reverse of the amulet.

Amulets, including blessed medals, rosaries, etc., continue to be employed by Christians. The fact that St. Christopher has lost status and authority with official Roman Catholics has not meant that he has been abandoned by the public. The image of the demoted saint, who is believed to have powers to protect the traveler, can still be seen mounted on the dashboards of automobiles. Unfortunately, according to traffic officers, on occasion the saint has betrayed his trust. In some severe-impact accidents the talisman has become a lethal missile and killed or injured those it was supposed to protect.

Roman Catholic shrines are veritable storehouses of bits and pieces of bones of holy men and women or of artifacts associated with them. For example, in the Bom Jesus Basilica in Goa, India, the perfectly preserved body of St. Francis Xavier who came to India in the sixteenth century as a missionary is enshrined. At least, most of the body is there. Both big toes were bitten off by fanatical female devotees. At the request of a pope, one arm was severed and sent to Rome. The saint's pillow went to the Duke of Tuscany, who in return for the relic provided the exquisite casket in which the body now rests. Why would anyone want these body parts or the pillow? The answer is simple: They are believed to be invested with magical or holy power. They are tangible items that supposedly convey the spiritual force of the holy man.

But, one may ask, are not such collections of body parts things of the past? In 1987, as part of the process of the beatification of Father Junipero Serra, the pope requested that bone fragments of the dead California priest be sent to Rome. Obviously, nothing has changed. The superstitions remain. If miraculous power resides in the relics of a saint-to-be, then some of those relics should rest in the papal sanctuary in Rome.

Amulets in the New Age Movement

The so-called New Age came into being during the 1950s and 1960s. These were years characterized by disaffection with sociopolitical systems, young people feeling empty and anchorless, experimentation with drugs, search for meaning outside traditional religions, establishment of centers for meditation, psychological experimentation, sexual freedom, and interest in the religions of the Far East. These changes impacted upon universities. The effects ranged from the abandonment of established dress codes to students' attending class in bare feet and varied casual attire, from co-educational dormitories to widespread and free experimentation in sex, made possible by new birth control methods. In the wider community the young and middle-aged wore headbands and beads, sought new experiences, or tried to achieve new awareness through peyote, the sacred mushroom, and Lysergic acid and other drugs. Ideas from India were fused with notions stemming from American Indian culture. As an outcome of the societal revolt came a new mysticism and a belief in occultism. The New Age was in the process of becoming.

American Indian Amulets

Apparently American Indians sensed an intimate oneness with nature and the earth. Stones and rocks of various texture, color, and composition were given specific meaning. Some were believed to have curative powers, others were worn or carried for protection. Arrowheads of different kinds of stone had different meanings. Some were for killing, some were for stunning prey, some were for ritual and were shot into the air as prayers.

G. F. Kunz (1913) reported that studies have shown that iron pyrite crystals were used in incantation by medicine men who believed the stones possessed magical power. According to Captain John Burke (1982), Apache medicine men believed that the crystals could induce visions. Just how much the modern crystal craze owes to American Indian culture can be debated, but some aficionados refer to the secret lore of crystals that is supposed to have been derived from the American Indians.

Crystal Magic

Discussion of occult use of crystals recalls crystal ball fortune-telling. Of course, many kinds of shiny surfaces, including everything from puddles of mercury to mirrors to pools of water, have been employed by those who claim to have scrying powers. Seers declare they can discern the shape of things to come in the reflected light from such sources. Such claims opened doors to easy money as well as power over those who yearn for knowledge of the future and feel helpless and without control over life forces.

During the Middle Ages, the crystal or glass ball was the accepted vehicle for scrying. The crystal was prepared for use by incantations that often included religious formulae. Once the ball was consecrated or prepared, the seer would focus on the light emanating from it. His or her eyes would rapidly tire and in his or her mind images would begin to form—interpreted, of course, as coming from the magic crystal ball, or on occasion from angelic beings. It is doubtful whether any images appeared within the ball; more likely the image was in the eye of the beholder. The richness of the report depended upon the creative imagination of the scryer.

Today, the sale of individual crystals and crystal clusters is big business. The fascination with crystals can be attributed in part to claims of their various powers by some Indian shamans, in part to biblical notions, but most of all to the lack of critical thinking by those who trust in them. The present craze is reminiscent of other whimsies, now pretty well outmoded, wherein magical power was attributed to various metals or shapes. For example, during the first half of the twentieth century, copper bracelets were worn to provide relief or protection from arthritis and other muscular pains. As one might expect, no change in the sufferer's condition occurred and the copper provided protection against rheumatic pains only for those who would not have had such pains anyway.

A more recent fad suggested that there was power in pyramid forms. Razor blades placed beneath pyramid structures were supposed to remain sharp for thousands of shaves. Tests demonstrated that these claims were false. Food placed beneath a pyramid form was supposed to dehydrate (like a mummy) rather than decay. Pure nonsense! Giant pyramids of light, tubular metal were suspended over beds to improve sexual performance. One can only speculate that whatever improvements in energy, approach, technique, and so on, that may have taken place beneath these pyramids were in the minds of the true believers. Some people sat beneath pyramid constructions to meditate and to gain insights which they were convinced could not be attained otherwise. When I said that I had been inside the pyramid of Cheops as well as in other Egyptian pyramids and that no changes occurred in my life, true believers suggested that changes of which I was unaware may have taken place! Then came crystal power. The power terms associated with pyramids were transferred to crystals, and of course enhanced with new language.

Any discussion with those who believe in the magical power of crystals automatically focuses on belief in "energy." Devotees of crystal power believe each person has his or her own unique psychic energy, and each crystal has its own unique psychic energy. Clear quartz crystals have one kind of energy, rose quartz another. Colored crystals—amethyst, emerald, ruby—give off different energies. These energies can be refracted or transmitted. Different colored crystals will react with individual personal energies. By handling crystals, a person will be able to detect resonating relationships, for crystal energy can be transmitted to humans to heal, strengthen, and enliven. Consequently, at psychic trade shows one encounters individuals standing with closed eyes moving their hands across a selection of crystals to determine which crystal "likes" them or which emits relational psychic vibrations. Crystal salespeople explain that personal psychic energy vibrates with the energy of a crystal in an individualistic way. By holding, stroking, touching, or waving hands over a collection of crystals, the individual can sense what the crystal can do for him or her.

Psychics who teach the use of crystal energy use terms from modern science and technology. They speak of the electromagnetic fields or frequencies of crystal. They refer to the commercial and scientific uses of crystals and draw notions from crystallography—the scientific study of crystals. By purporting to teach students how to harmonize their own electromagnetic fields with that of the crystal, they enter the area of superscience or perhaps superstition science. For example, Brett Bravo (1987), a teacher of crystal energy, points out:

Quartz crystal, for instance, is used in state-of-the-art watches, computers, radios, and other types of communicative equipment. It gives off a very consistent pulse. Colored crystals, such as rose quartz, amethyst, emerald, ruby, etc., are preprogrammed, and they refract or transmit energies according to their color.

She claims to have studied the biblical use of sacred "healing stones."

Crystals are supposed to have healing power. Some New Age crystal healers have adopted ideas close to those of religious groups that deny the reality of illness, sickness, and pain—even death. New Age teachers inform their clients that individuals are responsible for who they are and what they are. In other words, we are accountable for our personal health and well-being, regardless of genetic heritage. Physical illness is supposed to result from mental states, from feelings of disease, from disharmony within the self, from destructive or harmful patterns—all of which can be changed. Individuals are supposed to be able to self-heal through crystal power, which enables one to break through the restricting activity of the subconscious and tap deep inner feelings. Crystals make possible the recognition of blockages and of that which produces stress and illness and disease. Thus, through the release of mental power through the use of crystals one is supposed to be able to self-heal all manner of disease.

How Is It Done?

As they stand in front of clients who are seated with eyes closed, crystal healers encourage relaxation. As the client listens to soothing words, the crystal healer waves large chunks of crystal above and around the client, all the while assuring the person that magical healing is taking place through the power of the crystals. Perhaps the persuasive words have an effect on those who have mild neurotic disorders or who are under stress, but the waving of crystals about a person has about the same power to heal genuine ailments as waving spoons or twigs or wisps of straw. Any change in feeling results from the client's belief in the change.

Some avoid claims about the power of crystals to heal disastrous diseases but only suggest that crystals may serve to aid the healing process. Jill Taylor claims to have used crystal energy as a supplement to successful treatment of breast cancer, and Helene Taber, whose eyesight is deteriorating, told reporter Jane Ryan (1987) that she bought a one-pound amethyst because she was informed that the mineral was supposed to be good for the eyes. She said, "I am losing my vision. This is not like going to

Tijuana to find a miracle cure. I don't believe this [the crystal] is going to do it. But the mind is a very powerful thing if you have something to focus on, like Norman Cousins and his humor videos." No vision change has occurred for Helen Taber.

Some claim that crystals have calming powers. By holding a crystal in the hand and concentrating attention on it, tensions are eased. The crystal functions as a focal point, like a mandala, distracting attention from personal problems. Some say they have a feeling of confidence and security when they have crystals in a handbag or in their pockets, for the stones are believed to have protective powers that ward off evil, similar to the powers Christians attribute to religious amulets like crosses, crucifixes, and medallions.

Instructors in the use of crystal energy, who label themselves "crystal therapists," engage in a form of magical thinking as they assure patients of the wondrous healing powers of crystals. Some of these "therapists" claim different kinds of crystals have power to heal special ailments. Investigative reporter Frank Spencer (1987) learned that clear crystals are used as cure-alls. Topaz, on the other hand, is supposed to be "useful for cramps, pregnancy, post-partum, and helpful during hormonal balancing associated with the change-of-life." The emerald is "of a yin energy, working on anxiety as a chemical-neural balancer" and is supposed to "regulate blood pressure" as well as "expand feelings of peace, kindness, and oneness." Tourmaline, Spencer was told, could "draw out negative, dead useless energy," acting as a "vacuum cleaner to suck out bad energy." Finally, "the ruby is supposed to vanquish cancerous cells and relieve manic-depression" as well as "help cure baldness."

Crystal therapists place stones at various so-called key points on the reclining bodies of their patients. Different-color stones are employed for different body parts. The reasons given for placing a particular stone on a particular spot are simplistic. Through experimentation, we are told, the crystal therapists have learned that certain body parts respond to the vibrations or the energy in crystals of certain color or shape or form. When the crystals are in place, the client is led into guided meditation during which suggestions are made to increase belief in the magical process. Martha Smilgis (1987) reported that crystal healer Brett Bravo provides clients with "a 28-day ritual of positive thinking with each crystal." For example, she instructs, "with topaz, you hold the stone over the solar plexus for two minutes and repeat, 'This blue stone is vibrating to calm my nervous system'." Other healers, in addition to providing incantations, encourage clients to reveal personally troublesome issues. Aided by crystals, the healer provides psychological guidance.

It is not surprising to find that crystal healers have borrowed terminology from modern psychotherapy. For example, any competent licensed therapist will inform clients that changes in behavior or attitude "require work." Crystal therapists insist that work is also required to acquire and properly employ crystal power. Glenn Lehrer has borrowed the notion of "archetypes from Jungian psychology and states that each crystal has an "archetypal" memory of its own DNA." From yoga, crystal power teachers have borrowed the concept of self-centering or focusing on being oneself, collected, and unified. From New Age thinking comes the notion of energy which can originate in the earth and surge upward through the body, or begin in the sky and stream downward through the body so that the body becomes an energy channeler. The meeting of these heavenly and earthly acquired energies within the body balance the self, thus enabling crystal power to become effective. Then, by using meditative practices, one focuses on, or centers the self on, a particular crystal—thinking, projecting, incorporating one's thoughts and intentions. Inhaling and exhaling through the mouth so that the air moves over the crystal is supposed to project one's thoughts and wishes to the magic rock.

It is not difficult to understand what is taking place. After relaxation exercises, one feels relaxed. The relaxation comes from the exercise, not from the rock, as crystal healers claim. By projecting hope and wishes into the crystal, the client engages in magical thinking, believing, and hoping that miraculous results will occur—much the same way the Christian does when engaging in petitionary prayer.

Naturally, these precious, sensitive crystals must be properly treated. To learn the best techniques for preparation and use, one may consult an "expert" who, for a price, will convey the secrets of mining the power of the crystal. To begin, the crystal should be washed, but not in ordinary tap water, which may contain contaminants added by well-meaning public health authorities for sanitary reasons or to protect human health. Only spring water or perhaps ocean water may be used. Of course, it is important to ignore the fact that these waters may be polluted by everything from seepage of toxic wastes to oil spills to sewage. Next, the properly washed crystal should be exposed to the rays of either the sun or the moon for at least twenty-four hours. Thus washed or purified and penetrated by sun or moon rays, the crystal is ready for programming. The process is simple. The crystal is cradled between the two hands and as the owner makes a wish, he or she blows upon the crystal. Now the crystal is ready to exude its magic power.

Many crystal enthusiasts are also caught up in the recent reincarnation movement. If one has lived many lives, then what happened in previous existences may have direct consequences for the present life. It comes as no surprise to learn that through crystal power one can be made aware of self-destructive patterns that may have been repeated over and over again. Through awareness and crystal power, changes can be made to produce a better and healthier life.

Some crystal enthusiasts believe that ancient peoples possessed esoteric knowledge that has been lost during the passage of time. For example, Katrina Raphaell (1985) suggests that inhabitants of ancient Atlantis may have used crystals for telepathic communication. Of course, we have absolutely no factual information about Atlantis nor about the so-called wisdom some imagine these people may have acquired. Atlantis was mentioned by Plato and there are scholars who suggest that Plato may have been using an imaginary locale to make a point. Some modern archaeologists think that Santorini, which is now under excavation, may be ancient Atlantis. If Atlantis did exist, it preceded the time of Plato, and according to what we know from the study of ancient civilizations, the Atlanteans' knowledge and understanding would have been at a relatively primitive level. This is not to suggest that our early ancestors were stupid, but it is clear that they did not have the sophisticated information that we have acquired during the past 2,000 or so years, nor did they have the means we have for testing claims of the supernatural. In any case, despite the claims of the psychics, the site of Atlantis is not known to us and no reliable researcher, scholar, or scientist accepts the imaginary concepts concerning Atlantis projected by so-called psychics. Raphaell's Atlantis is a product of conjecture not fact.

Crystal power appears to have no limits. Attached to automobiles, crystals are supposed to enhance engine performance. Mounted on dashboards, they ensure safe driving, having replaced St. Christopher. Buried in the soil of property for sale, they increase the chances of selling. Cherished by lonely people, they become substitutes for human companions. Carried by shoppers, they provide guidance in purchasing. Worn about the neck, they ward off evil, thereby supplementing or replacing such amulets as the cross or crucifix. Placed in drinking water, the crystal purifies the liquid. Crystals are said to be harbingers of a new age of peace and prosperity for humankind. Crystal harmony, crystal healing, crystal therapy, crystal hope are all solidly anchored in magical thinking. An appropriate slogan might be "Wishing will make it so!"

Amulets and the Psychic Response

The ancient Israelites used the Urim and Thummim to get responses from Yahweh. Today other sacred amulets are used for the same purpose. For example, an amulet is suspended by a thread on a light string. When I have been with Muslims, the Koran was suspended. Christians have used a crucifix, a cross, a blessed medal. Jews have used the Star of David. Crystal believers use a crystal.

The participants agree upon a code. If the suspended amulet turns clockwise, the answer is yes; if it moves counterclockwise the answer is no. Should the amulet swing in a circular pattern, the answer is yes, but if it sways back and forth in a straight line, the answer is no. There is no limit to the kinds of questions that can be asked, except that, as with the biblical Urim and Thummim, they must be able to be answered by either yes or no. Many years ago, when I was in Jerusalem with a group of Muslims who did not like President Nasser of Egypt, they suspended the Koran and asked if Nasser was a good man. The answer was, predictably, no. An Ethiopian Christian priest who suspended and questioned a scapular medallion discovered to his satisfaction that his work was approved since the medallion spun clockwise.

What causes the amulet to respond? It is a well-known medical fact that the body responds to environmental conditions or stimuli with what are recognized as automatic muscle movements. Some muscle movements are also triggered by the subconscious. As I hold the thread that suspends the amulet and ask it to respond, my subconscious mind directs what are to me imperceptible automatic muscle responses. If the Muslim who held the cord by which the Koran was suspended had liked Nasser, the book would have turned in a clockwise fashion. Obviously, the subconscious mind informed the muscles how to respond, and despite the fact that the man was convinced that all he was doing was holding a thin cord between his thumb and forefinger, he was actually causing the book to turn. Similarly, if the priest with the scapular medallion had been convinced that his project was a waste of time and energy and doomed to failure, his automatic muscle response would have echoed this conviction.

Some hypnotherapists have utilized a similar technique to enable patients to tap their subconscious to recall where some object has been left. In the panic of having lost his or her keys or wallet or papers or a book, the client has forgotten what he or she has done with the object. The pendulum (nonpsychic therapists don't use magic amulets) enables tapping the subconscious memory in response to questions that serve as instruments of guided recall. The patient holds the pendulum and asks, "Did

I leave it here?"

Of course, for some people the pendulum may refuse to move. These are people who are critical of such ideas or skeptics for whom the whole business is simply nonsense. For these people the pendulum may swing erratically or in a direction opposite to what is expected or willed. It has been suggested that these are people who do not like to be told what to do. It must be pointed out that no reputable therapist will base treatment on what occurs when a client is playing with a suspended amulet.

Amulets as Symbols

Amulets may become symbols. Whenever the use of certain amulets becomes widespread, they may be transformed into symbols representing the group that employs them. Similarly, a symbolic design, representing group identity, may be used as an amulet. The examples that come immediately to mind are the Christian cross and the Jewish six-pointed Star of David. Christians wear crosses as identity symbols and the cross symbol touches human life from birth to death. When Roman Catholic clergy baptize infants they make the sign of the cross. Catholic Christians use the sign of the cross during religious services. At death, coffins often have crosses attached as part of the trappings. Tombstones may be marked with a cross or a star.

The cross may serve as an amulet. Persons in danger make the sign of the cross as a protective gesture or may wave a cross to ward off demonic forces. As my Roman Catholic father died, his believing sister waved a blessed crucifix across his face over the nostrils, ears, and mouth—orifices from which she had been taught the soul escapes from the body. (I confess that as I watched her, the thought occurred to me that there was a lower orifice through which a soul might escape.) The cross is represented in medieval sketches as a power against evil forces. Today, many individuals wear the cross for protection as well as for identification as a member of a religious group.

The six-pointed star is so intimately associated with Judaism that any misuse of this symbol can be construed as anti-Semitism. For example, in October 1987, General Mills produced a cereal box design for their product Count Chocula which depicted a likeness of the vampire Count Dracula based on the character as portrayed by Bela Lugosi in the 1931 film *The House of Dracula*. In the film, Dracula wore an amulet which, in a computer-enhanced image, took the form of a six-pointed star. The amulet was reproduced on a chain worn around the neck of Count Chocula on the cereal box picture. Modern Jews often wear the six-pointed star on a chain around the neck. What sinister implications might be suggested by the presence of the star worn by Count Chocula? Once the matter was pointed out, officials of General Mills hastened to announce that they were not anti-Semitic, that the imagery was an unfortunate oversight, and that it would be removed from future cereal boxes. In other words, the management was sensitive to complaints from the Jewish community and had no intention of implying that Dracula was Jewish (*The Los Angeles Times* 1987).

A five-pointed star, the pentagram or pentacle, was sometimes used as a Jewish symbol. Reporter Robert W. Stewart (1988) referred to a newspaper article from 1872 that described the first Jewish synagogue built in Los Angeles. The plan included carved stone spires that surmounted two buttresses, " 'the finial in the center will be surmounted by a five-pointed star set in a circle'. . . ." Stewart commented, "According to some scholars, the five-pointed star was occasionally used as a Jewish symbol into the late 19th century." Today the pentagram is in popular thought almost exclusively associated with magic or with Satanism. Whereas the Jewish star is presented with the point or angle at the top, in Satanism the pentagram is often turned so that two points are at the top, representing Satanic horns, and the Satanic face can be drawn in the triangle that ends with the point at the bottom. Some bigots have twisted the Jewish star so that two points appear at the top in an attempt to make it into a Satanic symbol.

Of course, any symbol can be twisted into an emblem of hatred or bigotry. Once the swastika symbolized good luck and was associated with the Christian cross. It can still be found in Indian Hindu temples, where it is a benevolent symbol. Under the Nazis it was transformed into a national symbol of tyranny, racism, cruelty, and totalitarianism.

The five-pointed star also appears fifty times on the flag of the United States. Each star represents a state. It is also used commercially as insignia for Texaco products and by the Chrysler corporation. The meaning is in the eye of the beholder, and those who find the demonic in the pentagram usually ignore the nondemonic use of the symbol.

Perhaps there is little harm in beliefs associated with charms and amulets, whether they be religious or secular. Indeed, some psychotherapists have suggested that they might have beneficial effects by helping nervous or panicky persons achieve a sense of calm. On the other hand, when followers of the voodoo priestess Alice Lakwena of Nairobi, Kenya, and her Holy Spirit Movement marched to liberate Uganda, assured that the oil rubbed on their chests would ward off bullets, were slaughtered, the use of this so-called magical substance became destructive, obscene, and inhuman.

When the magic of an amulet fails and the anticipated results are not experienced, the resulting emotions can be turbulent and unsettling. The person may believe that he or she has failed personally. Rejection by the amulet or the power it represents—whether it be psychic energy or power associated with some faith system—can produce deep depression.

Magic used for entertainment is one thing. Magical acts are performances; many of them are humorous and amusing. They lift the spirits through laughter and fun. They can contribute to mental growth by encouraging inquiry by those who are being tricked and want to know how the tricks are done and what principles lie behind them.

But magic that becomes a substitute for critical thinking and that encourages belief in supernatural powers inherent in stones or metals, oils, blessed medallions, or items associated with so-called holy people and things can only be destructive. The desperate search for quick and miraculous solutions to grave human problems may move the needy person away from legitimate mental health resources and make them pawns in the hands of greedy and unscrupulous would-be counselors. Those seeking magical healing of body ailments may delay proper medical treatment to the detriment of their health. It is comforting to know that the crystal craze will fade as have others before it. But one may wonder what will come next. On the other hand, because of church teachings, it is certain that religious superstitions associated with amulets, icons, and other such artifacts will continue.

References

Burke, John G., *The Medicine-Men of the Apache*. Ninth Annual Report of the Bureau of Ethnology, 1887–1888, Washington, D.C., 1892.

Bravo, Brett, *The Crystal Sourcebook*. Sante Fe, N.M.: Mystic Crystal Publication, 1987.

Davenport, Cheri, "Brett Bravo Unlocks Crystal Energy," *Whole Life Monthly*, October 1987, p. 33.

Dihle, Albrecht, *The Theory of Will in Classical Antiquity*. Los Angeles: University of California Press, 1982.

Eichrodt, Walther, *Ezekiel*. Philadelphia: Westminster, 1966.

Ireland, Jill, *Life Wish*. New York: Little Brown, 1987.

Kunz, George F., *The Curious Lore of Precious Stones*. Philadelphia: Lippincott, 1913.

Latourette, Kenneth Scott, *The First Five Centuries*. New York: Harper and Brothers, 1937.

Lehrer, Glenn, *The Archetypal World of the Mineral Kingdom*. Kristallos Rarities, San Rafael, Calif., 1987.

The Los Angeles Times, "Magic Fades for Uganda's Guerrilla Voodoo Priestess," January 2, 1988.

Owens, Joseph, *Human Destiny: Some Problems for Catholic Philosophy*. Washington, D.C.: Catholic University of America Press, 1985.

Raphaell, Katerina, *Crystal Enlightenment*. New York: Aurora Press, 1987.

Rubenstein, Richard L., *After Auschwitz*. New York: Bobbs-Merrill, 1966.

Ryan, James, "Mystical Qualities Fuel Crystal Craze," *The Houston Chronicle*, July 12, 1987.

Smilgis, Martha,"Rock Power for Health and Wealth," *Time*, January 19, 1987.

Spencer, Frank, "The Natural Beauties Have Assigned Tasks," *The Hartford Courant*, May 3, 1987.

Stewart, Robert W., "Site Yields Stones From First L.A. Synagogue," *The Los Angeles Times*, January 21, 1988.

The Magic Wand of Dowsing

> Strike the rock, and water shall issue from it.
> Exod. 17:6

Dowsing, or water-witching as it is sometimes called, refers to the use of a dowsing rod or divining rod to search for subterranean water supplies or mineral veins. In practice, the dowser holds one fork of a tree branch (witch hazel, willow, and alder branches are commonly used) in each hand with the base or junction of the fork pointed upward. As he or she (there are a minority of female dowsers) approaches the spot where water is located beneath the ground surface, the branch, which has been held upright, begins to dip automatically towards the ground. The gravitational pull cannot be controlled by the dowser and is said to be strong enough to peel the bark from the two extremities held tightly in the dowser's hands.

Experienced dowsers may talk to the rod or to whatever power they believe is back of the rod's action. They may ask how deep the well must be dug to get water and the rod will respond by dipping downward a number of times, each dip representing an interval, such as ten feet, to designate the depth, or by dipping after a certain number of paces are stepped off (usually each pace constitutes ten feet). The wand may provide additional information, such as how many gallons per hour can be expected, whether or not the presently designated spot is the best place to dig, and so on. The answers given are claimed to be reliable and accurate. For example, Christopher Bird (1971, pp. 19ff.) states that a water diviner saved the Misquamicut Club in Watch Hill, Rhode Island, from possible closure. James Kidd, a dowser, discovered an abundance of water at a depth of twenty feet after geophysicists had informed the club that no fresh water sources existed in the area. Mr. Kidd inquired of his forked stick, "How deep do we need to go?" The answer came in the number of paces it took to move from a point where he felt no pull on the divining rod to the place where the rod dipped toward the ground with maximum pull.

The relationship between dowsing, the Bible, and the occult is tangential. Some dowsers relate their activities to Moses' use of a magic rod to produce water in the desert of Sinai. Some dowsers believe their ability is a divine gift. Christopher Bird reported that when a peasant water-witcher in Czechoslovakia was asked whether just anyone could dowse for water, he replied, "By no means, this talent is granted by God to only a few" (p. 254). When Vogt and Hyman (1959) researched the subject of water-witching, they were told by several American diviners that "Moses was the first water witch" (p. 13). Newspaper articles on dowsing often include references to Moses. It would appear that the dowser's skill, which regularly comes under criticism by professional hydrologists, can be authenticated by reference to the Bible! What does the Bible really say?

The Moses Story

The legend of the exodus from Egypt was an important theme in biblical history. References to the event are often made in connection with current events involving tyranny or suppression of human rights. For example, during the sixth century B.C.E., immediately following the time of the Babylonian exile, a Jewish writer composed an intercessory hymn in which he recalled Yahweh's salvation of the Israelites in the time of Moses (Isa. 63:12). In more recent time, Martin Luther King Jr. voiced Moses' cry "Let my people go," as he sought equal rights for blacks in America (cf. Exod. 8:1).

The passages that refer to Moses producing water in the desert are a small part of the total narrative concerning the escape of the Hebrews from Egypt. The entire account must be classified as a wonder story or as religious fiction laced with the miraculous and the incredible.

According to the story, the Hebrew people, who had sought refuge in Egypt during a time of famine, had become enslaved. Yahweh, their god, raised up a savior named Moses, who, like other hero figures, had had a miraculous escape from enemies as an infant and was not recognized as a rescuer until he reached maturity.

To convince the Egyptian pharaoh that the Hebrew slaves should be released, Yahweh provided Moses with a magic wand that could miraculously be transformed from a staff into a serpent and then back again into a staff (Exod. 4:1–4). Moses' hand also had magical powers; it could suddenly become leprous and then be magically healed (Exod. 4:6–7). Moses could pour out pure water from the Nile River and cause it to become blood (Exod. 4:9). This marvelous Judean temple tale was composed, it is believed, during the tenth century B.C.E. in the time of King Solomon. In it, Moses is clearly portrayed as the hero, the magician with god-given powers. Moses possessed and wielded the magic wand. Aaron, his brother, was his spokesman before Pharaoh (Exod. 4:10–17). Similar relational motifs occur in another account, written after the death of Solomon by priests in the northern kingdom of Israel (cf. Exod. 4:17, 7:15,17, 9:23, 10:13, 14:16, etc.). Later, the two versions were merged, but the combined story was also to undergo changes.

During the sixth century B.C.E., religious leaders from Judah were exiled in Babylon. There the priesthood initiated a revision of their sacred literature. One of their most dramatic alterations in the Moses story concerned the role of Aaron, the patronymic founder of the Aaronic priesthood. As they rewrote the exodus fiction, the priests transferred the magic wand from the hand of Moses to the hand of Aaron. In the new version, it was Aaron's magic wand that was transformed into a serpent (Exod. 7:8–13), and it was Aaron's rod that turned the waters of the Nile into blood (Exod. 7:20, 21b–22) and that brought on the plague of frogs (8:5–7) and the plague of gnats (8:16–19). The story of Aaron's role as Moses' spokesman or prophet (Hebrew *nabi*) was retold (7:1–7). In the minds of the priestly revisers, although Moses was the lawgiver, Aaron, as high priest, was the divinely appointed interpreter of law. Therefore, whereas Moses had in the past enunciated the laws, the present priesthood, as descendants of Aaron, were to be the present interpreters of that law. They rewrote the exodus event to enhance the role of their progenitor and to reinforce the power of the priesthood as the legitimate custodian of the divine will.

Nor is it surprising to discover that reinterpretations continued to be made. Paul, the rabbinic student who became a Christian, allegorized the story of Moses and the rock. He informed converts in Corinth that they were the new Israel, and having become such, the experience of the "old" Israel was now theirs, but in a wondrously new and different way. He wrote:

> I would not have you ignorant, brothers, that our fathers [ancestors] were all under the cloud cover, and all passed through the sea, and all were baptized [immersed] into Moses [into the Mosaic baptism] in the cloud and in the sea. And they ate the same spiritual food [manna] and drank

the same spiritual drink; for they drank from the supernatural rock that followed them, the rock that was Christ. (1 Cor. 10:1-4)

Paul accepted a current Jewish legend that told how the water-bearing rock followed the Hebrew wanderers through the desert, providing a convenient, ever-present source of water. The legend must have been concocted by some Jewish realist who worried about a million Hebrews dehydrating in the Sinai desert. Now, in Paul, the life-giving rock is the Christian messiah. The new converts are the desert wanderers. The rock, the messiah, provides the water of salvation for the converts.

What was good enough for Paul is good enough for fundamentalist interpreters. For example, Arthur W. Pink in *Gleanings in Exodus* (1962) comments:

> The first thing to be noted here . . . is that the rock is to be *smitten*. This, of course, speaks of the death of the Lord Jesus. It is striking to note the *order* of the typical teaching of Ex. 16 and 17. In the former we have that which speaks of the incarnation of Christ; in the latter that which foreshadowed the crucifixion of Christ. Ex. 17 is supplementary to Ex. 16. Christ must descend from Heaven to earth (as the manna did) if He was to become the Bread of Life to His people; but He must be smitten by Divine judgment if He was to be the water of life to them! (p. 138)

The homiletic approach to biblical literature has provided, from the time of Paul to the present, what can only be called weird and wonderful interpretations of that which is already weird and wonderful!

During the Middle Ages, magic wands and the invocation of the divine name went hand in hand with the search for buried treasure. Whatever its earliest antecedents, dowsing became a popular and accepted practice. Some called on the name of Yahweh or Adonai because it was believed there was power in those names. Others used the trinitarian formula: "In the name of the Father and the Son and the Holy Ghost (or Spirit)."

The Exodus Event

It was no small thing for Moses to lead a rabble (the Hebrew term *erev rab* is derogatory) of over one million Hebrews (600,000 males, plus women and children) carrying kitchen utensils, unleavened bread, and jewelry into the Sinai wilderness (Exod. 12:34-39). Anyone who has ventured into that bleak and forbidding area can only be impressed with the stifling heat and the barrenness and aridity. When the people complained, Moses employed his magical powers. The Egyptians mounted a pursuit of the fleeing Hebrews. Moses used the magic wand to part the waters of the Sea of Reeds (in Hebrew, *yam suf*) so that dry land appeared, providing a walkway for the Hebrews (Exod. 14:16). When the Hebrews had safely crossed, Moses the magician caused the waters to return and submerge the Egyptian pursuers (14:26). When the Hebrew nomads found bitter and undrinkable water, Moses the sorcerer tossed bits of a tree into the waters, transforming them so that they became sweet and drinkable. At a later date the magician prophet Elijah sweetened the polluted waters of 'Ain Sultan at Jericho and parted the waters of the Jordan (cf. 2 Kings 2:14, 19–22). Obviously a good story bears repeating (see chapter on The Control of Natural Events).

When the people were hungry, Moses the magician conjured up quails that conveniently flew, exhausted, into the Hebrew encampment. He provided manna which tasted like biscuits made with honey (Exod. 16:13–31). This wonder story is recounted a second time in all of its details (Num. 11:7–34). When no water could be found, Moses used his magic wand to strike the rocky surface of Mount Horeb and cause water to gush forth (Exod. 17:7–34).

Explanations

Efforts have been made to provide naturalistic explanations for these miraculous events, but some of the biblical accounts are simply unbelievable. For example, the notion of over 1,000,000 persons traversing the Sinai Desert cannot be accepted. Gaalyahu Cornfeld (1961) has noted:

> The entire population of all the Bedouin tribes of the Negev who had settled and multiplied there for many centuries before the advent of the new State of Israel in 1948, did not exceed 70,000! When a tribe numbering, say, 5,000 families migrated with their flocks, it formed a wide column stretching over a front of 12 miles and 3 miles deep. (p. 143)

If we assume that the exodus actually took place, then the numbers reported in the Bible must be drastically reduced. The biblical story itself provides a suggestion of exaggeration: according to Exod. 1:15, when the Pharaoh spoke to the midwives, there were only two in service, clearly too few to take care of births for over one million Hebrews!

At one time it was assumed that Moses parted the Red Sea. The error was due, in no small part, to a mistranslation that appeared in the King James Version (cf. Exod. 13:18). As we have noted above, the Hebrew words *yam suf* should be translated Reed (papyrus) Sea or Sea of Reeds, suggesting marshy growth. Reeds do not grow in the Red Sea. Those who accepted the notion that the Red Sea was involved suggested that a strong wind had caught the waves and held them back as the fleeing Hebrews crossed over; then the winds died down and the waves were released to swamp the Egyptian chariots. An alternative suggestion was that a massive gas bubble was formed beneath the north end of the Red Sea, buckling the earth so that it rose above the surface of the waters, and it was over this raised sea bottom that the Hebrews escaped. Then, as the gas leaked through cracks, the surface of the earth bubble subsided, allowing the waters to rush back on the Egyptians. Obviously, these explanations are what might be seen as rather desperate efforts to provide naturalistic explanations for the story about the parting of the sea.

A more recent and perhaps a more believable explanation suggests that the Hebrews did not go in a southerly direction towards the Red Sea, but in a northerly direction toward the Mediterranean Sea, following the Pelusium arm of the Nile. At the edge of the sea they traversed a small sand spit that separates the Mediterranean from Lake Sirbonis (or Lake Bardawil as it is sometimes called, honoring the crusader King Baldwin). Today, the waters in the lake are saline, but inasmuch as they once formed an outlet of the Nile, it can be assumed that in ancient times papyrus may have grown there. When the Hebrews crossed, the sand spit was above sea level, but some disturbance, perhaps a subsea earthquake or a volcanic explosion, such as that which destroyed Santorini, produced a tidal wave that caught the pursuing Egyptian soldiers. Because some of the landmarks mentioned in the exodus account can be related to this route, this last explanation is the most credible of the naturalistic explanations.

For some, any questioning of the biblical account of this wonder story is destructive. In Simon Kistemaker's *Interpreting God's Word Today* (1970), the reader is warned, "If miracles in Scripture are eliminated, not much of Biblical revelation is left. If the miracles of the crossing of the Red Sea and the divine call of Samuel are not considered valid, then the rest of Scripture can no longer be considered trustworthy either" (p. 190). Kistemaker declares "that Scripture is trustworthy in every respect, including the historical accounts." Douglas White in *Holy Ground: Expositions From Exodus* (1962) comments: "Let no man question this miracle. We need no scientific explanations." Blind belief approaches invite closing of the mind to the realities of this world. Despite the demands for mind closure, scholarly scientific research into biblical literature continues, and while the numbers of Hebrew escapees from Egypt are obviously exaggerated and unbelievable, some details of the flight may have a potential basis in fact.

Quail, like those that fed the hungry Hebrews, are known to migrate from Europe across the Mediterranean on their way to Arabia and Africa. They fall exhausted along the Mediterranean shore of the Sinai Peninsula, where they are captured by the Bedouin. It seems logical to assume that knowledge about such exhausted quail is a basis for the legend of the miraculously provided birds of the exodus.

Manna, a product of the northern Sinai, is a secretion from two kinds of insects that live in tamarisk trees. In the spring, the female secretes drops of varying size that dry and drop as flakes to the ground. Bedouins gather this substance, which they call *man* or sometimes *man min sama*, that is "manna from heaven." In other words, there is nothing miraculous about the finding of manna by the migrant Hebrews; it is a natural phenomenon. However, there would not be sufficient exhausted birds or manna to feed the hungry hordes of people of the biblical exodus.

The emphasis on the northern exodus route negates the significance of traditional Mount Sinai, which is located in the southern Sinai. The site of the sacred mountain was determined by the Byzantine Queen Helena on the basis of a visionary revelation. A monastery was constructed there during the fourth century C.E., and this is the mountain and monastery to which pilgrims and visitors come. Much of the northern Sinai peninsula is limestone, and water has been found in some spots by breaking a limestone sheath. (The harder granite is found in southern Sinai, the presently accepted site of Mount Sinai, which would make this feat impossible). Some have suggested that Moses struck a limestone sheath and found the water beneath.

The bedouin of Petra have a different explanation. At the mouth of the "Siq," the waterworn cleft in the Nubian sandstone of the mountain that leads to the locale of the ancient city, is a spring called *'Ain Musa*, "the spring of Moses." According to local tradition, this was the place where Moses struck the rock with his wand, producing the spring and carving the Siq. The tradition points to the nearby mountain *Jebel Haroun*, "the mountain of Aaron," where Aaron is supposed to have been buried and where there is a shrine consecrated to Aaron. The Petra legend is interesting but has no relationship to the exodus route or tradition. To date, no naturalistic explanation has been found that provides the basis for the Hebrew story. Perhaps the fact that water has been found beneath limestone sheaths comes closest to naturalist explanation, although the limited amount of water that would be involved in such a case would not last long or be useful to a mobile multitude.

According to biblical tradition, Moses was associated with Yahweh on an intimate conversational basis. When the people complained of thirst, the prophet asked Yahweh, "What shall I do?" Yahweh told him to take his magic rod and "I [Yahweh] will stand in front of you on the rock of Horeb, then you shall hit the rock and water will come out of it so that the people can drink" (Exod. 17:6). It was Yahweh who guided Moses to the water-bearing rock and it was Yahweh who told him where to strike with the wand.

As we have noted, present-day dowsers also pose questions pertaining to their projects. Exactly to whom or to what the diviners' questions are directed is not clear, but the rod seems to comprehend and respond.

In a second and later biblical account of the finding of water in the desert (Num. 20:2–13), Moses was told to address the rock, to speak to it, to command it to yield its waters. In this account the rock is not located on Mount Horeb. Moses struck the rock twice. Now, exactly what Moses and Aaron did in this case to upset Yahweh is not clear but the god was furious. Perhaps Yahweh was offended by the fact that Moses simply struck the rock, rather than address it and utter a magical incantation as he had been instructed to do. In any case, both Moses and Aaron were accused of disobedience and lack of faith. Their punishment was a prohibition against entering the "promised land." Because the transgression appears to have been so trivial, it has been suggested that there may have been a more serious sin "which the sacred writer deliberately refrained from recording" (Butzer 1951, p. 238).

Does the Magic Wand Really Work?

Based on accounts by those who swear by dowsing, the success rate is often ninety to ninety-five percent. Indeed, water-witchers have claimed the ability to locate oil deposits, determine where ancient wrecks lie beneath the sea, and even provide medical diagnosis! (Shepard 1968, p. viii). But anecdotal accounts and folklore are not sound evidence. Few would question that on occasion dowsers have been successful. But when excessive claims are made and the success rate and the details become incredible, it is time for rational scientific testing and investigation.

Vogt and Hyman (1959) discuss several controlled experiments designed to test the validity of claims of dowsing. These include field tests conducted by the American Society for Psychical Research in 1949, and a test by P. A. Ongley of New Zealand in 1948. In both tests the dowsers failed. Laboratory tests in which, for example, oil or water is concealed in containers and the diviner is expected to use the divining rod to determine which container actually contains the substance also failed to substantiate the claims of the dowsers.

James (the Amazing) Randi, the well known skeptic and sleight-of-hand artist, reported on a test that was photographed for Italian television. Four dowsers attempted to locate and trace the flow of water in buried pipes that were fed from a water supply truck. The dowsers had predicted one hundred percent success; they were ninety-five percent wrong!

In another test of water dowsing in Australia, the diviner predicted one-hundred percent success, but was one-hundred percent wrong. Metal dowsing also proved to be a miserable failure. The dowsers explained that their lack of success was due, on the one hand, to a huge aluminum deposit somewhere beneath the ground, and on the other, to jewelry worn by some of the onlookers. In such ways do mystical powers interfere with the prowess of the endowed!

A popular television program, "20/20," experimented with dowsing on September 25, 1987. A number of holes were dug and in one of them a five-gallon plastic jug full of water was deposited. The holes were refilled. Five dowsers, each confident of his skill, attempted to find the water. All five failed. When asked about the failures, one suggested that possibly a negative psychic force hovered over the hole in which the bottle was deposited and thus thwarted the dowsers' efforts!

One can only conclude that dowsers' tales of success in locating subterranean water or oil or any other hidden substance or object are as exaggerated as the biblical story of Moses and the exodus.

Sexual Overtones?

Are there sexual overtones to dowsing? The idea was briefly explored by Vogt and Hyman. In their search through psychoanalytic literature, they discovered an essay by E. Servadio, published in 1935, that dealt with the subject (E. Servadio, "La baguette des sourciers: Essai d'interpretation psychoanalytique," *Revue francais de psychoanalyse*, 8, 488–500). Vogt and Hyman comment:

> Of course, the witching performance is seen as a sexual act. The rod allegedly symbolizes the penis or clitoris. Its motion is like an erection and is often acccompanied by emotions akin to sexual excitement. The object of the act—the penetration and exploration of the earth—is interpreted as a symbolic penetration of the mother (with which the earth has been universally identified by analysts). (p. 169)

As Vogt and Hyman point out, there has been some evidence presented to support this hypothesis. However, I would suggest that the notion of the universality of the mother earth concept can be challenged. In ancient Egypt the earth god was Geb, a male deity whose sexual partner was Nut the sky goddess (Larue 1988, p. 30). The psychoanalytic theory is based on a misconception, namely, the assumption that because in Western culture the mother earth notion is widespread, it is universal.

Vogt and Hyman point out that in the Ozarks there is a general association of virility with the power to dowse. They say that "for the most part, however, the sexual connotation of water witching seems to reside in the obvious analogy of the rod to a penis." In other words, there is really no reason to attribute any sexual connotation to the act of dowsing, and only in local folklore is the connection made. Nor is there any evidence that the word "rod" in the Bible has sexual meaning.

Personal Encounter

In 1967, I was on sabbatical leave in the Middle East. I was introduced to pendulum dowsing as a form of gaining hidden information. The Koran, the sacred book of Islam, was suspended by a cord. As I held the cord from which the book was suspended in my right hand (the left hand is taboo), questions were asked. If the book revolved slowly clockwise, a positive answer was symbolized; a counterclockwise rotation meant "no." In these same interesting sessions a Christian priest of the Ethiopan church suspended a holy medallion which also revolved in response to questions.

One participant introduced two stainless steel rods that could be extended like a portable television antenna and that were bent at right angles at one end and set loosely in handles that allowed the rods to swing freely. It was the owner's intention to use this device to seek buried treasure on unexcavated sites of ancient city mounds. We tested the rods over coins laid on the floor.

With regard to answers to questions provided by the suspended Koran or holy medal, there appeared to be no set pattern. For example, if one asked if the president of Egypt was a good or bad man, the Koran gave mixed answers, depending upon who was holding the cord. Several years later, I again met the man who owned the rods and asked about his treasure-hunting adventures. He admitted, with some embarrassment, that so far as he was concerned the device was a failure. He found no treasures.

When my skepticism surfaced during the testing there was much jocularity. It was clear that the participants "sort of believed" and perhaps "hoped the powers were there." So far as I could tell, the most convinced person was the priest.

References

Avi-Yonah, Michael, and Emil Kraeling, *Our Living Bible*. Chicago: Creative World Publications, 1972.

Barrett, Sir William, and Theodore Besterman, *The Divining Rod*. New York: University Books, 1968.

Bird, Christopher, *The Divining Hand*. New York: Dutton, 1971.

Butzer, A. G., "Exposition: Numbers," *The Interpreter's Bible*, Vol. 2. New York: Abingdon Press, 1951.

Cornfeld, Gallyahu, ed., *Adam to Daniel*. New York: The Macmillan Co., 1961.

Erdman, Charles R., *The Book of Numbers*. Westwood, N.J.: Fleming H. Revell, 1952.

Kistemaker, Simon, ed., *Interpreting God's Word Today*. Grand Rapids, Mich.: Baker Book House, 1970.

Larue, Gerald A., *Ancient Myth and Modern Life*. Long Beach, Calif.: Centerline Press, 1988.

Pink, Arthur W., *Gleanings in Exodus*. Chicago: Moody Press, 1962.

Randi, James, "A Controlled Test of Dowsing Abilities," *The Skeptical Inquirer*, IV:1, 1979, pp. 16–20.

Shepherd, Leslie, "Foreward," *The Divining Rod*. New York: University Books, 1968.

Smith, Dick, "Two Tests of Divining in Australia," *The Skeptical Inquirer*, VI:4, 1982, pp. 34–37.

Vogt, Evon Z., and Ray Hyman, *Water Witching U.S.A.* Chicago: The University of Chicago Press, 1959.

White, Douglas M., *Holy Ground; Expositions from Exodus*. Grand Rapids, Mich.: Baker Book House, 1962.

The Control of Natural Events

God's voice thunders magnificently.
He does great things which we cannot comprehend
For to the snow, he says, "Fall upon the earth,"
And to the shower and the rain, "Be torrential."

Job 37:5–6

Rain, rain, go away,
Come again some other day.

Children's chant to
dispel rain at playtime

Predictions, forecasts, television imagery, all contribute to our ability to cope with weather changes. We can trace the paths of hurricanes and can prepare for torrential rains. But we cannot control the elements. Jet streams and high- and low-pressure areas operate outside of our capabilities. Storms, droughts, fierce winds, or powerful waves can induce terror. Fear prompts prayers for deliverance of life and property from the ravaging forces of nature.

Of course, there are and always have been those who claim to have the power to affect the weather. By prayer or incantation or by the performance of some ritual, they believe they can cause rain to fall during a drought, divert the direction of destructive storms, or bring pleasant days for important events. The notion is not new. It is a familiar theme in the Bible.

The Jewish Scriptures

When the Hebrews entered Canaan, they were confronted with a so-phisticated culture with its own pantheon and theology. The economy of the land was primarily agricultural, so that it is not surprising that one of the important Canaanite deities was Ba'al, the god of fertilizing rain whose symbol was the bull. Ba'al and Yahweh became rivals. Through the translation of inscribed clay tablets found during the excavation of Ras es Shamra in Syria, the scholars have come into possession of sacred texts associated with the god Ba'al. He is described as a "rider of the clouds," whose voice was heard in the thunder. His return from the realm of death after the summer drought was marked by the coming of the annual autumn rains. Accordingly, the Canaanite new year began with the revivification of Ba'al, announced by the sound of the god's voice in the thunder, the gathering of clouds, and the first sprinkles of rain. The Canaanite ritual which enabled the god to act included a moment when the priest opened the windows in the temple on earth in the assurance that this magical gesture would result in the god opening the windows of heaven and permitting the rain to fall.

When Yahweh became the national god in Judah and Israel, Yahwism absorbed certain elements of the Canaanite faith. The Jewish new year begins in the fall, just about the time the autumn rains begin in Palestine. Yahweh was recognized as a "rider of the clouds" in Ps. 104:3, and his voice was the thunder (Job 37:2–4; Ps. 29:3–4), and so on. In the temple courtyard, bulls supported a huge basin of water (1 Kings 7:25) and were among the animals featured on the panels of the bronze wagons that supported the washbasins (7:29).

When the kingdom of Israel separated from Judah in the tenth century B.C.E., King Jeroboam established two Yahweh centers, one at Bethel in the south and the other at Dan in the north. In each, as symbols of Yahweh, he placed golden calves or bulls. Yahweh was not only the national war god who protected his people, but also a nature or fertility god, responsible for rain, drought, the fecundity of the soil, crops, herds, and human families.

A dramatic portrayal of the conflict between Ba'alism and Yahwism is narrated in 1 Kings 18. Yahweh, not the absence of Ba'al, so the story goes, had caused a severe drought (17:1) which resulted in a famine (18:2). To demonstrate to King Ahab that it was Yahweh and not Ba'al who was in charge of the weather and fertility, Elijah met in a contest with the prophets of Ba'al on top of Mount Carmel.

Ba'al's prophets performed their limping dance around the altar. They called upon Ba'al to respond, presumably asking the god that having made his annual move from the realm of the dead to the world of the living he should now manifest his presence by thunder and causing rain to fall. There was no response.

Then Elijah took center stage. On the altar were the firewood and the cut-up parts of a bull that had been sacrificed by the prophets of Ba'al. In a rite of sympathetic magic Elijah poured water from twelve jars (four at a time) on the wood and the bull parts. He then called upon Yahweh. Yahweh responded with a bolt of lightning that set the wood afire and consumed the bull offering. After supervising the murder of all the prophets of Ba'al, Elijah waited on top of the mountain until his servant announced that a rain cloud could be seen approaching across the Mediterranean. A rainstorm ensued and the drought was ended.

Elijah had demonstrated three things. First, that by sympathetic magic like produces like: the ritual pouring of water on earth resulted in divine action causing water to fall from the sky. Second, that Yahweh, not Ba'al, was the god of rain and fertility. Third, that whereas the priests of Ba'al were unable to cause rain to fall, he, a priest of Yahweh, could cause rain.

Hebrew heroes demonstrated magical control over nature. Moses and Aaron with their magic wands were able to cause a variety of horrible plagues in Egypt (Exod. 7:19–21, 8:5–7, 8:16–17, 10:13–14). With that same magic wand, Moses could cause Yahweh to send hail, thunder, and fire on Egypt (Exod. 9:23–24), and by simply stretching out his hand he could cause these visitations to suddenly cease. With a wave of his hand, he caused three days of darkness (Exod. 10:22). By stretching out his hand over the sea, Moses caused Yahweh to send a strong east wind that parted the waters, creating a dry causeway over which the fleeing Hebrews passed. When the Egyptians attempted to follow, Moses raised his hand again, and the waters came together and drowned them (Exod. 14:21–29). When Moses tossed ashes in the air, the Egyptians and their animals broke out in boils (Exod. 9:8–10). When the fleeing Hebrews encountered bad water at Marah, Moses threw bark into the water and it became drinkable (Exod. 15:23–25). No other biblical person came close to equaling the control over nature exercised by the legendary Moses.

When Elijah was in hiding from King Ahab at the Cherith brook, he had water to drink but no food. By means of natural magic, however, he had meat and bread delivered to him by ravens! (1 Kings 17:6). When the brook dried up he took up residence at the home of a widow and her son in Zarephath village. Here, Elijah magically produced flour and oil. The poor widow, who had only a handful of flour and a small amount of oil, was ordered by the prophet to use her meagre supplies to feed him first and then herself and her son. After she obeyed him, the prophet transformed ordinary household vessels into magical instruments simply by announcing that "neither the flour jar nor the oil container will ever be empty until the Yahweh sends rain to the earth" (1 Kings 17:10–16). On another occasion, Elijah summoned destructive fire from heaven to destroy one hundred men (2 Kings 1:9–12). When he wished to cross the Jordan River, he simply rolled up his mantle and struck the water, and the water parted so he could walk over dry shod (2 Kings 2:8).

His disciple Elisha also was able to control nature. He summoned two vicious she-bears to tear to shreds forty-two boys who had mocked him and called him "old baldy" (2 Kings 2:23–24). Like Moses, by throwing salt in it, he magically purified the impure water of the Ain Feshka spring at Jericho that caused death and miscarriage (2 Kings 2:19–21). When he wished to cross the Jordan River, he followed the example of his mentor and struck the surface of the water with Elijah's cloak so that the water stopped flowing and he was able to cross (2 Kings 2:14).

Yahweh, as controller of fertility, was believed to be able to prevent rain from falling, to bring disease to plants, to cause insects to devour agriculture, to cause animal death, or to bring on devastating storms. Through the prophet Amos, Yahweh boasted of numerous malicious and destructive deeds:

> Three months before the harvest, I held back the rain from you
> I would send rain on one city and none on another.
> One field would receive rain, and the field that received no rain withered
> So that two or three cities wandered to a single city, to drink water,
>   but were not satisfied . . .
> I struck you with blight and mildew
> I wasted your gardens and vineyards.
> Your fig and olive trees were devoured by locusts . . .
> yet you did not return to me, says Yahweh.
>
> Amos 4:7–9

Despite these agricultural disasters, the people apparently continued to worship Ba'al as the fertility god. Amos claimed that the drought and destruction of crops by disease and insects were caused by Yahweh, who was angry because the people had rejected him by seeking life and fruitfulness from Ba'al, the traditional god of fertility.

Amos believed that as Yahweh's prophet, he and only he had prevented further disaster. He stood alone between Yahweh and the nation and persuaded Yahweh to change the divine intent to destroy, first by locusts then by fire:

This is what Yahweh Elohim revealed to me. He was creating a swarm of locusts just when the late planting was sprouting. . . . When it was about to completely devour the crops of the land, I spoke, "Lord Yahweh, forgive, I beg you. How can Jacob [Israel] stand? He is so small. Yahweh changed his mind in this matter and said "It shall not be." (7:1–3)

The next threatened devastation was by fire. Whether the reference is to a prairie or forest fire raging out of control, or what is more likely, to the searing heat of the sun during drought, is not clear. The promised heat would be so intense that Amos could imagine it drying up the cosmic ocean, "the great deep" (*tehom rabbah*). Once again the prophet intervened: "Lord Yahweh, stop! How can Jacob survive, he is so small?" Yahweh responded "Neither shall this happen" (7:4–6).

Obviously, Yahweh was open to appeal. Amos's appeal was to Yahweh's sense of mercy or decency. On an earlier occasion, when Moses intervened to prevent disaster, he appealed to Yahweh's ego, to the deity's desire to protect the divine reputation. The desert-wandering Hebrews had complained about their miserable situation and Yahweh became furious, threatened to decimate them with disease, and ultimately abandon them entirely, leaving them unprotected in the wilderness. Moses challenged the decision and asked how this act would appear to Egyptians and to the other nations who would learn of Yahweh's failure to sustain the very people he rescued. To preserve his reputation Yahweh changed his mind (Num. 14:10–25). It is clear that the Jewish writers who composed the Bible ascribed human emotions to their god. Yahweh responded as one might hope a powerful ruler or overlord might. In each threatening situation, a human intervened and the divinely ordained disaster was averted.

Sympathetic magic is recorded in Jewish Scriptures without reference to the deity. For example, Jacob bargained with his father-in-law to act as sheep- and goatherder, provided he could have possession of any lambs and kids that were mottled rather than of solid color. Laban cleverly removed from the flock all mottled adult animals. As a husbandman, he knew that like tends to breed like. The flock Jacob was assigned responsibility for was uniformly hued.

Jacob thwarted Laban's scheme by peeling strips of bark from tree branches, producing a striped or mottled effect. He then placed the branches where the animals could see them when they drank and bred. The result was mottled offspring (Gen. 30:25–43). Of course, this story is nonsense. Like other, similar, biblical notions it reflects the superstitions of the ancient past.

The Christian Scriptures

Jesus is supposed to have been able to control natural forces. When he and his disciples were in a boat on the Sea of Galilee, a violent wind churned the waves, threatening to capsize the boat. Jesus commanded the waves, saying, "Peace, be calm!" and they obeyed him (Matt. 8:18–27; Mark 4:35–41; Luke 8:22–25). Indeed, Jesus' control was so great that the water of the turbulent sea supported him as he walked on its surface, as once again he caused the wind to die down and the troubled waters to subside (Mark 65:48–51).

When Jesus looked for fruit out of season on a fig tree, he was piqued, cursed the hapless tree, and caused it to wither and die (Mark 11:13–14; Matt. 21:18–19). The gospel writers made no comment on the unreasonableness of Jesus' expectations and behavior. On the contrary, they reported that Jesus encouraged illogical and frivolous belief in the power of faith. He is supposed to have said:

> Have faith in God. Honestly, I tell you, whoever says to this mountain, "Be uprooted and thrown into the sea," and is without doubt in his heart, but believes that what he says will happen, it will be accomplished for him. Therefore I am telling you, whatever you ask for in prayer, just believe you will receive it and you will. (Mark 11:22–24)

The passage differs a bit in Matthew's gospel. Here Jesus says:

> Honestly, I tell you, if you have faith as [small as] a grain of mustard seed, and you say to this mountain, "Move from here to that place over there," it will move. Nothing will be impossible for you. (Matt. 17:20–21)

The Gospel of Luke substitutes a mulberry tree for the mountain. In this account Jesus told his followers that with faith they could command the tree to "be uprooted and planted in the sea," and the tree would obey the command (Luke 17:6).

The Apostle Paul seems to have known of these teachings for he made reference to them in 1 Corinthians 13:2. He suggested that the supernatural readjustment of real estate meant nothing if one was without love.

Through such teachings another dimension of magical thinking became part of Christian thought. Prayer, which in many instances was little more than a manipulative effort to sway the deity, was as much a part of traditional Judaism as of other ancient religions. One praised the deity for the same reasons as one flattered a powerful person—in the hopes of gaining his good will. One thanked the deity for everything from pleasant weather to good business deals, because without acknowledgement of these benefits, the god could not be trusted to continue providing them. When in trouble one sought help and intervention from the deity, often asking forgiveness for whatever misdeeds one may have done, because misfortune was associated with sin and error. Now the New Testament introduced the belief in the magical power of faith.

There is absolutely no evidence that any mountains were moved, either in Jesus' day or since that time, by someone wishing it to be so or believing blindly that they could accomplish such a feat. In other words, neither wishing nor praying will make it so, no matter what degree of faith one might possess. The claim is pure nonsense. Of course, there is an abundance of evidence to show that there have been Christians who have been eager and willing to attribute natural events to the power of prayer or faith.

Modern Times

What could be more natural than that Christians would believe what Jesus was supposed to have taught and promised concerning the power of faith, and on the basis of that promise would continue to try to intervene and beseech the deity to send rain, or stop storms, or redirect tornadoes or hurricanes, or preserve loved ones during an earthquake? Throughout the history of the Christian church such appeals have been made. If the anticipated disaster failed to occur, it was assumed that God heard and answered the prayer. If disaster occurred, it was assumed that the deity had reasons for ignoring the petition and the divine refusal could be interpreted as a message.

A fundamentalist evangelist who became a candidate for the 1988 presidential race claimed he had diverted a storm that threatened to wreak havoc on the East Coast of America. The Rev. Pat Robertson, a Yale graduate in law, apparently believed that he, like Amos, stood alone between the forces of nature, which he assumed were under the control of God, and which threatened the East Coast. He announced that his prayers alone persuaded God to alter the course of the tempest. His claims raise questions about the development of critical thinking skills in higher education! No meteorologist or weather expert gives any credence to Robertson's boast. The direction taken by the storm can be explained naturalistically. Pat Robertson has attempted to take credit where no credit is due. He is not alone in making such claims.

After a five-year drought in the area of Juazeiro de Bahia in Brazil, the first sprinkle of rain, in March 1985, was interpreted by Roman Catholics as a response to prayers for intervention to St. Joseph. Clearly it is important to have powerful allies in high places.

In the dry month of August 1987, Xipe Totec Indians performed an ancient Aztec ritual seeking to produce rain. The ceremony included dancing and blowing on a seashell horn. No weather changes resulted.

Then there are modern rainmakers, or "weather modification specialists," as they prefer to be called. They operate during droughts in the Midwest, Oklahoma, and Texas. They may use small electric generators to spew particles into the atmosphere in the hopes of inducing high-domed thunderheads and rain. They may engage in cloud seeding using silver iodide particles. Whether or not the rain, if it comes, is the result of these activities is a matter of debate.

Some natural phenomena are interpreted by insurance companies as "acts of God." The phrase is employed to mark destructive events that cannot be attributed to human causation. For example, the devastation resulting from earthquakes, hurricanes, or tidal waves, or from fires started by lightning are all treated as "acts of God." Perhaps a more precise description might be "natural disasters."

However, for believers, natural events or incidents that bring deliverance to endangered persons are "acts of God." When the early Mormon settlers, facing the hardships of early pioneers, planted their crops in Utah in the spring of 1847, swarms of crickets began to consume the early growth. Human efforts to stop the invasion by driving the insects into ditches filled with water and by attacking them with fire were not effective. Then the sea gulls came—first a flock of seven, then ever-increasing numbers. They descended on the crickets, ate, regurgitated, and ate again. The crops were saved. There can be no question that without the intervention of the gulls the future of the struggling community would have been in jeopardy. For the naturalist, there are natural explanations for the arrival of the gulls so far inland; for the believer, the arrival of the birds was an act of God. Of course, this historical report, based on the records of those present at the time, was never attributed to human intervention as in the Pat Robertson claims. The Mormon interpretation of the event is a "faith explanation," or in the words of insurance companies "an act of God."

References

Inman, William H., "Rainmakers Still Popular," *The Los Angeles Times*, September 15, 1983.
Tormey, Don, "Aztec Dance Seeks Rain," *The Los Angeles Times*, August 12, 1987.

Biblical Monsters and Giants

Dreams and fantasy breed monsters. In dreams, experiences recent or remote are transmogrified to asume new and wondrous forms. Somewhere in our human bodies are chemicals that when released produce hallucinatory images that appear to be real for the moment, but upon our awakening, are recognized as nothing more than mental constructs. To what extent such conceptual fabrications were accepted by our ancestors as real cannot be known, but in the past, as in the present, there are those who have had difficulty distinguishing between the real and the imagined.

Perhaps well-known creatures contributed to the descriptions of chimeric beings. For example, certain lizards might have provided models for some frightening dragons. Of course, the goat, one of the most familiar animals of the ancient Near East, was the source for the face of the demon. The bull was the symbol of sexual vigor. In each instance, the familiar was transformed to become the extraordinary.

It is possible, as some psychoanalysts have suggested, that the mental images of monsters or other weird and wonderful creatures are distorted representations of repressed feelings and desires, of wish fantasies, or of the struggle between instinctual needs and desires (the id) and the restricting influence of the conscience (the superego), or perhaps repressed unacceptable feelings, neurotic fears, and so on (Mully 1980, pp. 37–46). For those engaged in such inner struggles, the imagery and the fantasy become reality—a reality that perhaps can be appreciated and accepted by others who have had similar experiences. When such experiences occur in a religious context, they become the basis for belief in monsters, demons, and other earthly or unearthly beings. The sanction of religion legitimates these fabrications and they become part of cultural belief systems and religious folklore. To doubt is heresy. For the true believer, the monsters represent reality, even though there is no evidence of their existence.

Biblical monsters have no more substance than those created by other religious groups or by present-day science fiction writers. The dragon figures of China, the monsters of Hinduism, the multiform god and demon figures that populate religious mythology are all artistic and mental distortions. They persist as anomalies in our present scientific world because they enjoy dogmatic authority provided by temple, church, clergy, and scriptures. For the educated church or synagogue member they are often an embarrassment. Biblical monsters and demons and dragons are considered real only because they appear in the Bible. Synagogues and churches, by sanctifying ancient biblical writings, have moved them beyond the pale of critical and scientific examination. But not for all of us!

Monsters in the Bible

The Hebrews believed in sea serpents and monsters that lived in the depths of the oceans and seas. The priests who wrote the creation myth stated in Genesis 1:21 that Yahweh created the giant sea monster (*tannin*). Inasmuch as this particular myth was written when the Hebrews were under Babylonian control, perhaps the sea monster image was borrowed from the figure of Tiamat in the Babylonian creation myth. Tiamat was an oceanic goddess representing the forces of primeval chaos, whose body was split in two to form the earth and the firmament (Larue 1988). Job used the same term, *tannin,* when he was being tormented by his god. He asked the deity, "Am I the sea (*yam*) or a sea monster (*tannin*) that you set a watch over me?" (7:12). The need to place a guard over the sea and the sea monster suggests borrowing from both Babylonian and Canaanite sources. Just as Tiamat was the goddess of the sea who had to be overcome before creation could ensue in Babylonian mythology, Yam was the sea god, described as a sea serpent, against whom the Canaanite god Ba'al struggled for control of the land. Both Tiamat and Yam required constant supervision.

As non-Hebrew deities battled for control in primeval times, so the Hebrew god, Yahweh, struggled against supernatural forces. Hebrew poets recalled Yahweh's fight with Rahab, the dragon (Job 9:13, 26:12–13; Ps. 89:10; Isa. 30:7). The sixth-century B.C.E. prophet known to scholars as Deutero-Isaiah, whose poetic composition was attached to the Book of Isaiah, called on Yahweh to deliver the exiled Hebrews:

Awake! Awake! Put on strength, O arm of Yahweh
Awake as in ancient time, in days gone by.
Was it not you who chopped Rahab in pieces,
    and pierced the dragon?
Was it not you who dried up the sea, the waters of the abyss
Who made the ocean depths a road for the ransomed?
Isa. 51:9–10

    The primeval sea monster was also referred to as Leviathan, a name derived from a root meaning to coil or wind. A psalmist wrote:

By your might you split the sea (yam)
and smashed the heads of the sea dragons (*tannin*)
You crushed the heads of Leviathan
and gave him as food to desert tribes.
Ps. 74:13–14

Just as the Canaanite god Ba'al defeated the sea god, Yam, so Yahweh defeated the primeval waters, depicted as a monster. Just as the primeval Canaanite dragon, Lotan, who was defeated by Ba'al, had seven heads, so the biblical Yam and Leviathan have multiple heads. It is obvious that the Hebrew writers and the Hebrew people were influenced by Canaanite theology and adopted Canaanite primeval battle motifs that were subsequently applied to Yahweh, for there is no biblical description of the encounter between Rahab and Yahweh or between Yahweh and Leviathan. Both monster stories reflect mythic imagery borrowed by the Hebrews from their non-Yahwist neighbors. Of course, the Hebrew writers utilized the references for their own purposes, and Rahab and Leviathan became symbols for Egypt.

    A completely different dragon story, set in Babylon, is found in the Eastern Orthodox version of the Book of Daniel, but placed in the Apocrypha by Jews, Catholics, and Protestants, in the book called Bel and the Dragon. According to the tale, the Babylonians worshipped a dragon as a living god. Daniel boasted that he could kill the creature without using a sword or club. On obtaining permission to try, he concocted a mixture of tar, fat, and hair and fed it to the dragon, which soon died. The populace was incensed at the loss of their god and Daniel was tossed into a lion's den with seven hungry lions that had not been fed so that they might devour Daniel. Nor had Daniel been fed. So the deity dispatched an angelic messenger to the prophet Habakkuk in Palestine. Habakkuk had just prepared breakfast for his field workers. Now the prophet and the food were magically airborne and transported to the lion's den in Babylon, where Daniel received the food. As one might expect, on the seventh day the king found that Daniel had miraculously survived. Daniel was set free and the king was immediately converted to Judaism.

The account is pure fiction. It has been suggested that the dragon was probably a huge snake, inasmuch as serpent worship was not uncommon in the ancient world (see chapter on The Cult of the Serpent). An interesting parallel to the Daniel story is found in the fiction once associated with Ethiopian royalty. According to the story, the Ethiopians once worshipped a monstrous serpentine dragon. At the advice of the king it was served a goat that had been fed poisonous food. Consequently, the dragon died. It was then that communication was made with King Solomon, who not only gave the Ethiopians the "true" faith, but also impregnated the King's daughter (the Queen of Sheba), from whom the royal Ethiopian family claimed descent. The royal legend was obviously a combination of material drawn from two biblical stories: the first was the tale of Daniel and the dragon; the second was the account of the visit of the Queen of Sheba to Solomon (1 Kings 10:1–13).

Present-day believers in the Bible ignore or are ignorant of the Canaanite and Babylonian origins of the biblical references to sea serpents, monsters, and dragons. Because these creatures appear in the Bible, they automatically had or have a reality for these people. Wherever in the world the Bible has been taken, belief in sea monsters has been taken, too. There are dozens of local legends about sea and lake monsters. Attempts have been made to enlist science to substantiate the existence of sea monsters. It has been suggested that somehow creatures from the age of dinosaurs escaped extinction and continue to exist in the unprobed depths of lakes or in the sea. To give credence to this supposition, it is pointed out that the coelacanth, a fish long believed to be extinct, was found to exist in our present time. But a relatively small fish is something quite different from the huge serpentine creature supposed to live in Loch Ness, Scotland. Despite fuzzy photographs and reported sightings, none of the numerous reports of sea or lake serpents has proven to have basis in fact. In other words, sea monsters and dragons belong in the literary realm of fiction. Efforts to provide scientific support for the existence of these wondrous creatures can be classified as "fiction science."

The author of Job presents an image of Leviathan that becomes the prototype for dragon features. When God bullied Job into silence with a series of challenges, he demanded:

> Can you pull Leviathan up with a hook?
> Or bind his tongue with a cord? (41:1)

He continued:

> Who can strip off his outer coat?
> Who can pierce his double-layered armour?
> Who can press apart his jaws,
> Ringed with fearsome fangs?
> His back is covered with rows of shields
> So tightly sealed to one another
> That there is no space between them.
> His sneezes are flashes of lightning
> His eyes burn like the dawn.
> Flames issue from his mouth,
> Sparks leap forth.
> Smoke as from a scorching pot or burning reeds
> Comes from his nostrils.
> Fire bursts from his throat,
> Flames from his mouth.
> His neck is strong,
> Violence precedes him
> His fleshy folds are bound together
> Firm and immovable.
> His heart is hard as stone
> As hard as a nether millstone.
> When he rears up he terrifies the gods
> When he crashes down they are beside themselves.
> A sword cannot touch him, it is ineffectual
> As are spear, dart and javelin.
> Iron he treats like straw,
> Bronze like rotten wood.
> An arrow cannot make him flee
> And slingstones are like straw to him.
> He treats clubs like straws
> And laughs at the javelin's rattle.
> His underbody is like sharp pottery shards
> Like a threshing sledge dragged through mud.
> He stirs the deep as if it were in a caldron
> And leaves behind him a shining wake
> Like ointment in a pan.
>
> Job. 41:13–32

Out of such imagery are dragons and sea monsters created and authenticated, because the description is given in the Bible.

"There Were Giants on Earth"

The ancient Jews believed in giants. According to the Priestly sections of Exodus, which was written in the fifth century B.C.E., when Moses sent a group of men on a reconnaissance mission in Canaan, some of them reported:

> The land we reconnoitered devours its inhabitants. The people we saw there were of gigantic stature. We saw the Nephilim there beside whom we appeared as grasshoppers, both in our own eyes and in theirs. (Num. 13:32–33)

An editor added a note to explain to the reader that the Nephilim were "sons of Anak, who come from the Nephilim" (13:33). An editor also added a note to the seventh-century B.C.E. Deuteronomic story of the division of Canaan, stating that in the territory that had belonged to Abraham's nephew Lot, "The Emim formerly lived there—a great and numerous people, as tall as the Anakim and like the Anakim they were also known as the Rephaim, but the Moabites called them Emim" (Deut. 2:10–11). Clearly, at some time after the fifth century the identity of these giants had been forgotten, and the editors felt a need to add explanatory notes.

The earliest mention of the Nephilim occurs in the tenth-century B.C.E. myth of the cohabitation by the sons of the gods (*elohim*) with earth women:

> The Nephilim were on earth in those days when the sons of the elohim had intercourse with the daughters of men who bore children to them. They were the mighty men of old, men of renown. (Gen. 6:4)

Obviously, various Hebrew myths were circulated at different times. The earliest reference to the Nephilim suggests that they were the product of divine-human intercourse. The later references may reflect this myth and suggest that the early inhabitants of Palestine were giants like the Nephilim. The Anakim were a tribal group in Palestine (Albright 1928, pp. 237–239).

Scholarly efforts to make sense of the spies' report suggest that the massive stone dolmens of the megalithic period may have so overwhelmed the Hebrew invaders that they assumed that giants must have erected them (Wright 1938, pp. 305–309). Or again, perhaps the Hebrews were small in stature in comparison with the Canaanite inhabitants of Palestine. As desert wanderers they may have had a restrictive diet as compared to the rich diet enjoyed by the inhabitants of the "land of milk and honey" they contemplated invading.

The actual size of one giant, the Philistine who was killed by David, is given as six cubits and a span (1 Sam. 17:4). The cubit was approximately eighteen inches, and a span was half of that distance or nine inches. The giant was therefore supposedly nine feet, nine inches tall—an excellent candidate, no doubt, for the position of center on the Philistine basketball team! According to 2 Sam. 21:19-22, there were a number of Philistine giants from Gath, including Goliath, who was killed by Elhanan (see Larue 1983). So far Palestinian tomb excavations have failed to produce any evidence to support the height of giants as given in the Bible. In view of the fact that David was relatively small (when he donned Saul's armor, it was so oversized, he couldn't walk in it, cf. 1 Sam. 17:38-39), perhaps the writer of the story exaggerated the size of the Philistine. No doubt the Philistine's height was extended by the plumed headdress worn by Philistine warriors.

Og, king of Bashan, was also described as a huge man. An editor of Deuteronomy noted:

> Only Og, king of Bashan, was left as the sole survivor of the Rephaim. His bedstead of iron is still in Rabbah of the Ammonites. It was nine cubits long and four cubits wide as measured by the common cubit. (Deut. 3:11)

A bed frame of iron, a valuable metal in early times, reflects the royal wealth. The thirteen-and-a-half-by-six-foot bed was truly "king-size." It has been interpreted as referring to a dolmen (Johnson 1962) or to a stone sarcophagus (Bailey 1976, p. 184).

Biblical folktales about giants are like the folktales of other cultures. They are fiction about the mysterious past designed to explain some aspect of the present. A culture hero defeats the giant or the monster and the people are freed from a fearful threat. Appeals are made to natural phenomena or to artifacts to support the claims. In reality, there is no basis in fact. To those of small stature, the size of large people is magnified. Among the small, light, slender jockeys, tall basketball players, football players, oversized wrestlers, and so on, appear as giants. It is possible that the early Hebrews were of small stature and anyone of exceptional size automatically became a giant. On the other hand, giant stories abound in fiction, why not in biblical fiction?

References

Albright, William F., "The Egyptian Empire in Asia in the Twenty-First Century B.C.," *Journal of the Palestine Oriental Society*, 1928, VIII, 223–256.

Bailey, Lloyd R., Trans. of "Deuteronomy," *The New English Bible with the Apocrypha*. New York: Oxford University Press, 1976.

Costello, Peter, *In Search of Lake Monsters*. New York: Coward, McCann and Geoghegan, 1974.

Day, John, *God's Conflict with the Dragon*. Cambridge: Cambridge University Press, 1983.

Halpin, Marjorie M., and Michael M. Ames, eds., *Manlike Monsters on Trial*. Vancouver: University of British Columbia Press, 1980.

Johnson, R. F., "Og," in *The Interpreter's Dictionary of the Bible*. New York: Abingdon, 1962.

Larue, Gerald A., *Ancient Myth and Modern Life*. Long Beach, Calif.: Centerline Press, 1988.

———, "Who Really Killed Goliath?" *Free Inquiry*, Vol. 4, No. 1, 1983/84.

Mully, Wilfrida Ann, "The Unwanted Possession: The Origin of Monsters from a Psychoanalytical Point of View," in *Manlike Monsters on Trial*, edited by Marjorie Halpin and Michael M. Ames. Vancouver: University of British Columbia Press, 1980.

Smith, Susy, *A Supernatural Primer for the Millions*. New York: Bell Publishing Co., 1966.

Sprague, Roderick, and Grover S. Krantz, eds., *The Scientist Looks at Sasquatch*. Moscow, Idaho: University of Idaho Press, 1977.

Wright, G. Ernest, "Troglodytes and Giants in Palestine," *Journal of Biblical Literature*. 1938, LVII, pp. 305–309.

Life Beyond Life?

He who believes in the Son has eternal life; he who does not obey the Son shall not see life, but the wrath of God rests on him.

John 4:36

No one knows just how or when belief in an afterlife arose. One may conjecture that there was a time when our most primitive ancestors did not believe in any form of existence beyond the present. The dead were dead. As with animals, so with humans; bodies were left where they fell. Perhaps, like some animals, primal humans mourned the loss, but life was for the living and the existence of the family or the group was of greater significance than care about the dead. If one assumes that the dead were buried, then it is probable that due to the migratory life patterns of early humans and the impermanence of camping sites, archaeologists have not been able to uncover any solid evidence of burial customs.

When humans began to live in settled communities, there is evidence that they buried and protected the bodies of the deceased. For example, some fifty thousand years ago in Palestine, cave-dwelling humans at Mount Carmel buried their dead beneath the floors of the caves in which they lived. Later, in communities such as that found at Rehov har Bashan in Tel Aviv, the dead were buried beneath the floors of dwellings. One might speculate that the purpose was to keep the dead family member close to the living. There is some evidence that food was shared with the dead, so perhaps the dead were considered to have an existence or a life of their own in the grave, while maintaining links to the world of the living. Ultimately, places of entombment were located away from the homes of the living and the cemetery, the necropolis, or city of the dead, came into being, an institution that is still with us.

Just how notions of the continuing existence of the dead came into being can only be matters of conjecture. It has been suggested that perhaps the source of belief in the afterlife may have been in dreams. The records of human history, from the beginning of the third millennium to modern times, provide numerous reports of dreams about death or about those who have died. The dream may include conversations with the dead. Sometimes the dead person informed the dreamer that he or she was not dead, but just in hiding. In other instances, the dead may have invited the living to join them. Such dreams represent the dreamer's attempt to cope with loss through denial, inasmuch as in the dream the dead person is not truly dead. Even today people experience dreams in which dead friends or family members are envisioned. Some become convinced that the dead are not truly dead and are seeking to communicate with the living.

To us, a dream is just a dream, but our ancient ancestors may not have been able to distinguish between dream and reality. When a deceased family member appeared during sleep and seemed to be communicating with the dreamer, our forebears had no way of knowing that dreams, with all their vivid details, are the products of our own minds. The dreamer, as the creator of the dream, is all parts, all roles, and all conversations of the dream. For our ancestors, the dream and reality merged. J. S. Lincoln in his study of *The Dream in Primitive Cultures* (1935) has noted that what the dreamer "perceives in the dreams, is not recognized as images created by his own mind, but is regarded as having a reality of its own and an existence which is independent of the dreamer" (p. 27).

The dream may feature popular concepts of the afterlife. For example, the Sumerian-Babylonian story of Gilgamesh relates a dream of the afterworld that includes commonly held notions of what lay beyond this earthly existence. Some modern dreamers envision an afterworld which reflects aspects of their present environment, and they, too, accept what they dream as a relatively accurate portrayal of an existence beyond death.

Perhaps early beliefs in the afterlife grew out of hallucinatory experiences. All of us know that on occasion the mind seems to play tricks. We conjure up an afterimage of something that has been seen earlier. For example, recently I spent a weekend with friends in a mountain condominium. They own a large dog, part wolf, named Kenzie. In the evenings, Kenzie would stretch out in front of the fireplace—a huge mound of flesh and fur with magnificent pointed ears alert and eyes watching every move. Upon return to my home, there were several occasions as I was seated by the fireplace, reading, when out of the corner of my eye I could almost see Kenzie lying in about the same location in front of the fireplace he would have been had we been in the mountains. Of course, there was nothing there. The flickering shadows produced by the fire apparently triggered memories of the mountain sojourn. The powerful mental imprint of the animal produced a recollection of an experience, and for a moment the experience was relived.

There is nothing particularly supernatural or uncanny about this sort of remembering. Many people have it. Quite often, after some loved person has died, they imagine they hear a familiar voice, and because the memory of the voice is so vivid, they are almost persuaded to respond. Indeed, out of emotional need or out of habit, some do respond. A few years ago I conducted a grief seminar in which an attending psychiatrist shared his reactions following his wife's death. At certain moments, when he was alone and relaxed, he would be startled by what he thought was her footstep or the sound of her voice. In his loneliness and out of habit, he would call out to her. Of course, he knew that there was no one there, but he refused to ignore the power of past associations. At times he held one-sided conversations with her just as if she were present. The conversations helped him cope with his loss.

Our ancient ancestors may also have experienced afterimages. Perhaps because they were not always able to distinguish between what they fancied they saw and reality, they truly believed that the dead were still alive or at least had power briefly to manifest themselves. If such power was attributed to the dead, it is not surprising to discover evidence of beliefs that the dead could have influence in the world of the living. Consequently, there was fear of the dead. Efforts were made to please the dead and to thwart any mischief an unhappy dead person might seek to cause for the living.

Another source of belief in an afterlife is related to the fear of dying and death. Death means the termination of all that has been experienced in life. The notion of not being can be frightening. Belief in an afterlife represents a denial of and resistance to the finality implied in dying and death. If there is a life beyond this life, then what we do in our lifetime and what we experience may have a larger dimension of meaning. Without such a belief, life itself can be construed as meaningless.

Often we think in terms of rewards and punishments, and we may ask what is the reward for having lived, for having struggled through infancy toward maturity, for having grappled with disease and misfortune, for having achieved successes and contributed to human welfare? What is the importance of life if it is simply a momentary spasm in the endlessness of time and space? It was this sort of question that prompted the writer of Ecclesiastes to declare that existence was meaningless (*hebel*). This same attitude is expressed in the writings of modern existentialists. Afterlife beliefs challenge this attitude. Despite the fact that there is no proof that life beyond death exists in any form, physical or spiritual, many find comfort in believing that there is life beyond death. Afterlife beliefs ease the sting of death and may imply rewards for enduring the burdens of mortality. Promises of rewards and punishments for what is done in this life provide solutions (simplistic though they may be) to issues of injustice, poverty, suffering, and class discrimination. The belief, despite the lack of evidence, that cosmic justice or divine justice is operative in the universe, can induce individuals to endure and accept their lot in life no matter how mean and unsatisfactory that lot may be. If one can assume that, despite poverty, disease, unjust treatment, and deprivation of essentials for a good life, as long as one lives as a decent human being, one will be rewarded for that behavior in another existence, and if one can believe that the cruel, the unjust, the manipulators of society that deprive others of their full status as humans will ultimately be punished, then one can argue that life is fair. When the problem of justice assumes theological dimensions, as it does under the title of "theodicy," or the justice of god, the believer proclaims trust in a just god who will in the end set the balances straight. One lives in trust and by faith.

Of course, there is absolutely no evidence to support such beliefs. There is no proof that evil that is not identified and dealt with in this life is punished in an afterlife. There is nothing to demonstrate that human decency earns approval or merit for the future. Good and evil are social and personal realities that require recognition and reward or punishment or curtailment in our present existence.

The great danger in belief systems that promise rewards and punishments in the afterlife is that they tend to support the status quo. It could be argued that the organizations that teach and encourage belief in an ultimate justice are really concerned with maintaining present injustice, inasmuch as they discourage social rebellion against discrimination and maltreatment. By persuading believers that evil will be punished in a future existence, religious dogma may discourage indulgence in evil and destructive behavior. But at the same time, such teachings promote attitudes of resignation to evils by suggesting that back of evil and misfortune, there may be a divine plan of retribution whose nature is hidden from humans. Belief in an afterlife may give solace to the underprivileged, the undernourished, the oppressed, and the enslaved, as they hope for freedom and better conditions in another dimension. But these same beliefs discourage efforts to effect the changes that can eliminate poverty and mistreatment of minorities or handicapped persons. They encourage and indeed produce an apathy that is nothing more than an easy escape from reality.

The Locale of the Dead—the Earliest Beliefs

A perfectly normal question arising out of belief in an afterlife is: if the dead continue to exist beyond this life, where is the locale of that existence? The fact that in some cultures food offerings were made at the grave of the dead suggests that those people believed that the burial place was where the dead remained after life ended. For example, the Egyptian belief in afterlife developed around the myth of Osiris, the first ruler of Egypt, the divine son of the sky goddess Nut and the earth god Geb. Osiris was murdered and dismembered by his jealous brother Seth. Isis, Osiris's wife-sister, reconstituted and mummified his body, and through sacral rituals enabled Osiris to become king of the underworld. His reconstituted body was now immortal. Horus, his son, became king of Egypt, and like subsequent pharaohs claimed divine status similar to that of Osiris. At death, each ruler was mummified. Magical, empowering funerary rituals performed at the tomb enabled the dead pharaoh and perhaps certain deceased nobility to enter an afterlife where they would associate with the gods. The pharaohs were believed to become immortal and one with Osiris. Rulers could be imagined riding in the divine sun-boat or dwelling among the stars or in some paradise. Their mummified bodies remained in the tomb, but the spiritual self (the *ka*, the spiritual "other" of the dead person) experienced the wonders of the afterlife. The treasures buried with pharaohs and nobles were to be enjoyed by the *ka* in the tomb. Just how this stored wealth was to be utilized by the *ka* is not clear. The cave tombs of Egyptian nobility contain wall paintings portraying life in ancient Egypt, and it has been suggested that the *ka* could enter the scenes and enjoy the portrayed activities.

The *ka* of the dead pharaohs required nourishment. Food was entombed with the mummies and food offerings were made outside the tomb by relatives or priests. Indeed, as E. Wallis Budge (1972) pointed out, there is clear evidence in the mastaba (prepyramid) tombs, that out of fear of lack of food and water for the dead, funerary offerings were regularly presented at the tomb site by paid clergy. If the offerings were not made, it was feared the dead might cause suffering, disease, and death in neighboring villages. Just how the deceased were supposed to consume the food is not known. Perhaps the *ka* of the dead could absorb the *ka* of the offerings. The dead person having consumed the spiritual dimensions of the offerings, the physical food became the property of the priests.

The common people could entertain no such grandiose illusions. Their graves were simple, and the staples buried with them represented their possessions in the earthly life. From time to time, family members might visit the graves with food offerings to replenish what was placed in the tomb. I have witnessed Muslim families in Upper Egypt doing that very thing, even though such a custom is not part of accepted Muslim religion. These women gathered at the grave of a deceased relative, performed mourning rites, and poured out liquids on the ground. Ancient patterns persist and attach themselves to the new.

In Mesopotamia the condition of the dead was visualized differently. There the literature depicts the grave as a gloomy, underground environment presided over by a queen and a king of the dead. The dream in the Gilgamesh epic portrayed the dead as dwelling in darkness, feathered like birds, with clay for food. Even those who had held high positions on earth were slaves in the underworld. Thus, while the body decayed in the grave, the essence of the person continued on in some sort of ghostly way in a not very pleasant environment.

Despite the Mesopotamian notion that the afterlife would not provide a desirable existence, the unearthing of the third-millennium "royal" graves at Ur by Sir Leonard Woolley (1963) has suggestd that there were those who believed that people "could take it with them," since the tombs provided a rich harvest of bejeweled gold and silver artifacts (pp. 52–90). In addition, the persons buried in the magnificent tombs were accompanied by retinues of servants, guards, and animals. A more recent and more feasible explanation of these rich burials is that they are related to sacred marriage or fertility rituals pertaining to myths associated with new year celebrations (Saggs 1962, pp. 374ff.). In other words, they do not reflect Mesopotamian beliefs concerning afterlife.

The pre-Israelite Canaanites developed sophisticated notions about death. The god of the realm of the dead was Mot, a word which is the equivalent of the Hebrew word for death: mawet. During the summer season, when the sun blazed down on Palestinian fields, it was assumed that Ba'al, the rain god, the lifegiver, was in the clutches of Mot. The coming of the autumn rains signified the resurrection of Ba'al and the beginning of the new year. The netherworld was a dismal place of mire and filth whose mouth or entrance stretched from heaven to earth, always open and ready to consume (Driver 1955, pp. 105–107).

As in Canaanite thought, so also in Hebrew thought, both death (mawet and the place of the dead (sheol) could be personified. Jeremiah wrote:

> For death (mawet) has entered our windows
> and it has penetrated our palace.
>
> (9:21)

A wisdom writer warned his pupils to avoid those who plotted to despoil the rich and who said:

> Let's swallow them alive and whole like Sheol
> like those who descend into the Pit.
> (Proverbs 1:12)

The prophet Isaiah's warnings of disaster were mocked by those who claimed:

> We have entered into a covenant with death (*mawet* = Mot)
> and we have an agreement with Sheol
> so that when the overwhelming disaster strikes
> it will not affect us.
> Isa. 28:15

Sheol, the netherworld, comprised a community of those who once lived but who were now cut off from the living and from their god Yahweh (Ps. 88:3-5). The dead were said to be "gathered to their kindred" (Gen. 25:17, 35:29, etc.) and excavations of Hebrew cave tombs give clear evidence that from time to time the graves were opened to admit the newly deceased, just as in some Arab countries Muslim familial tombs are opened and closed for entombments.

Sheol was an unpleasant place (Job 18:18) of darkness and decay (*abaddon*), where the dwellers became energyless (*rephaim*) and kings and commoners rested together for eternity (Job. 3:13-19), oblivious of the earthly life (Ps. 88:12; Eccles. 9:5). In a dirge directed toward Israel's enemies, a poet depicted Sheol welcoming a deceased oppressive ruler:

> Below, Sheol is stirred up to meet you when you arrive
> It rouses the shades (*rephaim*) to meet you,
>   all of whom were leaders on earth,
> It raises the dethroned, all who had been kings of nations
> They all speak and say to you:
> You have become weak as we are, you have become like us.
> Your splendor, the music of your lutes is brought down to Sheol
> Maggots form the bed beneath you, and worms are your covering.
> Isa. 14:9-11

The shadowy existence in Sheol cannot be construed as a meaningful personal immortality. The dead in Sheol seem to have been able to retain a recognizable identity—at least for a time. Their mortal remains decayed and in time they were all but forgotten. The essence of the dead person, which was labeled as *elohim*, a god or power, could be conjured up for consultation by a necromancer or channeler (1 Sam. 28:13; see chapter on Channeling).

Resurrection and the Locale of the Dead

Although Ishtar, the Babylonian goddess of love and fertility, visited the world of the dead, the notion of resurrection never became part of Babylonian belief. Ishtar journeyed

> to the house from which none who enter ever leave
> over the road from which there is no return route.
> (Speiser, 1950, p. 107)

During her absence sexuality came to a standstill on earth:

> The bull does not mount the cow, the ass does not impregnate the jenny
>
> Nor does the man copulate with the young woman.
> (Speiser, 1950, p. 108)

Fortunately the goddess returned from the underworld and nature was restored to normal.

Notions concerning resurrection that developed in the ancient Near East had a Persian origin. These notions were to impact on Jewish belief. After the exile of the Judeans in Babylon (sixth century B.C.E.), Ayran ideas from Persia were incorporated into the theology of some Jewish groups. The tomb became a temporary dwelling place for the dead, and there arose a belief in resurrection and in an eternity in either Heaven or Hell.

Afterlife in Jewish Scripture

The revelations of the Aryan prophet Zoroaster, which gave birth to the official religion of Persia, postulated an end time for human history, together with a belief in an afterlife which included a final judgment when individuals would receive rewards and punishments according to their behavior in this life. This concept was adopted by certain Jewish sects. In Jewish Scripture it is represented in the Book of Daniel, which was written during the Maccabean period, around 165 B.C.E., when Jews were persecuted for their faith by the Greek ruler Antiochus Epiphanes.

The author of Daniel pretended to be writing during the time of the exile in Babylon (sixth century B.C.E.). Consequently, he had little problem in "predicting" historical events that had already occurred up to 165 B.C.E. When he attempted to go beyond his own time, like other foretellers, he failed miserably. He accepted the Persian notion of an end time when history would cease and the dead would be resurrected and judged. He believed that end time was very near—three and a half to four years off (12:12-13). The promise was:

> At that moment your people will be delivered
> Everyone who is written in the book
> Many of those who sleep in the dust of the earth will awaken
> Some to everlasting life
> But some to reproach, to eternal abhorrence.
>
> Dan. 12:1-2

For the first time, the notion of resurrection and judgment became part of biblical thought.

Some have argued that the idea of resurrection appeared earlier. For example, the prophet Ezekiel developed an allegory based on his vision of dry bones (Ezek. 37:1-14). The bones represented the Jews in exile who seemed to think that their identity as a people was dead. The revivification of the bones in the allegory symbolized the hoped-for reestablishment of the nation of Judah, and had nothing to do with the resurrection of dead individuals.

Jewish beliefs in resurrection and judgment underwent further development during the intertestamental period. For example, the Book of Enoch prophesied that the righteous would "shine as the lights of heaven," while sinners would enter into "darkness and chains and a burning flame" (103-104). The Psalms of Solomon stated that "they that fear the Lord shall rise to life eternal, and their life in the Lord's light shall never end" (3:16), but the inheritance of the wicked "is Sheol and darkness and destruction" (14:7). Other writers echo these beliefs.

On a terrace above the northwest shore of the Dead Sea a colony of monks, believed to be Essenes, wrote out their beliefs, now known as The Dead Sea Scrolls. They, too, believed that the end was at hand. They saw themselves as the community of the enlightened righteous ones who would battle the forces of darkness in the final eschatological struggle. They believed that the wicked would "suffer in the darkness of eternal fire" and they, the righteous, would enjoy "eternal peace, eternal light, eternal truth, eternal glory" (Burrows 1955, p. 270).

Thus, the stage was set for the New Testament, where the idea of resurrection from the dead is demonstrated in Jesus, whose brief sojourn in the tomb became the model and the hope for Christians.

Afterlife in Christian Scripture

The Jesus story differed from the earlier myths in that Jesus was an historical person who, according to kenotic theology, had divested himself of his divine status to become completely human (Phil. 2:5–8). Almost as preparation for his resurrection, the gospels record stories of the miraculous raising of the dead by Jesus. He restored life to the dead daughter of a synagogue leader simply by taking the child's hand and saying, "Get up, my child" (Mark 5:41–42 and parallels). In another instance, he interrupted a funeral procession, placed his hand on the bier and said, "Young man, get up" (Luke 7:11–14). The dead man came to life. Lazarus was dead and entombed for four days. It was assumed that the process of decomposition had begun. Jesus ordered the removal of the blocking stone from the tomb and commanded: "Lazarus, come forth." The dead man came back to life and emerged from the tomb (John 11:38–44).

Jesus' disciples also raised the dead. Peter brought a dead woman named Tabitha back to life by praying and saying, "Get up, Tabitha" (Acts 9:40). When a boy named Eutychus fell from a third-story window and was presumed dead, Paul put his arms around the boy and said that he was still alive (Acts 20:8–12). In this instance, it could be argued that the boy was simply unconscious and only needed resuscitation. In each story of the dead returning to life, it is assumed that the reanimated person would ultimately die.

The death and resurrection of Jesus is something quite different. According to Christian Scriptures, he was killed and then came back to live eternally. Belief in Jesus' resurrection is central to the Christian faith. The Apostle Paul wrote:

> If there is no resurrection, then Christ was not raised; and if Christ was not raised, then our gospel is null and void and so is your faith, and we turn out to be lying witnesses for God because we bore witness that he raised Christ to life, whereas if the dead are not raised, it follows that Christ was not raised, and if Christ was not raised your faith is void of meaning and you all remain in your old state of sin. (1 Cor. 15:13–17)

As one might expect, Paul went on to affirm his faith in the resurrection.

Inasmuch as Paul's letters are the earliest New Testament writings (from between 55 and 65 C.E.), his statements provide the first record we have about the revivification of the dead Jesus. He wrote to Christians in Corinth:

> First and foremost, I transmitted to you the facts which had been given to me: that Christ died for our sins in accordance with the scriptures; that he was buried; that he was raised to life on the third day, in accord the scriptures; and that he appeared to Cephas, and afterward to the Twelve. Then he appeared to over five hundred of our brothers at once, most of whom are still living, although some have died. Then he appeared to James, and afterward to all the apostles. Finally, he even appeared to me. (1 Cor. 15:3–8)

Paul's testimony contains much hearsay evidence plus a reference to a personal experience of the risen Jesus. In addition to Paul's list of witnesses, the reports of the resurrection (omitting Mark 16:9–20, which was not part of the original text) include that of the women at the tomb (Matt. 28:9–10), Mary Magdalene (John 20:11–18), and two disciples on the way to Emmaus (Luke 24:13–31). With the exception of Paul's personal reference, all reports are hearsay, and the accounts of Jesus' resurrection in the four gospels do not harmonize.

Additional evidence for the resurrection, including the empty tomb and the testimony of the Roman guards, is also hearsay. There are no firsthand data. What records we do have were written long after the event. Paul's written statement was composed at least thirty years after the crucifixion. The gospels came into existence some forty or fifty or sixty years after Jesus' death. Research into oral transmission has demonstrated the ways in which accounts assume new dimensions, add information, and take varying forms over time. So how do we evaluate New Testament testimonies?

Empty tombs abound in Palestine. As a participant in archaeological research, I have been in dozens of empty tombs. The style of the tomb or pottery fragments may help to date the tomb, but they tell us nothing about what happened to the body or bodies. As my Canadian New Testament teacher, Clyo Jackson, said, some fifty years ago, "The empty tomb proves only that the tomb was empty." The tomb cannot be used to validate Jesus' resurrection.

The testimony of the Roman guards appears only in Matthew's account. The report is not given by the guards. It is hearsay evidence, recorded and perhaps composed by the gospel writer in response to an accusation that the disciples or followers of Jesus stole the body or moved it to another locale. The account cannot be admitted as evidence of Jesus' resurrection.

Those who went to the tomb following the Jewish Sabbath were supposed to have been accosted by one or more angelic figures or by Jesus himself, depending upon which account one reads. If one believes in angelic extraterrestrial beings, the accounts may sound reasonable. But angels do not seem to manifest themselves in modern times. Despite the insistence of some that they do exist, if they do, they are figures that belong to the distant past (see chapter on Extraterrestrials). The story of Jesus' manifestation to the women (Matt. 28:9) lacks completeness. Jesus suddenly appeared, and one must assume, as suddenly disappeared. In the Johannine story, when Jesus appeared to Mary of Magdala, she did not at first recognize him (John 20:14). The implication is that Jesus' human form (the tradition states that his body was resurrected) had somehow assumed new dimensions.

There are variations in the descriptions of the form of the risen body. Paul's vision, despite his claim "Did I not see Jesus our Lord?" (1 Cor. 9:1) appears to have been of a nonphysical Jesus or what many prefer to call a "spiritual" body. The report of his hallucination, recorded by the author of Luke and Acts, perhaps as late as 85 C.E., describes the encounter in which Paul and his companions saw a light, but only Paul heard a voice and carried on a conversation with the invisible Jesus (Acts 2:1–11). In other accounts, Jesus' materialization had physical attributes. He shared food (Luke 24:30), showed his crucifixion wounds, which could be touched (Luke 24:30–39 [although in John 20:17 he forbade Mary of Magdala to touch him]), gave advice on fishing (John 21:6), and in other ways manifested a physical presence. He could also suddenly appear and disappear (Luke 24:15, 31, 36, 50) and pass through walls or locked doors (John 20:19). He seemed no longer bound by laws of time, space, nor, as we shall see, gravity.

If one could accept the resurrection of Jesus as an historical fact, a more serious question would arise concerning the ultimate disposition of the risen body. The biblical response is that Jesus ascended into Heaven (Luke 24:51). He simply levitated, defied gravity, and rose up into the sky as the apostles watched (Acts 1:1–11). It was Paul's belief that Jesus would descend from this same Heaven to establish the divine kingdom of believers (1 Thess. 4:16), and that with Jesus' return, the dead would be resurrected (1 Cor. 15:52).

The notion of a Heaven in the sky was an acceptable idea some 2,000 years ago during the first centuries of our era. The telescope had not been invented. Copernicus was not yet born. The probing of space was far off in the future. Palestinian Jews believed what others also believed, that the earth was a flat disc arched over by a solid firmament, and that some-where above the earth the gods dwelled. Today the notion is simply non-sense. There is no Heaven to which Jesus could have ascended. There is absolutely no evidence of his resurrection, except in the minds and faith of those who choose to believe the gospel stories. The belief is naive and belongs in the category of other ancient myths that told of the comings and goings of divine beings between earth and the heavenly abode of the deities. Resurrection is a faith statement which denies the reality of death.

Paul was absolutely wrong in his belief that Jesus would soon return riding on the clouds of Heaven. He was wrong when he foretold the open-ing of the graves and the resurrection of the dead. If, as some fundamen-talist preachers maintain, that event is still to happen, then over the two millennia that have intervened since biblical times the bodies of believers will long since have disintegrated into dust. They will have to be miracu-lously transformed into spiritual entities as Paul claimed they would be (1 Cor. 15:52f.).

Since the time of the New Testament, no other claims of resurrection have been accepted. The dead remain dead. Resurrection remains as a Chris-tian myth.

Implications of Christian Beliefs

Christian beliefs in an afterlife postulate a dualism according to which the individual consists of a body and a soul. This notion was not present in biblical thought prior to the acceptance of Aryan theology following the exile in Babylon. Before that time, Jews appear to have accepted a belief in the psychosomatic unity of the person. One was not a body *and* a soul, one was a soul-body or a body-soul. At death the total unit entered a shadowy existence in the grave. As the body disintegrated, the dead became the energyless. The only immortality was in the continuation of the man's (as opposed to the woman's) family name and identity as a progenitor.

Some Christians argue that when the time for resurrection comes, the physical body, despite having rotted and disintegrated in the tomb, will be rejoined with the soul to constitute a physically identifiable person in the afterworld that most Christians assume will be Heaven. Others argue for a spiritual existence in paradise. The souls or spirits of evil persons or of those who have not accepted Jesus as lord and savior or who have not accepted some particular denomination's belief system will spend eter-nity burning in Hell as promised in the Christian book "The Revelation of John" (Rev. 20:12-15).

Reincarnation

The doctrine of reincarnation is one answer to the problem of human suffering and injustice in this life. It is a response to the question: "If there is such a thing as divine or cosmic justice, why do some good people suffer and why do some evil people prosper?" One answer lies in the concepts of karma and reincarnation. Each life is trapped in the vortex of a cyclic pattern which is known as the wheel of life. Each life develops along a spiral pattern moving toward personal escape in the absolute or the cosmic whole or the attainment of cosmic consciousness. As each life proceeds on that pathway, what is done in one life affects what occurs in the next, for the individual never loses personal identity. Therefore, what is happening in this life is the result of what the individual did in a past life. Who or what one is in this life (in some beliefs one may be reborn as an animal or an insect) depends upon how one lived in the preceding incarnation. There is no escape from the cycle. The only escape comes when one reaches nirvana, the state of cosmic enlightenment.

Like many other beliefs in afterlife, the reincarnation notion is based on an acceptance of dualism, that each person is composed of a physical body and a soul or mind or identity. It is possible for a person's soul or mind or identity to inhabit a different physical form in each reincarnation. When the physical form is discarded, the spiritual self enters a new body.

Religions that subscribe to such notions have developed high ethical principles to guide the individual towards the perfection or completion which is nirvana. They may also recommend an asceticism that moves one toward the perfect life and away from such harsh realities of this life as lust and greed, which are recognized as destructive or negative qualities. The belief in a rotational pattern of life may give rise to the sanctification of animal and even insect life. For example, among the Hindus of India, the cow and the monkey hold privileged positions that protect them from slaughter as food or nuisances or health hazards and that permit them to invade the streets and homes.

There is no verification of reincarnation (Edwards 1986). Claims of memories of past lives and past existences that have been investigated have not been substantiated.

Reincarnation in the Bible

From time to time it is suggested that the concept of reincarnation is reflected in both Jewish and Christian Scriptures. The example most often quoted is associated with the prophet Elijah, one of two Old Testament characters who escaped death.

The first to escape death, Enoch, is mentioned in the genealogical list prepared by ancient Jewish priests (Gen. 5). He is the single preflood character who did not die. It is written that he "walked with Elohim and he was not, for Elohim took him" (5:24). During the intertestamental period writings came into being that were attributed to the heavenly Enoch and are now published in the Pseudepigrapha. The writings are supposed to represent what Enoch learned and revealed after reaching his heavenly abode. The New Testament Book of Jude (14) contains a quotation from the Book of Enoch (1:9).

The prophet Elijah is also supposed to have bypassed death, and while still alive, to have ascended to Heaven (2 Kings 2:1-18). The witness to his miraculous translation was his disciple Elisha. The two prophets had just walked dry shod over the Jordan river, a wondrous event made possible by Elijah, who had compelled the river to stop flowing by striking the water with his rolled up tunic (2 Kings 2:8). The story continues:

> And as they continued to walk and chat, suddenly they were separated from one another by a chariot of fire and fiery horses. Then Elijah was transported by a whirlwind into heaven. Elisha witnessed it and shouted, "My father, my father! the chariots and horsemen of Israel!" Then he saw him no more. (2 Kings 2:11-12)

To guarantee that this was truly an ascension and not merely a freak accident of nature, fifty members of Elijah's prophetic school searched the area to see if they could find his body. They failed, and it was assumed that he was taken into Heaven.

Jewish theologians reasoned that if Elijah had been physically taken into Heaven, then he would not have suffered the fate of entombed bodies. He would not have decayed. He would be a whole person living in the presence of the Jewish god, Yahweh. Whoever added the final appendage to the Book of Malachi drew on this belief and stated that before the final day of judgment Yahweh would send "Elijah the prophet" (Mal. 4:5).

Inasmuch as messianic notions and end of the age ideas were current in Jesus' time, it was natural that someone should ask Jesus if either he or John the Baptizer were Elijah. Jesus seemed to identify John as the expected forerunner (Matt. 11:14). Sherman Johnson (1951) has noted:

> Here and elsewhere Matthew expresses the Christian doctrine that John is Elijah (cf. 17:12-13). He does not necessarily mean that he is identical

with the earlier prophet; he simply exercises his functions and fulfills the prophecies regarding him. (p. 384)

This suggestion makes good sense. Elijah was not thought of as a disembodied spirit that could be incarnated in some other life form. John was a whole person; Elijah remained in the heavenly environs.

On the other hand, the concept of body and soul was a part of the thinking of the Roman world. It is unlikely, but not entirely impossible, that some Jews may have entertained the notion of Elijah being reincarnated as an infant born to Elizabeth and Zechariah (Luke 1:57–60) so that he might mature as the forerunner to Jesus, who was born to Mary and Joseph and who in Christian thought matured as the Messiah. According to the writer of the Gospel of John, the Baptizer did not recognize himself as the forerunner (John 1:19–21). In any case, the possible relationship of the idea of reincarnation in the Bible to the present-day Western fascination with the idea is at best tangential.

Past-Life Regression

If one will live in an afterlife, is it not possible that one had a prelife, a pre-this-world-now existence? The idea, found in the reincarnation doctrines of Hinduism, has become part of current New Age thinking. Certain hypnotists claim that they are able to relax patients and by suggestion help them recall previous existences. The results of these recall experiences are singularly unconvincing.

Perhaps the most notorious case of past-life regression is that of Bridey Murphy, which burst upon the public in 1952. Despite claims that Ruth Simmons (Virginia Tighe) in her recall of her previous life as Bridey Murphy provided testable data concerning Irish customs that she could not possibly have known or experienced from this life (she was born in Chicago in 1923), it has been demonstrated that all that she revealed through her hypnotic regression was actually learned in her present life (cf. M. Harris 1986). The explanation for her belief that she was recalling past-life experiences is the phenomenon known as cryptomnesia. In cryptomnesia, information acquired from a wide variety of experiences and sources (including radio, television, overheard conversations, etc.) are stored in memory but are not readily available for normal recall. When this information does surface, sometimes spontaneously, the sources have been forgotten. Under hypnosis, a subject can, if asked, recollect where the information originated—that is to say, subjects who, under hypnosis, are able to tell a great deal about former lives, are also able, when questioned, to provide the sources for the information, all of which are from present life experiences. In the most famous cases of so-called past-life regression, it has been possible to demonstrate that what the person is recalling is not a former life, but information stored in the mind and reformulated as personal experiences. This is cryptomnesia.

Many New Age past-life regressions seem to be contrived. In one of the many New Age past-life demonstrations, a hypnotized woman, having been led through various past-life regressions, claimed to have lived in ancient Egypt, and at another time, in another life, in Europe. When questioned, she was unsure of the location of the pryamids. In the same interview, a question was asked about Europe. The woman responded as if through her European identity, although at the moment she was supposedly in her Egyptian identity. Individuals claim to be able to place themselves in different historical epochs and to talk about their lives in those times. But what is "relived" appears to be mere fantasy built on fragmentary knowledge. Insofar as I have been able to determine on the basis of talking with people who were supposed to have "regressed" to time periods concerning which I have some detailed knowledge, the regression experiences did not at all reflect documented historical reality. One would have expected that if a person wished to make a so-called regression real and convincing, he would do his homework and at least read up on the epoch!

What appears to happen in the current wave of past-life regressions is that the hypnotized person (if he or she is truly hypnotized) enters a semitrance state. But the person is keenly aware of everything that is taking place in his or her present time and place. What the person describes as a previous life may reflect deep emotional needs, and appears to be a product of cryptomnesia coupled with a rich imagination and ability to fantasize.

Some envision their past life as one of servitude or unhappiness—which is often very close to the way in which they contemplate their present life. Some with a hunger for authority or power envision themselves in a dominant role. The romantic fantasies of people who live prosaic lives are reflected in their supposed past existence. Past lives are often like daydreams.

Some psychics claim to be able to envision the past lives of their clients. They tell those who come to them for counseling or advice about past relationships that may explain present situations. For example, an employee who suffers under a tyrannical supervisor might be told that in a past life she was a male, married to this person (who was then female), and their relationship was unhappy because she had been intolerant and demanding. The present situation is simple karma. The wheel of life has rotated, and what occurred in past existences has affected what is taking place now. To the outside observer, the interpretation reflects the creative imagination of the psychic rather than any reality.

Ghosts and Apparitions

The word "ghost" refers to an apparition, generally of a person. Belief in ghosts rests upon hallucinatory or misinterpreted experiences of what are believed to be phantom persons that give the impression of formal identity. Usually ghosts are described as wearing clothing. Sometimes the apparitions breathe or speak or make sounds. Many reports of ghostly appearances coincide with fatal accidents, murders, and tragic deaths. In the minds of some, the ghost is believed to be the "spirit" of a deceased person freed of fleshly bonds but still retaining a shadowy identity with the flesh form. That is to say, that although the ghost is insubstantial, its walking produces creaking of floor boards; its anguish is expressed in moans and groans reflecting a physical body.

The significance of ghostly manifestations is variously interpreted. Sometimes they are believed to be warnings from the dead to the living. Some hauntings are seen as reprisals for mistreatment during the ghost's earthtly life. Sometimes ghosts appear to be friendly and helpful, at other times hostile and harmful. Still others seem to have neither malevolent or benevolent intentions, inasmuch as they are completely involved in their own memories.

Ghost stories are found in every culture. Those who claim to experience ghostly apparitions appear to be mentally and physically healthy. Quite often these people are dismissed as naive, or dupes, or liars, or as individuals who accept dreams and hallucinations as reality rather than as mental phenomena. On occasion, attempts are made to give scientific respectability to phantom appearances by reference to the so-called "personal energy" which remains after death, though without defining just what the term means. At other times theological meaning is given to apparitions by referring to them as "souls" of the dead.

Folklorist Andrew Lang (1897) noted that what he called "old ghost stories" were "much more dramatic than the new." The "old" ghosts had specific characteristics:

> As a rule their bodies were unburied, and so they demanded sepulture; or they had committed a wrong, and wished to make restitiution; or they had left debts which they were anxious to pay; or they had advice, or warnings, or threats to communicate; or they had been murdered, and they were determined to bring their assassins to the gibbet. (p. 110)

As Lang and others have suggested, there may be a link between dreams and the experience of ghosts, and as we have noted, our ancient ancestors may have had difficulty distinguishing between fantasy and reality. When the dead appeared in dreams and gave messages, it was believed that they continued to exist and were communicating with the living. Thus, in Egypt, when troubles afflicted the living they would leave messages at the tombs of dead relatives warning that tomb offerings would cease if the dead did not do something to relieve the bad fortune of the living.

Priesthoods encouraged their followers to believe in an afterlife and to believe that the dead had power in the world of the living. The proper interpreters of dreams were the priest. Today, in New Age situations, dreams about or experiences of the dead are treated seriously by those who claim to have the ability or power to decipher the significance of them—for a price. Nothing has changed, the practitioners still prey upon the gullible.

There is absolutely no scientific validation for the existence of ghosts. They exist only in the mind, in the imagination, in the mental conjuring of those who say they experience them. Many ghostly appearances that have been investigated are found to be misinterpretations of perfectly natural phenomena or events, including sheets of paper or cloth caught in bushes and disturbed by a slight breeze, shadow forms cast by flickering lights, and so forth.

Out-of-Body Experiences

There are those who have claimed to have experienced, or who claim to be able to create the experience, of separation of the self, the soul, the spirit from their physical body. They describe the feeling of the self or the psyche rising above the physical body so that it is able to view the physical body as if from the outside. They see the physical body lying on a bed (or whatever) while their true self is separated and apart. Sometimes the experience comes when the person is somnolent, almost drowsy, in a state akin to twilight sleep, somewhere between semiawareness and deep slumber. At other times the experience comes after a person has been in an accident or is in the hospital and is presumed to be dead (these occurrences are discussed next as near-death experiences). The basic presumption underlying out-of-body experiences is that the human, unlike other creatures, is composed of two parts: a body and a soul—a notion that is completely foreign to most of the Jewish Scriptures, wherein the individual is a psychosomatic unit, but which is basic to some Christian theology.

In out-of-body experiences, the person has the sense of rising out of the body. One woman spoke of finding herself at the level of pictures hung on the walls of the room. Some claim to travel about in this state, but no tests have demonstrated that they are able to describe accurately what is occurring in another room or building or location. Because this phenomenon is so closely related to near-death experiences, detailed analysis will be presented in the following section.

Near-Death Experiences

During the early 1970s, a wave of public interest and curiosity was engendered by the publication of reports by Dr. Elisabeth Kubler-Ross (1971) and Dr. Raymond Moody (1975, 1977) concerning near-death experiences. Some individuals who were presumed to be dead as a result of accidents, heart failure, cessation of breathing, etc., reported that during the "death" period they had out-of-body experiences that brought them into another dimension of time and space. Some of the "death experiences" occurred in hospital settings, where physicians in attendance, believing the patient was dying or dead, began resuscitation procedures. Of course, the individual was not dead, inasmuch as he or she lived to report on the near-death experience.

Although the subject became popular in the 1970s, interest in deathbed experiences goes back to medieval times (Zalewski 1987). Parapsychologists have investigated the subject, but so have others. Dr. Michael Sabom (1982), a Florida cardiologist, reported on near-death experiences, primarily associated with cardiac arrest. Dr. Kenneth Ring (1980), a University of Connecticut psychologist, reported on the study of 102 near-death experiences of people residing in the New England area.

Kubler-Ross claimed to have talked with more than one thousand men, women, and children about their near-death experiences. Moody, whose *Life After Life* was translated into more than twenty languages, based his comments on an eleven-year study of more than 105 cases. Both Kubler-Ross and Moody imply that their findings suggest the reality of a life after death.

Neither Kubler-Ross nor Moody have published their findings in a proper scientific manner that would make them available for analysis. Indeed, most of Kubler-Ross's reports are summary statements. Moody's case studies are selective and the sampling procedure is haphazard.

The reports contain amazing similarities and exhibit, in general, the following pattern. At the moment of "death," the person felt his or her spirit leave the body. In many cases, the spirit hovered above the body and viewed the scene below, watching as doctors and other health professionals labored to restore heartbeat and breathing. Relatives may have wept because the person was presumed to be dead. That is to say, the individual had a sense of being dead or of being considered dead. Such awareness has produced mixed emotional responses. For some, watching efforts being made at their resuscitation was disturbing, frightening. Others have reported feelings of detachment or of intense calm and peace. The sense of being separated from the body has also produced mixed emotional responses. In some cases, the farther the individual seemed to have moved away from the body, the greater the tranquility and the sense of becoming distant from pain. Others reported insecurity in the separation, as if the body might be taken over by some other spirit. When the individual's name was called by the attending physicians, some claim to have heard and to have tried to respond. Because they felt as if they were in a different world or a different dimension, they could not communicate.

Some experienced a period of life review, as if their whole life was rapidly replayed before them. Because of the awareness of death, some of these reviews included a preview of one's own funeral and mourning by family and friends. Others did not have the preview experience.

Light that became increasingly bright welcomed the spirit in a warm, friendly atmosphere. The only sensations reported were those of sight and sound. Sometimes the person was greeted by identifiable spirit forms who were relatives or hero figures or divinities such as Jesus or God. From this point on the stories vary.

Ray Canning (1965), in discussing the environment of the other world with Mormons who have had near-death experiences, discovered that the reports reflect much that is familar in our present environment, only magnified in splendor. The buildings and the flowers were more beautiful, the singing was superior, and so on (p. 32). Often the person greeted dead family members. Sometimes the individual claimed to have encountered a cultural or religious hero such as Jesus or Moses or God or Joseph Smith.

Finally, in the near-death experiences, it became necessary to return to the earthly body. In some instances, the individual was told that his or her work on earth was unfinished; in other cases the person simply felt that he or she must return. Some returned reluctantly. The sensations of returning to the earthly body were often rather simple, involving little more than feeling warm and taking a deep breath. In other cases, there was a sensation of the return of pain. Some reported experiencing a physical thump or bump.

Most reported changes in attitudes towards life and death following the near-death experience. They sensed a purpose in life. They became more caring, more compassionate, more empathetic. They moved with an assurance they did not have before. Death was no longer feared, for it was recognized as a doorway for transition to another life in a spirit world.

Almost nothing negative is reported from these visions. The life review appears not to engender feelings of guilt or failure. There is no judgment and no dividing path leading to Heaven or Hell, and there is no purgatorial in-between. However, not everyone experiences pleasant visions. For example, in an April 4, 1872, article in the *Virginia City Chronicle* it was reported:

> The negro, Sandy Hammons, who was shot in a fracas last Christmas near New Liberty, died to all appearances March 24th. Strange things happened to this negro which are worth repeating, for he has brought news from a quarter where there is as yet no telegraph or reporter. He was shot in the neck, and his entire lower body has been completely paralyzed ever since, while he was at all times sensible. Some days ago he died, as all his friends supposed, and he was laid out to bury, but came to life in time to escape the grave. After coming to, he said that he had been to see the devil, was in hell, and saw many of his old acquaintances; the devil told him he had no room for him then, but would be ready for him in a few days. He reports the devil a large black, savage-looking monster, armed with fiery lashes, which he lays on his unruly subjects. His dominions are all interspersed with lakes of fire and places of rest; the worst are punished the most, but all are punished according to their crimes. (Splitter Collection)

How are these experiences to be understood? Some would argue that they provide definite proof of an afterlife; others categorize them as hallucinations. The similarities in pattern among the stories are astounding. Some aspects clearly reflect cultural patterns and in general reflect standard beliefs in an afterlife as taught in churches throughout the Western world.

No satisfactory explanation for what triggers these experiences has been found so far. Among those suggested are the possibility that some of the hallucinatory experiences could be caused by therapeutic drugs administered to the patient at the time of physical crisis; that the panoramic life review is a result of a discharge of neurons in the eye creating an imagery of lights, colors, and dark tunnels; that the tunnel effect is a recollection of birth experiences when the infant passed through the vaginal canal to enter into a brightly lit room where it was welcomed by caring persons. These suggestions have not been generally accepted.

A cerebral anoxia theory suggests that a failing heart rate and lack of oxygen to the brain could induce visionary experiences. However, not enough subjects entered hypoxia to support this idea. Another physiological hypothesis proposes that a massive release of endorphins, triggered by the closeness of death, could produce relaxed, peaceful feelings. This has remained no more than a proposal.

Psychological explanations have not fared well, including the theory that the near-death experience represents a "depersonalization" in which the prospect of death induces a defensive psychological reaction. This reaction produces feelings of well-being, of bodily detachment, panoramic review, and mystical transcendence, all of which are to be recognized as ego defenses insulating the individual from the harsh reality of immediate annihilation. A psychological expectation theory suggests that the death visions reflected an anticipation of imminent death and afterlife. It is clear that no single hypothesis serves to explain near-death experiences. The subject remains under study.

We know that imagery is not absent from the deathbed. Kubler-Ross reported the words of a man who described his fight to stay alive for a few more days in these terms:

Last night I put up a fight for several hours. There was a big train going rapidly down hill toward the end, and I had a big fight with the train master. I argued and fought with him. And I ordered him to stop this train one tenth of an inch short. (Kubler-Ross 1971, p. 59)

Kubler-Ross interpreted the experience as a form of bargaining for more time. In another case, a woman suffering from a serious kidney ailment related her experience:

A big cloud came over me and I had the idea that I had a kidney operation and didn't need those doctors. When I woke up they were gone. (p. 59)

Kubler-Ross recognized that this visionary experience reflected the woman's fantasy that she did not need the doctors to save her life. Kubler-Ross wrote: "Considered to be psychotic and hallucinating, she was rejected for dialysis."

In these two cases, the ailing body and the mind cooperated in making real the fact that an illness was terminal and that the time of death was near. The posture of denial, which is recognized as a legitimate coping stance, could no longer be maintained. Body and mind, through a visionary experience, forced the confrontation of the reality and proximity of death. There was nothing supernatural in either situation.

What the mind fantasizes is always an individual experience. Coincidence of visionary content may be partially explained by cultural conditioning or perhaps genetic memory, although there is no scientific evidence to support the later concept. The accounts represent personal fiction, products of religious imagination that assume factual or reality status for those experiencing the visions. They are symbolic rejections of the fact of death, and for those who fear death provide assurance that human existence, unlike other animal existence, does not cease with death, but continues on in a spiritual sphere of being.

What is not verified is the existence of an afterlife. Our culture is dominated by religious beliefs that project a hope, that often becomes an assurance, of afterlife, constituting a denial of the finality of death. For those who choose not to live with unsubstantiated hope, and who find no assurance in near-death experiences or past-life regressions, existence is oriented towards life in the present, not in a postlife future.

The Biblical Connection

Of course, for some people, biblical passages seem to support the validity of out-of-body experiences. Someone appended to the writings of Qoheleth, the teacher, in the Book of Ecclesiastes a warning to recogize the "creator" before old age and death came (12). In the description of the infirmities of old age, which include failing eyesight and hearing, insecurity, the loss of teeth (grinders), and sexual desire, the writer warned against the moment of death when "the silver cord is severed or the golden bowl is broken or the pitcher is shattered at the fountain or the water-wheel broken at the cistern" (12:6). Orientalists immediately recognize the silver cord as that which suspends the golden lamp. When it is cut, the lamp falls and breaks just as surely as a clay pitcher can be smashed at a well or a water-wheel can break down. There are those who find psychic or spiritual meanings in the silver cord, arguing that it represents the cord that ties the body to the soul. Death constitutes the breaking of the spiritual cord. Those who experience out-of-body sensations have not completely severed the cord that binds soul and body, and should they feel insecurity in being away from their physical self, that fear reflects the understanding that some other spirit could enter the body and take possession. Of course, this belief rests on a passage lifted out of context and completely misinterpreted! The Bible does not support this notion.

The Apostle Paul, on the other hand, implies that he has had some sort of out-of-body experience. When he wrote to the Christian group in Corinth he told them that:

I know a man in Christ who fourteen years ago was caught up into the third heaven—whether in the body or out of the body, I do not know, God knows. And I know that this man was caught up into Paradise—whether in the body or out of the body, I do not know, God knows—and he heard things that cannot be told, which man may not utter. On behalf of this man I will boast, but on my own behalf I will not boast. (2 Cor. 12:2-5)

Paul's oblique reference to his personal experience is so vague that there is no way to develop an understanding of his experience. It is clear that he believes in a layered Paradise and that he reached the third layer (Muslims believe in a seven-layered heaven). The notion of a third heaven was current in Jewish thought in Paul's time (Apocalypse of Moses 40:2; 3 Baruch 4:8), so the reference would be understood by his audience. Paul was unable to state whether he went to this heaven physically (as Mohammed was to do later, on horseback) or spiritually. It is obvious that Paul believed in out-of-body experiences, and inasmuch as Paul's Corinthian correspondence is part of Christian Scripture, then out-of-body experiences have an authoritative base as real experiences in Christian Scriptures. Once again the Bible can be used to authenticate the supernatural.

Living Without Belief in an Afterlife

She was a woman in her early seventies. She had been raised as a Methodist, and her question was asked with timidity and yet with intensity: "Do you thnk there will be harps in heaven?" For once I gave the proper response: a question rather than a statement. "Why do you ask?" She replied, "Well, I hate harp music and I don't want to go there if that is what they are going to be playing!" What boredom! An eternity of harp music when you hate the instrument and the way it sounds! She was a good, kind, thoughtful, and caring person, but the reward for her Christian belief and decent lifestyle threatened to be an eternal punishment. I explained to her that this is what people believed who lived 2,000 years ago and for whom harp music was the best they knew. She seemed satisfied.

Qoheleth, the teacher, found the endless routines of life boring and meaningless: "Emptiness of emptiness, everything is empty [of significance]. What gain does a man have for all of his labor under the sun?" (Eccles. 1:2-3). How would he have thought of eternity? Perhaps much the same way as the Methodist woman: "If that is what it is going to be like, I don't want it."

Afterlife beliefs are responses to human fears about death and personal annihilation. They also serve as social controls, as implicit warnings that what one does in this life has implications for the life to come. To do evil and escape judgment today could result in an eternity of punishment after death. Notions about reincarnation provide the hope of some possible variation in the next incarnation, but even in those notions, the idea of an endless procession of rebirths before one can escape the cycle and be absorbed into the whole constitutes a punishment-reward concept that controls human behavior through implicit warnings that what one does in this existence determines one's fate in the next.

How Does One Live Without Belief in a Hereafter?

In everyday existence, the nonbeliever lives a life not too dissimilar from that of his believing neighbor. Nonbelievers and believers make the same sort of choices in terms of lifestyle. It is often assumed that without the threat of punishment in an afterlife a person would probably live a to-hell-with-everything-and-everybody existence, greedily enjoying pleasures, ruthlessly exploiting others, indifferent to the future of humankind and the environment. Of course, anyone can choose such a way of life, whether or not he or she believes in an afterlife.

On the other hand, a nonbeliever, a Humanist, can also choose to live this life to the full, seeking that which enhances the human spirit and contributes to the future. Art, music, the dance, the theater, great literature, glorious sunsets, magnificent forests, amazing wildlife, beautiful fauna, and so on, enrich the spirit and the mind. Warm companionship, love and friendship, work that contributes to human welfare, enliven and give meaning to the precious moments of existence. Where there is pain and suffering, the caring person, whether or not he or she entertains belief in a future life, reaches out in compassion. Where others hunger and are in poverty, the full human responds as best he or she can. Morals, values, and ethical principles are drawn from the highest and noblest ideals of philosophers, psychologists, poets and painters, realists and dreamers, theologians and skeptics, and most of all, lovers. The nonbeliever, the Humanist, chooses not out of fear of punishment but out of love and of commitment to life and living, so that one feels within the self a sense of achievement and fulfillment, believing that because one is here and is committed the world will, at death, be just a little better than it was at birth.

Such a commitment to life, to justice, to decency, to human betterment, to self-fulfillment can be identified as the Christian way, the Jewish way, the Buddhist way, the Muslim way, the Humanist way, and so forth. What is different between the Humanist way and that of traditional religions is that although the Humanist path parallels that of the highest ethical concepts entertained by religions, the path is chosen because it is good and satisfying rather than out of a fear of the consequences in an afterlife.

In other words, one may live a fine, meaningful life without belief in a hereafter. One chooses to live so, the only reward being an internal awareness and satisfaction experienced in the here and now.

References

Brichto, H. C., "Kin, Cult, Land and Afterlife—A Biblical Complex," *Hebrew Union College Annual,* Cincinnati, XLIV, 1973, pp. 1–54.

Budge, E. Wallis, *The Liturgy of Funerary Offerings.* New York: B. Blum, 1972 (reprint of 1909 edition).

Burrows, Millar, *The Dead Sea Scrolls.* New York: Viking Press, 1955.

Canning, Ray R., "Mormon Return-From-the-Dead Stories, Fact or Folklore," *Proceedings of the Utah Academy of Science, Arts and Letters,* 42, 1965, pp. 29–37.

Driver, G. R., *Canaanite Myths and Legends* (Old Testament Studies No. 3). Edinburgh: T. & T. Clark, 1955.

Edwards, Paul, "The Evidence Against Reincarnation: Part One," *Free Inquiry,* VoL 6, No. 4, 1986, pp. 24–30; "Part Two," Vol. 7, No. 1, 1986, pp. 38–48.

Guignebert, Charles, *Ancient, Medieval and Modern Christianity: The Evolution of a Religion.* New York: University Books, 1961.

Harris, Melvin, "Are Past-Life Regressions Evidence of Reincarnation?" *Free Inquiry,* Vol. 6, No. 4, 1986, pp. 18–23.

Jacobson, Niols O., *Life Without Death?* trans. by Shiela LaFarge. New York: Delacorte Press, 1973.

Johnson, Sherman E., "The Gospel According to St. Matthew: Introduction and Exegesis," *The Interpreter's Bible.* New York: Abingdon-Cokesbury Press, 1951, Vol. VII, pp. 232–625.

Kubler-Ross, Elisabeth, "What Is It Like to Be Dying?" *American Journal of Nursing,* 71, 1971, pp. 54–60.

Kung, Hans, *Eternal Life?* trans. by E. Quinn. New York: Doubleday, 1985.

Lang, Andrew, *The Book of Dreams and Ghosts.* London: Longmans, Green & Co., 1897.

Lincoln, Jackson Steward, *The Dream in Primitive Cultures.* London: The Cresset Press, 1935.

Moody, Raymond A., *Life After Life.* Covington, Georgia: Mockingbird Books, 1975.

———, *Reflections on Life After Life.* Covington, Georgia: Mockingbird Books,

1977.

Osis, Karlis, and W. Haraldsson, *At the Hour of Death*. New York: Avon Books, 1977.

Ring, Kenneth, *Life at Death, A Scientific Investigation of Near-Death Experiences*. New York: Coward, McCann and Geohegen, 1980.

Sabom, Michael B., *Recollections of Death, A Medical Investigation*. New York: Harper and Row, 1982.

Saggs, H. W. F., *The Greatness That Was Babylon*. New York: Hawthorn Books, 1962.

Siegal, Ronald E., "Accounting for Afterlife Experiences," *Psychology Today*, January 1981, 65–75.

Speiser, E. A., trans., "Descent of Ishtar to the Nether World," in James B. Pritchard, *Ancient Texts Relating to the Old Testament*. Princeton, N.J.: Princeton University Press, 1950, pp. 106–109.

Splitter, Henry W. Collection, Archives of California and Western Folklore, Center for the Study of Comparative Folklore and Mythology, University of California, Los Angeles.

Woolley, Sir Leonard, *Excavations at Ur*. London: Ernest Ben, Ltd., 1963.

Zaleski, Carol, *Otherworld Journeys: Accounts of Near-Death Experiences in Medieval and Modern Times*. London: Oxford University Press, 1987.

The Cult of the Dead

Beliefs in an afterlife, attempts to contact the dead, beliefs that the dead can exercise influence in the community of the living, gave rise to a partly formalized, partly unformalized Christian cult of the dead. The veneration of the dead has two aspects. The first is concerned with the ways in which the living might influence the dead. The second is concerned with the ways in which the powerful or influential dead might benefit the living. This is to say that something more than memorial celebrations are involved.

Roman Catholicism has fostered the belief that individuals who, having failed to reach some sort of perfection of belief and behavior in this life, and who die without having all sins forgiven, are destined to spend time in Purgatory. Purgatory, as the name implies, is a place of purgation. Venial or minor sins such as dishonesty or acts committed when one was not aware that they were sinful separate the soul from God. Time spent in Purgatory is designed to purify or cleanse the soul to make it acceptable for entrance into Heaven and into the presence of God. Mortal sins such as suicide or murder may condemn the perpetrator to an eternal Hell from which there is no escape.

This theology of the afterlife is drawn, in part, from the notion of final judgment. For example, Paul the apostle warned Roman Christians: "We shall all stand before the judgment seat of God" (Rom. 14:10). He wrote to the congregation in Corinth: "We must all appear before Christ's judgment seat so that each may receive good or evil, according to what he has done in the flesh" (2 Cor. 5:10). Roman Catholic interpretations of Paul's correspondence suggests that there is no escape from this judgment; one is destined for Heaven or Purgatory or Hell.

To shorten time in Purgatory, the devout Roman Catholic may arrange to have masses said for the dead—for him or herself or for others. Belief in the effectiveness of such masses rests on a passage in the twelfth chapter of 2 Maccabees, a book written during the first century B.C.E. that is supposed to be an abridgement of a five-volume work dealing with the Maccabean revolt, written by Jason of Cyrene (2 Macc. 2:19–23). The larger book has never been found. The writer of 2 Maccabees, who may have been a Pharisee, reports the Jewish struggle against the imposition of Greek concepts as a sacred history. The writer betrays a theological intent designed to assure readers that the afflictions suffered by the Jews were permitted by their God for disciplinary reasons (6:12). He introduces, as essential elements of his account, visions, intrusions of angelic figures, important festivals, and acts of worship. Although the book provides a general outline of the struggle between Jews and Syrian Greeks, the preferred historical account is to be found in 1 Maccabees, which largely omits a theological interpretation (Larue 1968, pp. 422–426).

The hero of 2 Maccabees, Judas Maccabeus, prayed for forgiveness for Jews who died in battle but on whose bodies were found amulets sacred to pagan gods, which the writer noted "explained why they had fallen" (12:39–42). In addition, Judas took up a collection of 2,000 drachmas of silver that was sent to Jerusalem to provide a sin-offering for these same dead Jews. The author of 2 Maccabees noted:

> In doing this he acted properly and honorably, taking due account of the resurrection. For if he were not expecting that the fallen would rise again, it would have been superfluous and foolish to pray for the dead. But inasmuch as he was looking to the wonderful reward reserved for those who die godly deaths, his intent was pious and holy. Therefore he made atonement to free the dead, from their sin. (12:43–45)

It is clear that there were Jews who believed that the fortunes of the dead could be affected by prayers and offerings made in their behalf by the living. Because Judas Maccabeus is supposed to have prayed for dead Jewish warriors who had violated their faith, and because 2 Maccabees is included in the Roman Catholic canon of sacred scripture, modern Roman Catholics have a biblical basis for prayers for the dead whose lives may have been less than perfect.

As one might expect, the Roman Catholic Church has capitalized on the belief in the importance of prayers for the dead. One example will illustrate the promotional techniques employed. The Sacred Heart Spiritual Society is centered in Walls, Mississippi. Promotional literature promising masses for the dead for those who enroll in the society is accompanied by an illustrated enrollment folder containing a portrait of Jesus bearing a heart on his tunic. The heart is bound by a chain of thorns. From the top of the heart flames emerge. A cross is depicted rising from the flames. Thin black lines radiate from the heart through a golden aura. The literature refers to the masses for the dead as acts of "remembrance," but also states that

> When you enroll a loved one in the Sacred Heart Spiritual Society, you are beseeching God that this Soul may be granted a sharing in the infinite fruits of the Holy Mass that is offered daily for all enrolled in the Spiritual Society. We recall that through a centuries' old tradition and teaching, the Church instructs us that our prayers, sacrifices, almsgiving, and especially remembrances in Holy Mass are of great benefit to the Souls of the Just in purgatory. We also know that we here on earth, along with our departed loved ones, are all members of Christ's Mystical Body. Since Holy Mother Church teaches us to believe in the Communion of the Saints, we know that these departed loved ones can be of mutual benefit to one another. Because we have no way of knowing whether they are in the cleansing realm of purgatory or are already enjoying the Beatific Vision of God and because we also know that their time for good works is over, we can lovingly offer our prayers, alms, sacrifices, and Holy Masses for them.

The appeal is compelling. It is based on belief in the magical power of prayers and masses for the dead, on human love that can only desire the best for others, on the importance of remembrance, and on guilt feelings that many may carry if they think they may not have done enough for the deceased. There is also a secondary benefit: by doing the proper thing in enrolling another in the society, an act of love may be chalked up on the donor's benefit in the divine book of judgment. Just how the church knows that the masses are of benefit to souls in Purgatory can only be explained by reference to the Judas Maccabeus legend.

The Cult of the Saints

Statuary of Mary, Jesus, and other religious figures abound in Catholic churches. Believers kneel before these images in acts of veneration that usually include prayers for their intercession at divine headquarters. Thomas Byrnes (1985) recalls his Roman Catholic instructions:

> We must not pray to the statue itself but to the blessed individual it represented, which wasn't easy, especially when May-crowning Mary or laying a written petition at the feet of St. Anthony or St. Jude. What's more, we were not to expect the saints themselves to bestow the favor asked. Their job was to intercede for us, and with us. (p. 60)

The practice clearly reflects human hierarchical patterns. Associations with powerful individuals and authority figures can open doors for personal requests. What is more natural than to project earthly social patterns into the realms of the heavenly? God obviously listens to influential people.

The belief in the intercession of saints has only the vaguest biblical support. For example, some biblical personalities appear to have had special influence with the deity. King Abimelech of Gerar took Abraham's wife as a sex partner after having been assured by Abraham that Sarah was Abraham's sister. Yahweh prevented consummation of the sexual act and told Abimelech, "I know that you have done this in the integrity of your heart . . . now return the man's wife for he is a prophet, and he will pray for you and you shall live" (Gen. 20:6–7). Abimelech could not redeem himself. Only a man of unusual power could pray for him and protect him from divine retribution by committing a crime in which he was virtually entrapped by Abraham, who was a liar!

The righteous Job, the innocent pawn in a test devised by Yahweh and his son Satan, refused to admit that he was unrighteous, despite the theological arguments of his three "friends" who came to comfort him. At the conclusion of the cruel experiment, Yahweh stated that Job was correct in his comments about the deity and that he (Yahweh) was furious with the three counselors, whose ideas were in error. To protect them from their deserved punishment, they were required to make a burnt offering and to ask Job to pray for them. This they did and "Yahweh accepted Job's prayer" (Job 42:1–9).

For Christians, the most powerful intercessor is Jesus. He is supposed to have said:

> Truly, truly, I tell you, if you ask anything of the Father in my name, he will give it to you. Up until now you have requested nothing in my name; ask, and you will receive so that your happiness may be complete. (John 16:23–24)

Jesus' name becomes a magical formula, assuring a hearing and response by the Father (John 15:7,16). Consequently, prayers to God usually end with a phrase like "in the name of Jesus Christ, our Lord and Savior."

Over the centuries preserved body parts of saints and martyrs were accumulated. Festivals, parades, pilgrimages, and special holy days came into vogue. The veneration of cultic objects was augmented by church teachings concerning magical powers inherent in the bones and artifacts (see chapter on Faith Healing).

During the centuries after the death of Jesus, numerous New Testament figures became saints, including the disciples (except Judas), those associated with composing the gospels (Matthew, Mark, Luke, John), Paul the Apostle, Stephen the Martyr, and so on. These and other heroes of the faith were chosen and elected to the roster of saints because of martyrdom; social work, as with St. Vincent de Paul; kindliness, as with St. Francis of Assisi; great devotion to the church, and so on. They become links between the church on earth and the Christians in Heaven. During the third century C.E., the Christian philosopher Origen pointed out that the greatest Christian virtue is love of neighbors. If Christians love and help one another while on earth, one can only imagine how much they will do so after death when they are with Christ. Perhaps the most venerated saint is Mary, the mother of Jesus (see chapter on The Cult of the Mother Goddess).

At first, martyrs and heroes of the faith were canonized by popular consent or by a bishop. This power was withdrawn during the twelfth century C.E. on the grounds that such election lacked infallibility. Although veneration of those already sainted was permitted, from that time on only the pope could sanction veneration. In 1634, during the reign of Pope Urban VIII, veneration was permitted for saints who had been canonized prior to that time only after investigation and formal beatification. Once canonized, the saint may be venerated and may become the patron of a congregation, and is entitled to wear a halo.

Some saints became specialists. For example, St. Denis, who was martyred by decapitation and is said to have picked up his head and walked away, became the saint in charge of alleviating headaches!

The acquisition of sainthood is presently a long and tedious process, as those who seek to have some favored person elevated have discovered. In recent years efforts have been made on behalf of Father Junipero Serra, despite claims that he was responsible for the mistreatment of Indians in the eighteenth century. The first steps have already been taken.

Father Serra was born in Majorca, Spain, in 1713. In 1769, in San Diego, California, he founded the first of a chain of nine Franciscan missions. Subsequently his order established twenty-one missions between San Diego and Sonoma. In 1985, the pope declared Serra "venerable," which signified that he had "lived a life of heroic virtue." In December 1987,

Pope John Paul II announced the beatification of Father Serra, which is the second step toward sainthood and which will allow the label "blessed" to be applied to the "apostle of California." Beatification requires the authentication of a miracle having occurred through intercessory prayer to the proposed saint. Serra's miracle was the cure of Sister Boniface Dry-daof of St. Louis, a seventy-two-year-old nun of the Franciscan order who prayed for his intervention when she was near death from lupus (a disorder of the connective tissue) some twenty-five years ago. The third step toward sainthood, canonization, calls for a second miracle, although this requirement may be bypassed. Miraculous cures must be authenticated by medical documents demonstrating that the healing was not the result of medical intervention and cannot be explained naturally.

Efforts are also underway to sanctify Mother Mary Angela Truskowska who in 1855 founded The Congregation of the Sisters of St. Felix (Felician Sisters) in Poland. In 1982, Pope John Paul II recognized her life as one of heroic faith, hope, and charity, and declared her a servant of God. During the mid-1970s, Lillian Halasinski of Dunkirk, New York, after praying to Mother Angela to intervene for her, was healed suddenly of a painful illness that kept her bedbound and unable to walk. If the investigating tribunal accepts the cure as something occurring outside of natural healing, Mother Angela may be advanced on the next step toward sainthood. Not surprisingly, the sisters of the order encourage parishioners to pray to Mother Angela for her intercession (Briggs 1989).

The move towards beatification does not just happen. In Father Serra's case, a public relations firm was hired and more than $750,000 was raised to pay for investigations and ceremonies.

One can only wonder at the efforts made to sanctify the very mundane lives of the rich and famous. Ross Benson (1989) reported the suggestion that Princess Grace of Monaco (formerly the film star Grace Kelly, originally from Philadelphia) be canonized. Apparently some visitors to the tomb of Princess Grace have claimed that she can effect cures. These allegations began after a priest, Don Piero Pintus, commented during a mass for the princess in 1984 that she was so good she was a saint. The priest's request for the canonization of the princess was refused by the Vatican.

The Mormon Cult of the Dead

The Church of the Latter Day Saints performs baptisms on behalf of the dead. A living person acts as a proxy for the dead individual. The basis for the ritual rests on a letter from Joseph Smith, dated September 6, 1842, that expounded an earlier revelation concerning baptisms for the dead persons. The practice is based on several notions. First, the Apostle Paul made reference to such a practice in a letter to the Corinthian Christians:

> Otherwise, what do people mean by being baptized for the dead? If the dead are not raised by all, why are people baptized on their behalf? (1 Cor. 15:29)

Exactly what Paul was referring to in these two sentences has been debated, but apparently vicarious baptism was practiced, perhaps by converts who were concerned about the afterlife well-being of loved ones and believed that without baptism one could not enter the kingdom of the saved. The custom never became a tradition in the early church.

The second basis for the practice of baptism of the dead is that Jesus gave power to his disciples so that whatever they bound (or as Smith preferred to interpret the saying, recorded) on earth would be bound (or recorded) in heaven (*Doctrine and Convenants* 1978, 128:8). Thus, the unbaptized dead could be guaranteed entry into the bliss of heaven through the ministry of the living who acted in their behalf.

A third reason for the Mormon rite is that it is based on a revelation given to Joseph Smith in which the need to keep proper records of baptisms was stressed. The biblical Book of Revelation described the final judgment scene:

> And I saw the dead, the great and the small, standing before the throne, and books were opened; and another book was opened which is the book of life, and the dead were judged by what was written in the books according to what they had done. (Rev. 20:12)

According to Smith, the book of church records will be used in the heavenly judgment. Consequently, church records are carefully secured and protected. Thus, if one accepts the validity of the vision recorded in the Book of Revelation, and further accepts the validity of the revelation described by Joseph Smith, then the rite of baptism for the dead is essential for the unbaptized dead to be part of the heavenly kingdom.

Finally, baptism for the dead binds the living and the dead, to the benefit of both:

> It is sufficient to know that, in this case that the earth will be smitten with a curse unless there is a welding link of some kind or other between

the fathers and the children, upon some subject or another—and behold, what is that subject? It is baptism for the dead. For we without them cannot be made perfect; neither can they without us be made perfect. (*Doctrines and Covenants* 1978, 128:18)

This important ceremony, conducted in secret, that is, nonpublic, settings within Mormon temples, permits the dead, now baptized, to receive the "restored" gospel (i.,e., the Mormon version) in the afterworld, if they so desire.

Thus, in the Mormon cult of the dead, the Old World supernaturalism of the Bible has combined with the neosupernaturalism of a New World faith group to produce sacred and secret rites conducted in a modern occult scenario magically producing effects in the world beyond death.

The Dead and the Living

Earlier, in the discussion of beliefs in the afterlife, it was pointed out that following a death, the living may, from time to time, have experiences that convince some of them that the dead person is trying to communicate with them. The experience is a grief response and is a denial of the finality of death. The living may also, in seeking to remember and commemorate the dead, reveal beliefs in the potential of, or perhaps the hope of, communicating with the dead.

Each winter solstice, in cemeteries like the Forest Lawn graveyard in the Los Angeles area, small, decorated Christmas trees are set up on graves by grieving family members, and numerous cards are attached to the tree addressed to the dead and carrying messages from the living to the dead. These are truly expressions of grief and love and caring, but they give silent testimony to the hope and to the belief that somehow the spirit of the dead person is lingering in the vicinity of the tomb and is able to receive these very physical testimonies of love.

Occasionally, on new burials, small wooden crosses are erected, and floral wreaths are placed on the graves with messages for the dead attached. The dead are addressed directly and the notes contain words of love and affection.

Perhaps these rituals need to be separated from the idea of a formal cult of the dead. These are human grieving responses providing the living with means of effecting closure with the dead. They can be understood and accepted as outpourings of feelings. At the same time, they demonstrate denial of the finality of death and age-old belief patterns in the ability of the dead to receive messages from the living.

References

Benson, Ross, "Pilgrims Amazed by the Power of Grace," *Daily Express*, June 1, 1989.

Briggs, David, "Vatican Investigating Dunkirk Woman's Cure," *The Buffalo News*, June 17, 1987.

Byrnes, Thomas E., "Altar Boys Who Got All Fired Up," *The Catholic Digest,* February 1985, pp. 98ff.

The Doctrines and Covenants of the Church of Jesus Christ of the Latter-day Saints, Salt Lake City, Utah: The Church of the Latter-day Saints, 1978.

Larue, Gerald A., *Old Testament Life and Literatrure*. Boston: Allyn and Bacon, 1968.

O'Dea, Thomas F., *The Mormons*. Chicago: University of Chicago Press, 1957.

Pinsky, Mark, "Father Serra—Diocese Answers Critics of Potential Saint," *The Los Angeles Times*, November 24, 1986.

——, "Competing Tours to Serra Beatification Mass Create Friction," *The Los Angeles Times*, July 30, 1988.

Schanche, Don A., and Mark Pinsky, "Pope Won't Beatify Serra During Visit, Vatican Says," *The Los Angeles Times*, August 8, 1987.

Conclusion

The closing decade of the twentieth century is marked with insecurity and uncertainty. The belief that humans can take charge of their own lives and be successful has, for some, faded. The rational approach to life, the findings of science, the emphasis on giving personal meaning to one's existence fail to satisfy some. The strident voices of those who take refuge in the Bible and the 2,000-to-3,000-year-old notions expressed there has helped millions return to a belief in magic, disguised as divine truth.

What most fail to realize is that biblical magic was, in the beginning, simply a variant form of magic prevailing in the ancient Near East. Instead of going to an Aesclepian center for healing, one went to a Christian center. Instead of appealing to a local sorcerer to expel a demon, one turned to a priest who acted in the name of Jesus to do the same thing. As one mother goddess was discarded, a new mother goddess in the form of Mary emerged to take her place. The hallucinatory experiences of one ancient cult were replaced by the hallucinatory visions of another, and Jesus and Mary and angelic beings appeared to believers, and continue to manifest themselves in the experience of those who believe.

Occurrences that have absolutely no basis in fact are accepted as reality. Children who claim to have visions are accepted as uttering profound truths. Others, affected by these claims, state that they too have seen wraiths and manifestations of the holy. A whirling sun that approaches the earth and pulsates in the sky is accepted as a reality by a small band of people gathered about some spot where visions are expected. The fact that nowhere else on earth, and in no astronomical observatory, has any such unusual phenomenon been seen, and the fact that such a solar activity would wreak havoc on earth, are ignored. The fiction is more important than the fact. The mirage becomes a reality that is reported over and over again.

Magical stones, crystals, metals, herbs, powders, potions and pills, prayers, laying on of hands, and so on, prescribed by those who claim to have astral connections or to have discovered some psychic secret encourage the naive to invest faith and money in ridiculous cures, and perhaps ignore the best information that modern scientific medicine can provide. When clients of these magical healers die as a result of ignoring proper medical care, the pseudohealers hide behind dangerous laws that provide for religious freedom without protecting the believer from exploitation or from harm.

Rebellious youth has always been just rebellious youth. As far back as we can go in literary history we find stories of conflict between youth and the establishment. When youth employ shocking tactics and underscore independence by employing symbols that frighten the adult world, they are labeled Satanists and are supposed to be linked to the devil. When young people from disaffected families use drugs and alcohol to cloud their misery, and when they seek magical solutions in what they believe are ancient rites, they are again labeled children of Satan.

Most people are ignorant of our biblical heritage. The synagogues and churches have, for the most part, failed to impart the best of biblical scholarship to the public. In scholarly meetings, those who pursue analytical studies of religion talk to themselves. Their findings seldom appear in the popular press or in current magazines. Indeed, should any of their questions about "biblical truth" leak out, the voices of the fundamentalists and evangelicals are raised in protest, while the learned clergy remain silent. As one who taught in a private university and as a committed teacher who sought to share the best findings of biblical scholars with the classes I taught, I can testify to the uneasiness and in some cases the undercutting by religiously conservative colleagues, to protests by parents, and at the same time to wonderful support from students and some (not all) understanding administrators. But the noisy throng was always there, not interested in research and growth, but only in the promulgation of their own belief systems.

In this book, I have sought to touch on some of the common themes associated with the Bible, with faith systems, and with magical thinking in our present society. So long as the Bible is taught as a final truth, so long as the history of the composition of the Bible is ignored, so long as the environmental and world setting out of which the Bible came are ignored, the Bible will continue to be the most influential contributor in the Western world to magical thinking and to belief in the occult—rivaled only by the Koran, and the writings of Mary Baker Eddy, Joseph Smith, and other moderns who have accepted the basic teachings of the Bible.

It is time for the voices of analytical biblical scholars to be heard. It is time, a time long overdue, for the Bible to be recognized for what it really is—a collection of writings by people who lived in Palestine and the Mediterranean world some 2,000 to 3,000 years ago, with no more accuracy or authority concerning the nature of the cosmos, the world, or life than any other ancient writing. The Bible is a product of its time. Its occult superstitions are out of harmony with the modern world, and although its influence has motivated millions to live according to high moral and ethical ideals, its teachings have also encouraged war and violence and have served to evoke brutish and cruel responses among millions and millions of people. What is most troubling is what Bishop D'Arcy recognized as its supernaturalism, which not only interferes with progress in education but which continues to encourage magical thinking in an age of science. It is my hope that what is written here will encourage critical reading of the Bible and an analytical approach to claims of the paranormal.